great Wood Finishes

great Wood Finishes

A STEP-BY-STEP GUIDE TO BEAUTIFUL RESULTS

Jeff Jewitt

The Taunton Press

Publisher: **JIM CHILDS**

Associate Publisher: **HELEN ALBERT**

Assistant Editor: **JENNIFER RENJILIAN**

Copy Editor: **LARRY SHEA**

Designer: **MARY TERRIZZI**

Layout Artist: **ROSALIE VACCARO**

Photographer: **RANDY O'ROURKE**

Illustrator: **MARK SANT'ANGELO**

Indexer: **HARRIET HODGES**

Taunton
BOOKS & VIDEOS
for fellow enthusiasts

Text © 2000 by Jeff Jewitt
Photographs © 2000 by The Taunton Press, Inc.
Illustrations © 2000 by The Taunton Press, Inc.

Printed in the United States of America
10 9 8 7 6 5 4 3 2 1

The Taunton Press, Inc., 63 South Main Street, PO Box 5506, Newtown, CT 06470-5506
e-mail: tp@taunton.com

Distributed by Publishers Group West

Library of Congress Cataloging-in-Publication Data
Jewitt, Jeff.
Great wood finishes : a step-by-step guide to beautiful results / Jeff Jewitt.
p. cm.
ISBN 1-56158-390-1 (hb)—ISBN 1-56158-288-3 (pb)
1. Wood finishing. I. Title.
TT325.J417   2000
684'.084—dc21   99-046385

To my wife, Susan

Acknowledgments

There are many behind-the-scenes people that develop a book idea, encourage it, and eventually bring it to life. In no particular order I'd like to thank the following.

At The Taunton Press: Jim Childs, Helen Albert, Jennifer Renjilian, Mary Terrizzi, Anatole Burkin, Bill Duckworth, Tim Schreiner, Strother Purdy, Rosalie Vaccaro, and Carolyn Mandarano.

The following companies and/or individuals provided technical assistance, props, and or assistance in photographing: Jonathan Kemp at Behlen; Larry Ledbetter at Bartley Collections, Ltd.; John Austin at M. L. Campbell; Paul Smith at Fuji Spray Systems; Loren Simonsen at Devilbiss; Jeff Weiss at Target Coatings; Ed Woods and Jan Lampe at Columbia Forest Products; Campbell Hausfield; and Woodkote.

I'd particularly like to thank everyone at The Bartley Collections for providing me with much of the unfinished furniture that appears here.

Also, special thanks to Chris Minick and Michael Dresdner.

Finally, a heartfelt thanks to my photographer, Randy O'Rourke. Randy's eye for detail, sense of humor, and design skill are profoundly appreciated—even though he's a diehard Yankees fan.

Contents

SECTION 1
TOOLS AND MATERIALS

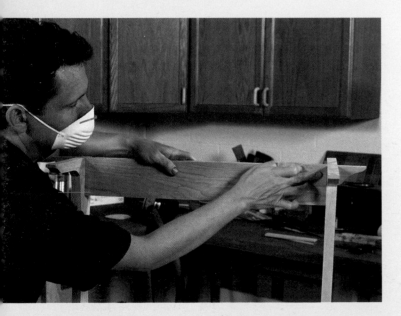

SECTION 2
THE BASICS

Introduction

The process of applying a finish has been described at various times as a secret art, a complicated science, and, by those who do a lot of it, downright frustrating. Good information is hard to find. You often have to to wade through elaborate processes or explanations when all you need is basic information. What type of finish should you use? What's the best way to apply it? How do you match the finish on another piece of furniture in your home? Professionals learn the answers to these questions by trial and error, but most people don't have the time or the knowledge to tackle projects in that fashion.

This book provides the answers to your finishing questions. In the first section, you'll find the best finishing tools and materials

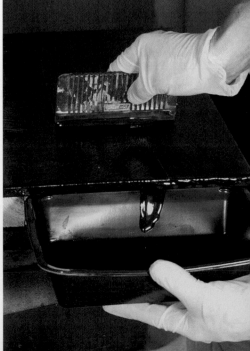

and explanations of how to use each one. In the second section, you'll find the basic step-by-step techniques for surface preparation, staining, bleaching, pore filling, glazing and toning, applying finishes, rubbing out, and waxing and polishing. You'll learn how to get the best results. The third section brings together the basic techniques you learn in the second section to show you how to create the most popular finishes.

Beyond the easy-to-follow step-by-step information, you'll find charts and tips to help you anticipate and solve finishing problems. While there is some gallantry in learning by mistakes, learning from this book makes more sense. It takes the guesswork and frustration out of finishing, and it gives you the knowledge you need to succeed.

YOUR TOOL KIT

While there is a vast array of finishing *materials*, there are relatively few tools necessary to apply them. These tools can be grouped into two categories: materials to finish and surface-preparation tools.

The most common surface-preparation tool is sandpaper, but a handplane or scraper can speed up the work and leave a very different surface. The choice of application tools ranges from rags, rollers, and brushes to spray equipment. The biggest difference between the tools is in the speed, quality, efficiency, and suitability of some tools in applying certain materials.

WORKING SMART

Whether you use a plane, a scraper, or sandpaper, it's best to prepare the surface of your project before gluing up, if possible. It's easiest to work on parts when they're flat.

SURFACE-PREPARATION TOOLS

Surface preparation is the process of taking the rough parts of a piece of furniture and smoothing them so that they appear more aesthetically pleasing and accept finishing materials uniformly. When you smooth wood, you remove the machining marks left by the tools used to shape, cut, and join the piece together. Surface preparation can usually be accomplished with abrasives (sandpaper), but for rougher surfaces, a handplane or scraper saves time. Most often, several surface-preparation tools are used in combination.

Planes

Using handplanes is the traditional method for smoothing wood. Handplanes are still prized by woodworkers who do period work, as well as those who prefer the texture and subtle nuances of a handplaned surface. Planes have several advantages:

They can be resharpened when dull, they produce shavings instead of dust, and most people find them immensely satisfying to use.

Planes do have some drawbacks, though. First, they only work well when properly sharpened, and the sharpening process can be daunting to a beginner. To sharpen planes, I grind a 25° bevel on the blade with a slow-speed (1,725 RPM) grinder and an aluminum-oxide wheel. This step puts a hollow grind on the blade and provides a steady surface for honing the blade by hand. I start the honing with a 1,200-grit waterstone and proceed to polishing with a 6,000-grit waterstone.

The second drawback is that planes require a degree of skill to use them effectively. Because they slice wood, they can be used optimally in only one direction, which causes problems on large panels where the grain changes or on glued-up panels made from different boards. The

Handplanes are available in a wide range of styles. Larger planes are generally used to remove milling marks, while smaller ones are used for final smoothing and detail work.

best way to learn how to use a plane correctly is to take a class or observe someone who knows how to sharpen and use planes. A lesson or two will save you countless frustrating hours of trying to teach yourself. Once you attain a modest degree of skill, planes are easy and enjoyable to use.

Scrapers

Scrapers are similar to planes in that they are cutting tools, but they are simpler to use and sharpen and they remove wood differently. A scraper is simply a piece of hard steel that has a small burr, or ridge, formed along its cutting edge. The burr makes the scraper similar to a plane blade with a steep cutting angle. This burr allows the scraper to be used in any direction, regardless of the grain of the wood or the presence of knots and changing grain. It also scrapes the wood shavings off as it cuts. If used aggressively, a scraper leaves a rough surface, but if used with a delicate touch, it leaves a smooth surface that needs little more surface preparation.

Scrapers are sold either as hand scrapers or cabinet scrapers. Hand scrapers are a

Planes vs. Scrapers

The low cutting angle of a plane blade cleanly severs wood fibers. A scraper's steeper cutting angle tends to break the fibers, resulting in a rougher surface.

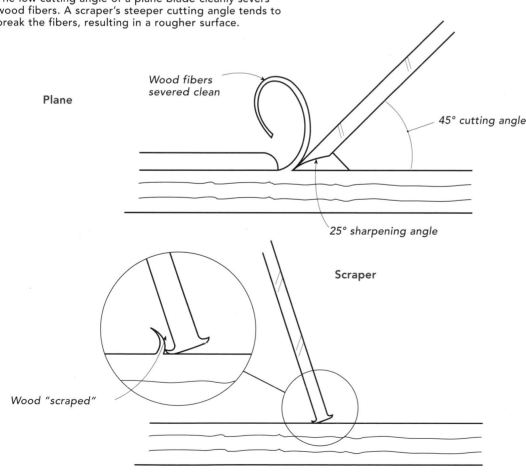

Plane

Wood fibers severed clean

45° cutting angle

25° sharpening angle

Scraper

Wood "scraped"

7

WORKING SMART

When buying a scraper for the first time, look for a thin one. They're easy for beginners to use because they flex fairly easily. For sharpening, you'll also need to buy a single-cut mill file and a sharpening stone.

Turning a Burr

Once the scraper has been filed, it's time to create the burr, or cutting edge.

1. Push the burnisher flat across the filed and honed edge.

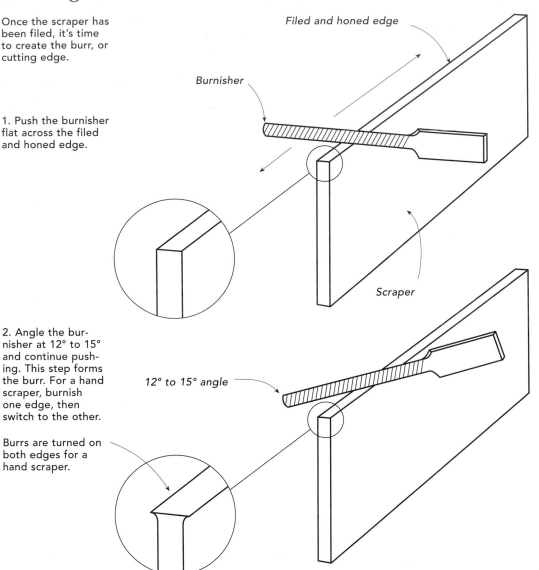

Filed and honed edge

Burnisher

Scraper

2. Angle the burnisher at 12° to 15° and continue pushing. This step forms the burr. For a hand scraper, burnish one edge, then switch to the other.

Burrs are turned on both edges for a hand scraper.

12° to 15° angle

flat piece of steel that you hold in your hand. They are sold in different profiles, hardness, and thickness. The profile determines the type of surface the scraper can be used on (flat or curved). Hardness affects the durability—how long before the scraper has to be resharpened. Thickness is mostly a personal preference, although thinner scrapers are easier for most people to use, and thicker scrapers can be used a bit more

aggressively. Hand scrapers are invaluable because they can smooth corners and areas that are impossible to reach with cabinet scrapers and planes.

Cabinet scrapers are also pieces of hard steel, but they are held in a fixed position in a metal body. They have flat soles and some are shaped like planes. Because of this design, they can be used to flatten a piece of wood and can be adjusted to remove a thicker shaving than a hand scraper.

Scrapers are available as handheld pieces of steel or fixed in a body like a plane. Different profiles can be bought or custom made, making smoothing moldings and other complex profiles a snap.

To sharpen a scraper, file the edge flat, then hone it on a fine oilstone or waterstone. Use a burnisher to turn a burr on the edge of the scraper. On a hand scraper, four burrs are turned (two one each side), while on a cabinet scraper only one is turned.

Abrasives

When most people think of smoothing wood, the first tool that comes to mind is sandpaper. It is far easier to use than planes or scrapers, it is widely available, and it comes in a variety of shapes, sizes, profiles, and grits. Abrasives, as sandpaper products are generically known, can be used by hand or on a machine. They smooth and polish bare wood, as well as the finishes that go over wood.

Sandpaper is composed of abrasive grits that are attached to a flat piece of paper with some kind of glue. These grits are designated with a number. The lower the

number, the coarser the paper. While different glues and paper affect the working qualities of the sandpaper, neither has as much effect on the final product as the grit. There are four main types of grit: garnet, aluminum oxide, silicon carbide, and ceramic.

Garnet is a naturally occurring mineral and is a good choice for hand-sanding. Garnet is available in coarse grits ranging from 80 to 220, so it is only used for smoothing bare wood.

Aluminum oxide is a man-made abrasive that is tougher and harder than garnet. It's available in a wider variety of grits and backings and generally performs better than garnet in machine-sanding. Grits range from 80 to as high as 1,200.

Silicon carbide is the grit of choice for sanding finishes. Because it can be used wet (with a liquid lubricant), a waterproof

Sandpaper Grading

The most common sandpaper grading system in the United States is called CAMI (Coated Abrasives Manufacturers Institute). The CAMI system allows a greater deviation in particle size (larger-grit particles may be present) than other systems, but this is not a problem when sanding wood because most wood doesn't need to be sanded past 180 grit. The European P system and the micron system—designated by the letter μ—are also used in the U.S. The P and μ systems use tighter grading tolerances, so these designations are better for sanding finishes, where stray, oversize particles on the paper could present a problem.

Abrasives are used by hand or on a machine. They're available in a wide variety of shapes and grits.

for demanding applications like belt sanders and is mixed with aluminum oxide to lower the cost. It's generally available only in coarse grits.

Both aluminum oxide and silicon carbide can be mixed with a talc-like lubricant called zinc stearate, which makes the sandpaper resist clogging and loading as you use it. These papers can be used on bare wood, but as a rule, aluminum oxide is better for sanding wood and silicon carbide is better for sanding finishes.

In the past, stearates have posed some problems with finish compatibility, particularly with water-based finishes. However, both finish and abrasive manufacturers have changed the composition of their ingredients so they are more compatible today. Nonetheless, I recommend using a nonstearated silicon carbide paper with a water-based finish. If you use a stearated paper, be sure to wipe the residue from the surface with clean rags and water.

glue and backing is used. This type of paper is easily identified by its grayish-black color. While coarse grits are available, the most useful ones for finish-sanding start around 220.

Ceramic is the most expensive and toughest of the grits. It's usually reserved

When sanding complicated profiles, moldings, or finishes, paper-backed sandpaper can easily cut through sharp edges and corners. Cushioned abrasives that incorporate grit into a nonwoven plastic fiber or sponge-like material are available. These products—synthetic steel wool (like Scotch-Brite pads) and sanding sponges—are first-rate problem-solvers. Because the backing is cushioned, the grit cuts less aggressively and will ride over sharp profiles instead of cutting through them. Cushioned abrasives have the added benefit of being easy to clean with water.

Steel wool is technically an abrasive and is sometimes mistakenly thought of as a surface-preparation tool. Steel wool is comprised of fine strands of steel woven into a pad. This product should not be used on bare wood because it will tear off and lodge in crevices.

BRUSHES

Brushes are probably the first tool that comes to mind when most people think of applying finishes. They are undoubtedly the oldest of the tools, and although some of the materials have changed, brushes aren't much different than they were hundreds of years ago.

For applying finishes, a good brush needs to hold a lot of finish, dispense it evenly on the surface, and leave few brush marks. For applying other products, such as stains, glazes, and paste wood fillers, these qualities may not be as important as bristle stiffness and durability. Knowing a little about brush types and construction can help you match the right brush to your finishing (see the illustrations at right). While most brushes have the same basic configuration, they can be divided into different groups by the type of bristle, the shape of the bristle, and the profile or overall shape of the brush.

Brush Anatomy

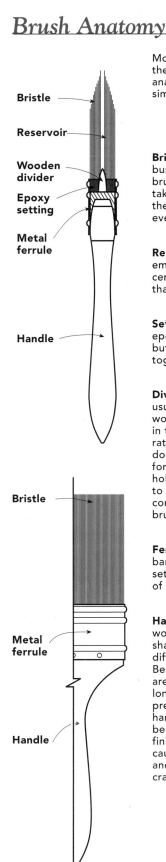

Bristle

Reservoir

Wooden divider

Epoxy setting

Metal ferrule

Handle

Bristle

Metal ferrule

Handle

Most brushes follow the same general anatomy and contain similar elements.

Bristle refers to the business end of the brush. Its function is to take up and release the finishing material evenly.

Reservoir refers to the empty space in the center of the brush that forms the divider.

Setting is usually epoxy and holds the butt ends of the bristle together.

Dividers are plugs, usually made from wood, that are placed in the setting to separate the bristle. This does two things: It forms a reservoir to hold finish, and it helps to shape the overall configuration of the brush.

Ferrule is the metal band that holds the setting to the handle of the brush.

Handle is made from wood or plastic and is shaped differently for different applications. Beaver-tailed handles are for comfort, while long, thin ones are for precise control. Not all handles are finished, because water-based finishing materials cause wood to swell and the finish would crack off.

Brushes are divided into two broad categories: natural (top left) and synthetic (bottom). Paint pads work like a brush with a very short bristle (top right).

Hog Bristle

There are two qualities that make hog bristle ideal for applying finishes. First, it's tapered so it has strength and resiliency. Second, it has natural split ends, or flags, at the tip that allow finish to flow on smoothly and reduce brush marks.

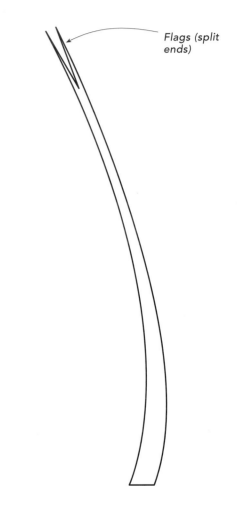

Flags (split ends)

Types of Bristle

Bristle can be divided into two categories: natural bristle like hog hair or synthetic bristle like nylon. Although natural bristle is the oldest and best choice for oil- and solvent-based paints and finishes, synthetic bristle is the best choice for water-based applications.

Natural The most widely used natural bristle is hog bristle from China. It has natural split ends at its tip called flags. The flags allow for a heavier loading of finish at the tip of the brush, and their fineness dispenses the finish with few noticeable ridges or brush marks. China bristle also has a natural taper from the base toward the tip. This taper gives strength and resiliency—called spring—to the bristle, which allows it to maintain its shape when used in intricate corners or edges. The qualities of bristle—its fineness, softness, and length—vary, but in quality brushes, different hog bristle may

Buying a Brush

When you're standing in front of a wall of brushes at the paint or hardware store, don't be afraid to take the wrapper off a couple of brushes and examine the bristle closely. There are several things to keep in mind when you buy a new brush.

Look for a chisel-tip profile. This is a sign of a handmade brush. There should be shorter bristle on the outside and longer ones in the center.

Check for flags on all of the bristle, both short and long. A lack of flags on the outside may mean that the chisel shape was mechanically cut into the brush after it was produced.

Bend the bristle back and forth. The bristle should have good springback and be neither too hard nor too soft to bend.

Disregard bristle color—it's meaningless. Black bristle is not inferior to white bristle, and natural as well as synthetic bristle may be dyed to look like something else.

If a salesperson comes over and glares at you, tell him you're looking for a chisel-cut, flagged, and tapered bristle with a solid wood divider that's not oversize to give a false impression of bristle fullness. Ask if he would mind if you sawed one of the brushes in half just to check. It's a sure way to let him know you mean business!

---

be blended together to create a brush with specific performance properties.

Other animal hairs are used in some specialty finishing brushes. Because of its softness, badger hair is used in brushes that blend and soften glazes. Badger hair is sometimes advertised in varnishing brushes as well, but most of those brushes are actually made of quality hog hair dyed to look like badger.

Another imitator is the camel hair brush. Camel hair is a very poor choice for a brush, so the hair on a camel hair brush is usually something else. In reality, these brushes are made from squirrel or other soft hair. Sable is used for small touch-up artist's brushes because of its ability to form a sharp, fine tip. Ox hair is used in some varnishing brushes because of its extreme softness.

Synthetic The first synthetic bristle ended up in toothbrushes because it was fairly thick and blunt-tipped. Nowadays, modern manufacturing methods are able to produce very fine, soft nylon bristle, as well as bristle with a man-made taper and flags built into the individual bristle filaments.

Cheap, blunt-tipped polyester brushes aren't good for applying finishes, but they can be used for paste wood filler, bleaches, and stains. Better-made synthetic-bristle brushes can be used with any finishing material, but they are the best choice for water-based finishes. Natural bristle absorb 100% of their weight in water, which makes the brush lose its shape and spring. Synthetic bristle absorb hardly any water, and as a result, the brush retains its shape and is easier to control. In addition, synthetic bristle clean up easily because they lack the microscopic "openings" (which trap finishing material) that natural bristle have in their structure.

Bristle Shape

The shape of the bristle also determines the suitability of a brush for certain finishing materials. Bristle—both natural and synthetic—can be blunt-tipped, tapered, or

Basic Brush Inventory

There are so many brushes available that it may seem overwhelming to determine what you need. You can narrow it down to a basic inventory, though. Here's what I recommend:

- Two good-quality rectangular chisel-tipped brushes for applying clear finishes. A 2½-in. brush is a good all-around size for large areas, while a 1-in. brush is good for detail work.
- Several average-quality brushes—either round or square—for applying stains and glazes.

- At least one 2-in. synthetic-bristle brush for applying water-based materials.
- Several artist's brushes, including a #1 and a #4 for touch-up and detail work.

An expanded inventory would also include:

- At least one or two fine nylon artist's brushes with a square edge (golden nylon).
- Several round, chisel-tipped brushes in a variety of sizes from 1 in. to 2½ in. These brushes are good for creative effects like softening and blending glazes, antiquing, and highlighting.

Bristle Shapes

Blunt-tipped bristle are found on cheaper brushes.

Flagged bristle allow finish to be laid down smoothly.

Tapered bristle are for precise, detailed work.

The fine bristle and sharp, square tip of the golden-nylon brush on the left is perfect for detailed, precise work, such as the inside of this small drawer.

flagged, or a combination, as in hog hair. Blunt-tipped bristle is found on both cheap synthetics and on natural brushes. The end of the brush is blunt and squared off, which is bad for applying clear finishes (it leaves noticeable brush marks) but not for working thick paints into the crevices of exterior wood. Some synthetics imitate natural bristle with a taper and/or a flag at the end. One of my favorites is a 1½-in. artist's brush with fine tapered golden-nylon filaments. The fine square edge of this brush is perfect for applying finishes to complex surfaces. Flagged and tapered hog bristle occurs naturally and produces a fine, smooth finish.

Brush Profile

The profile, or overall shape, is built into a brush during its production. Good brushes are made by hand. Different bristle lengths, amounts, and thicknesses are used to create brushes that have different shapes for different uses.

Bristle Profiles

A square-tipped bristle is good for applying paste wood filler and stains, but does not offer as much control as a chisel-cut profile.

A chisel-cut profile allows for finer, more precise work.

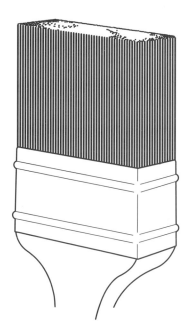

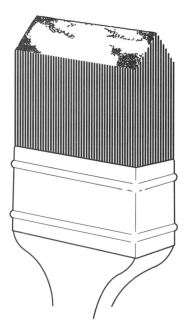

Cleaning a Brush

1. After working a soapy lather into the brush, bend back the bristle to force out any remaining finish.

2. Twirl the brush to spin out water.

3. Straighten the bristle with a brush comb.

4. Wrap the brush and lay it flat to dry.

Square-tipped brushes are inexpensive because the squared-off top can be mass-produced. Also called flat-trim or blunt-tipped, this profile works for general-purpose, noncritical work and exterior painting.

Chisel-tipped brushes are handmade, with shorter bristle lengths on the outside and longer bristle in the center. The chisel tip does a better job of putting down a smooth finish than nonchiseled brushes. Chisel-tipped brushes may be available as a rectangular profile or a round profile. The round profile uses about double the amount of bristle that a rectangular profile uses, and it holds much more material than other brushes. One disadvantage is that these brushes can be hard to thoroughly clean.

Caring for Brushes

You can choose the best and most expensive brush for finishing, but unless you care for it and clean it, it won't last very long. With proper care, a brush should last for many years.

Before using a brush, whether for the first time or after it's been stored for a while, whack the bristle against your palm or on the edge of a table to dislodge any debris or loose bristle. Next, dip the brush all the way up to the ferrule in the solvent for the particular finish you're using—mineral spirits for varnishes and oils, alcohol for shellac, lacquer thinner for lacquer, and water for water-based materials. This step coats the deepest part of the bristle near the ferrule with solvent so they're easier to clean later. Wipe off the excess solvent with a clean, lint-free cloth and then begin finishing. During finishing, never dip the brush into finishing material all the way up to the ferrule or the brush will be hard to clean.

After you're done finishing, brush any residual finish onto a scrap piece of wood or newspaper. Rinse the brush in the clean-up solvent and then, standing over a sink, squirt a generous amount of dishwashing soap onto the bristle. Work the soap into a lather with some warm water, and using the palm of your hand, swirl the bristle vigorously to work the lather up into the reservoir. Bend the bristle back to force out the finish near the base at the ferrule. Repeat this process until the bristle no longer feel slick or slimy.

Rinse well with water and spin the water out by twirling the handle between your palms. Comb through the bristle with a brush to straighten them. Wrap the bristle carefully in a paper towel to keep the profile intact, then lay the brush flat to dry. For small brushes and red sable touch-up brushes, you can dip the bristle in shellac to "lock" them in shape. To dissolve the shellac and free up the bristle for use, soak the brush in alcohol.

If a brush hardens with an oil- or water-based finish, you may be able to rescue it by soaking it in a nonmethylene chloride–based stripper for several hours, then wire-brushing it near the heel to break up and dislodge residual finish.

ROLLERS, PADS, AND FOAM BRUSHES

Paint rollers—the type used to apply paint to walls—can be used to apply finishes, but they rarely do a good job. They're better suited to thick paint and will drip when used for thinner materials like stains. I tried to use one to stain paneling in a large room and got more stain on the floor and my arms than on the wood. If you do use a roller, get one with as short a nap as possible.

Paint pads are much better suited for applying finishing products. They are in essence a brush with very short bristle. They're great for floors, and perform well with water-based products.

Foam brushes have become a favorite of some finishers. Though not really a brush or a pad, they're more like a piece of sponge that holds and dispenses finishes. They are popular for use with water-based finishes that typically foam or bubble when applied with a brush or pad. They can't be used with strong solvent finishes like lacquer or shellac, and they work best on flat surfaces. Though low in cost, foam brushes work well only once or twice, so I don't use them much.

RAGS AND CLOTHS

Rags and cloths are the workhorse applicators of finishing, yet most people don't really think about which ones are best to use. These applicators can range from the mundane paper towel to a more sophisticated pad applicator for shellac. Your choice should depend on the type of product you're applying.

General application of stains, oil finishes, and other products where most of the excess is wiped off can be done with paper towels, disposable rags, or any other absorbent cloth. Natural-cloth fibers like cotton and wool work best, and they should be clean and bleached white so they are free from dyes. If you do a lot of finishing, look in the Yellow Pages under textiles for a place to buy cotton T-shirt material in bulk. You can find synthetic heavy-duty paper-type towels in bulk, as well as boxes of rags, at hardware and paint stores.

For critical finishing tasks like the application of wiping varnishes or padding shellac, the cloth has to be clean, absorbent, and as lint-free as possible. For wiping varnishes there is nothing better than old cotton or linen tablecloths,

WORKING SMART

If you can't find lint-free cloth to apply finishes, you can "de-lint" new fabric. Dunk it in a tub of warm water, then put it in the clothes dryer with a lint trap. One cycle is generally sufficient.

T-shirts, socks, or other cotton garments. The repeated washing and drying of these items removes all of the lint, which would be trapped in the finish as you applied it. But I've even used paper towels with good success. Using old cotton clothes is also a great way to relieve men of the undergarments and socks that they've formed an intimate attachment to. For padding shellac, tightly woven cheesecloth is my first choice, though wool and cotton can also be used. Some retailers carry padding cloth or "trace" cloth for this purpose.

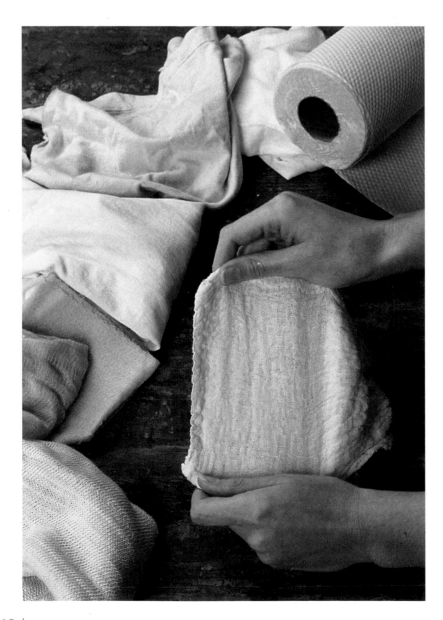

Any soft, clean, and absorbent cloth can be used for finishing tasks as long as it's not synthetic.

SPRAY EQUIPMENT

Of all the tools available, a spray system lays down material the fastest. It works not only on flat, level surfaces, but also on hard-to-finish items like chairs. Years ago, spraying was the domain of professional finishers and backyard auto-painters, but with the introduction of newer, nonflammable finishing products and inexpensive spray rigs, spraying has become a viable choice for woodworkers of all skill levels.

It's worth taking the time to learn a bit about the different types of spray systems and gun designs. Not only will this knowledge help you to choose the best design for your use, but knowing how your gun works will improve your technique and make cleaning and maintaining it much easier.

Spray Gun Anatomy

There are many different types of spray systems available, but they are all based on the same general idea. Liquid finish is atomized into tiny droplets when it's mixed with air from a pressurized air source. The liquid/air mixture is directed onto the wood by a gun that controls the way in which the liquid is atomized. When the atomized finish hits the wood, it flows back together to form a continuous film. Every spray gun works on this same basic principle.

A complete spray gun system isn't all that different in principle from an aerosol spray can. The valve at the top of the can is like the gun—when you depress it, it allows pressurized fluid in the can to flow up through a siphon tube. As the fluid

You can purchase an entire spray system or add a gun to a compressor. From top left to right: a medium-priced three-stage turbine with gun, a high-pressure gun attached to a compressor (below), and a low-end turbine with gun.

leaves the tip of the nozzle, it is broken up into hundreds of tiny little droplets.

Most spray guns follow the same general design. Air is forced into the gun through the air inlet. The pressure of the air is controlled by a regulator either on the compressor or positioned just before the gun; some guns have a set, nonadjustable pressure from a turbine. The amount of air is controlled by the air-adjustment

The Pros and Cons of Spraying

PROS

- **Speed and efficiency** You can lay down material faster with a spray gun than with any other tool.
- **Uniformity** A spray gun delivers a thin, uniform coating, resulting in a more even finish that requires less work to rub out.
- **Creativity and control** Spraying allows you to lay down subtle coloration where you want it, such as that used with toning and shading techniques.
- **Wider latitude in finishes** You can spray virtually any liquid finish, from fast-drying lacquers specifically designed for spraying to slow-drying oil-based varnishes. (Brushes and rags can't be used to apply products designed for spraying.)

CONS

- **Wasted material** Only a portion of the finishing material ends up on the wood. Brushes and cloths apply all the material.
- **Overspray** Spraying produces overspray, which must be exhausted from the workplace.
- **Expense** Spray equipment is more costly than brushes and cloths.

Basic Spray Gun Anatomy

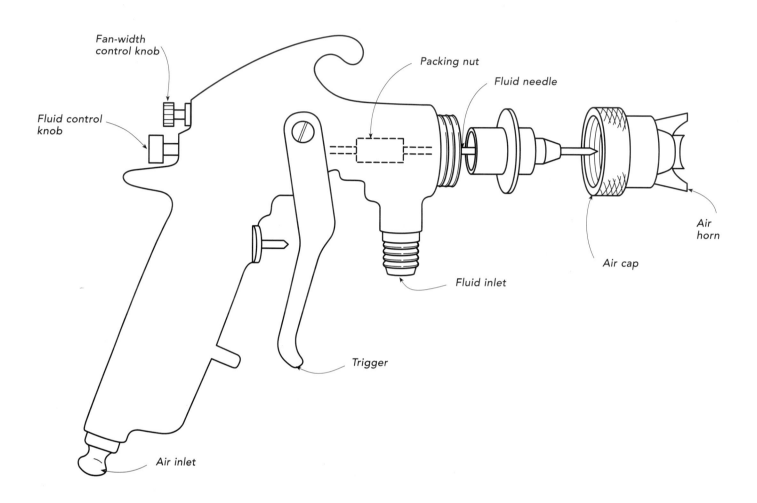

Fan-width
control knob

Packing nut

Fluid needle

Fluid control
knob

Air
horn

Air cap

Fluid inlet

Trigger

Air inlet

knob (which is omitted in some high-volume, low-pressure, or HVLP, guns). Fluid enters through the fluid inlet and travels through the fluid nozzle into the air nozzle, where it is mixed with air to atomize the fluid. The atomized pattern is controlled by air passing through the small holes in the air horn.

There are actually very few controls on a spray gun. Most of the steps involved for using any spray system involve thinning the finish to the correct viscosity and selecting the correct nozzle/valve for the finish you're spraying and then using proper techniques.

Viscosity control Most finishes are too thick to be sprayed, so you must thin the material with the appropriate solvent. Some materials need a lot of solvent (as much as 50%) to adequately atomize them, while others need very little or none at all. Most turbine systems sold to novice finishers have a chart and a device called a viscosity drip cup for determining finish viscosity. Having the correct viscosity prevents problems like orange peel, a pebbly look to the finish after it has dried.

Needles, nozzles, and air caps Needles and nozzles are provided with most systems and are matched to the type of finish being sprayed. Generally, smaller-aperture fluid nozzles are used with clear lacquers, while larger-aperture nozzles are used with oil varnishes and paints. These are usually sold with a matching air cap.

Gun controls Most quality guns have two threaded knobs (screws) at the back to control the rate at which the finish is released and the amount of air that's released. Turning the fluid control knob simply increases or decreases the amount of finish traveling through the gun. The results range from a light mist coat to a heavier full wet coat of finish material. The air control knob only affects the pattern of spray—from small and round to a wide fan-shaped pattern. Most HVLP turbine systems have a set flow of air that can't be regulated, but compressor drive systems can be regulated at the compressor or by a valve installed near the gun. For guns that do not have a pattern control knob at the back, the pattern is controlled by turning the air cap.

Variations There are, of course, variations on the basic anatomy. These variations affect how the finish is delivered to the gun (the feed) and the way in which the air supply is handled.

Gravity feed Fluid sits in a cup at the top of the gun and enters the body of the gun through the force of gravity. This design is efficient but takes getting used to.

Siphon feed Finish is sucked up into the body of the gun by air flowing rapidly through a passage within the body of the gun. You can recognize a siphon-feed gun by the hole at the top of its lid that draws in air. This hole must be kept clean.

Pressure feed Pressure is fed into the cup, pressurizing the contents and forcing it up the tube. This is the same design as an

From left to right: a small touch-up and detailing gun, a 1-quart production gun, and a gravity-feed gun.

aerosol can. Pressure-feed guns have a small tube that runs from the body into the top of the cup lid. This tube must be kept clean, and a small one-way check valve is usually installed on the tube.

In addition to the variations in the feed of spray guns, there are also variations in their air supply. The variations appear as bleeder and nonbleeder guns. Bleeder guns are part of most turbine systems. They have a nonadjustable supply of air that is constantly moving through the gun once the turbine is on. This constant air flow can be annoying because it kicks up debris around the spray area. However, it can be used to clean dust off the surface before spraying.

In nonbleeder guns, which can be found on higher-priced turbine systems, the air passes through the gun only when the trigger is engaged. You can recognize a nonbleeder gun by the presence of a small plunger right behind the trigger. This design is much better than that of a bleeder gun, and lightly depressing the trigger produces enough air to dust off the surface to be sprayed without discharging any finish.

Siphon-Feed vs. Pressure-Feed Cups

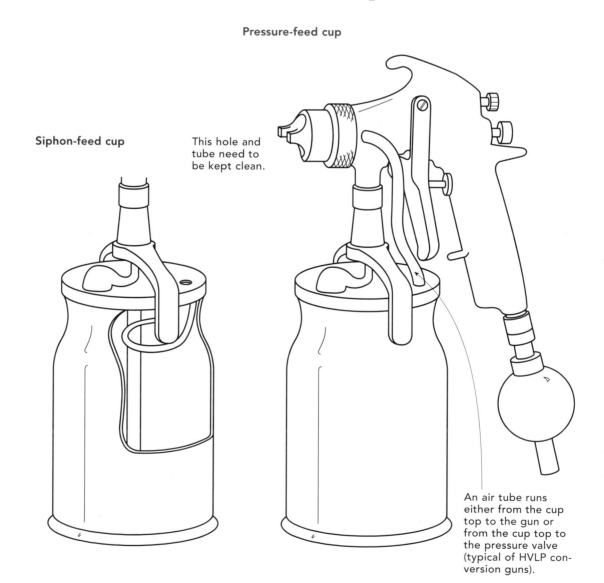

Pressure-feed cup

Siphon-feed cup

This hole and tube need to be kept clean.

An air tube runs either from the cup top to the gun or from the cup top to the pressure valve (typical of HVLP conversion guns).

Using Spray Systems

There are several steps to follow when using any spray system.

1. Thin the material to be sprayed so that your particular set-up can spray it.
2. Match the proper nozzle/valve combination to the finish you're spraying.
3. Adjust the controls on the gun and compressor (if possible) for optimum spraying efficiency and finish quality.
4. Use proper techniques for spraying.
5. Properly clean and maintain the gun after using.

Types of Guns

There are two basic types of guns available for spraying: conventional high pressure guns and newer HVLP (high-volume, low-pressure) guns. Both systems apply finish, but there are some basic design differences.

Conventional guns Conventional guns use the high pressure from a compressor to blast the finish onto the surface of the wood. These guns are capable of atomizing finishing materials well, which translates into smooth flowout and leveling of clear finishes as well as paint. They deliver excellent results but at a sacrifice of transfer efficiency. Only about a third of the finish sprayed ends up on the wood.

HVLP guns These relatively new guns were designed to improve transfer efficiency so less material is wasted and released into the atmosphere. Many of the solvents used in finishing products contribute to poor air quality, so HVLP systems have been adopted by many high-volume shops and are mandated by many state governments. In these systems, air is delivered at a higher volume but with less pressure so that less finish bounces off the workpiece and into the air. A typical HVLP system will at least double the transfer efficiency of a conventional system, and sometimes triple it.

HVLP guns can run off of two different sources: a turbine that is usually sold with the gun as a complete unit or an HVLP conversion gun that operates off of a conventional compressor. The conversion gun converts the continuous high pressure from a compressor to a lower pressure at the very end of the gun. Both power sources have the same effect—reduced overspray and bounce back of the finish. Until recently, conversion guns needed a rather large compressor to operate, but there are now many guns that will operate off of smaller compressors (typically 1 hp to 2 hp).

If you don't own a compressor I recommend an HVLP turbine-driven system. These systems are available in a range of prices. The inexpensive systems are comprised of smaller turbines and basic guns. These systems will spray most products but are incapable of delivering a fine, smooth finish with clear varnishes and lacquers, particularly the water-based ones. To get the best finish, I recommend at least a three-stage turbine to power the system.

This portable spray booth can be easily set up in a garage or basement.

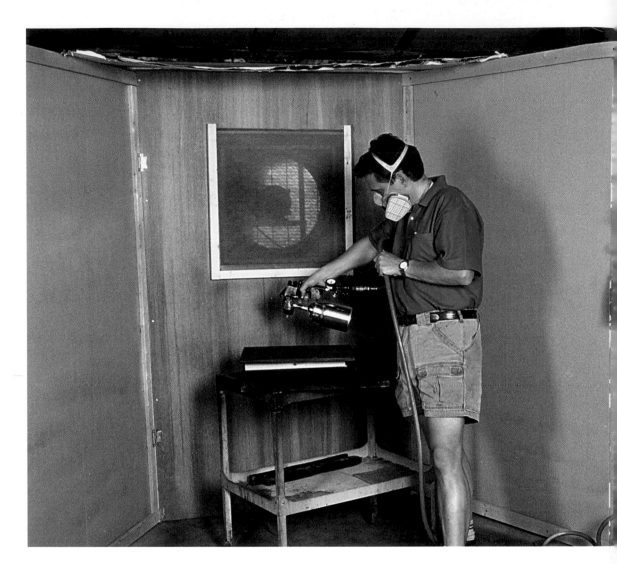

Spray Safely

To protect yourself from the solvents released during spraying, take precautions when spraying any finishing product. The best protection is a cartridge-style organic vapor respirator. These respirators feature cartridges that should replaced when you can smell the finish through the mask. You can find them at good paint stores, or look in the Yellow Pages under Safety Equipment for other locations.

Overspray in the air can create other problems, too. The build-up of atomized finish and solvent can be very dangerous if the solvent is flammable. Spraying in an enclosed space without proper ventilation is never recommended and can lead to a fire or an explosion. Here are some options for safe spraying:

- Spray outdoors.
- Spray within a well-ventilated area such as a screened-in porch. This is better than working directly outdoors because the piece you're finishing will be protected from debris and from direct sunlight, which impedes proper drying of finishes.
- Spray in an enclosed area, and exhaust the fumes with a fan.
- Spray in a spray booth specially designed to exhaust fumes, like those professional finishers use.

An explosion-proof motor and fittings exhaust flammable vapors from the spray booth. A bracket attached to the side panel keeps the assembly from tipping over.

Professional spray booths work the best, but they are quite costly and take up a large amount of space. I designed and use a smaller version that can be built for much less, can be set up easily in a garage or other room with a large door or window, and can be taken down and stored out of the way to conserve space (see Spray Booth Construction on pp. 26-27).

The heart of the system is an explosion-proof motor and nonsparking fan (16 in. is best), which is available as a complete unit (see Resources on p. 229). I always recommend an explosion-proof motor, even if you'll be spraying only nonflammable, water-based finishes. Fine dust that accu-mulates around the discharge opening and motor is a potential source of ignition.

The fan is mounted in a torsion-box-style assembly with furnace filters over it. Two "wings" constructed from rigid ure-thane insulation sheathing are attached to each side of the fan "wall," shown in the photo on the facing page. (You should check with a local electrical supply compa-ny for the proper electrical connections for the fan.) The whole assembly is set up with the back of the fan facing outside. A piece of cardboard or rigid insulation placed over the top significantly improves the efficien-cy of the booth.

Spray Booth Construction

To construct a spray booth that you can use at home, follow these steps. Even though this will help in exhausting harmful and flammable vapors, you still need to exercise caution. Do not exhaust onto sources of ignition, and be mindful of any restrictions that may apply to residential locations.

1. Draw the outline of the fan housing on the ½-in. and ¼-in. plywood and cut the opening for the fan in both pieces with a jigsaw.
2. Bolt the fan housing to the ½-in. plywood using 4 carriage bolts.
3. Cut the 1½-in. x 2-in. spacers from 2x4 studs and attach to ½-in. plywood as shown.

Booth dimensions

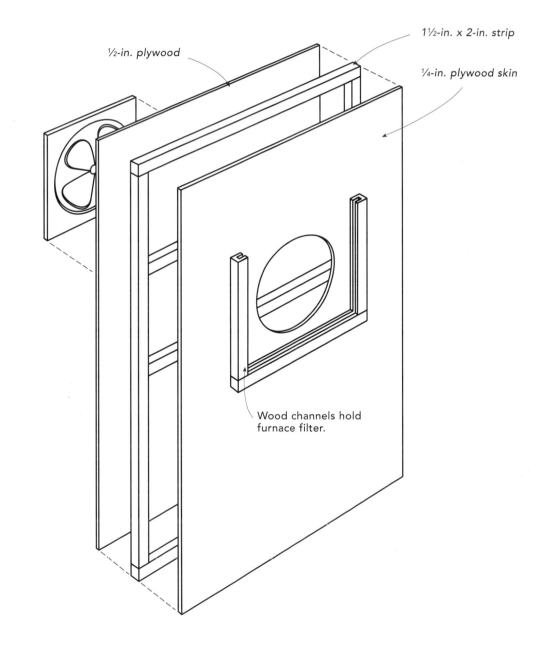

½-in. plywood

1½-in. x 2-in. strip

¼-in. plywood skin

Wood channels hold furnace filter.

4. Attach the ¼-in. plywood skin with screws over the spacers, aligning the hole over the fan opening.

5. Construct the back brace and attach it to the back using hinges.

6. Set the assembly upright and adjust the back brace so that the unit is vertical, then attach a rope to the back brace and back of the unit.

7. Attach the wings (stiffened with 1x3 furring strips) to the sides of the center assembly using hinges.

Overall view of booth

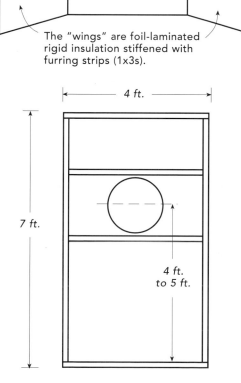

16-in. fan with explosion-proof motor

Furnace filter

The "wings" are foil-laminated rigid insulation stiffened with furring strips (1x3s).

4 ft.

7 ft.

4 ft. to 5 ft.

Back view

The fan

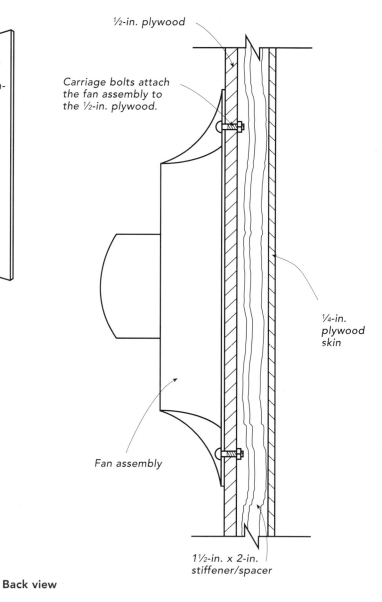

½-in. plywood

Carriage bolts attach the fan assembly to the ½-in. plywood.

¼-in. plywood skin

Fan assembly

1½-in. x 2-in. stiffener/spacer

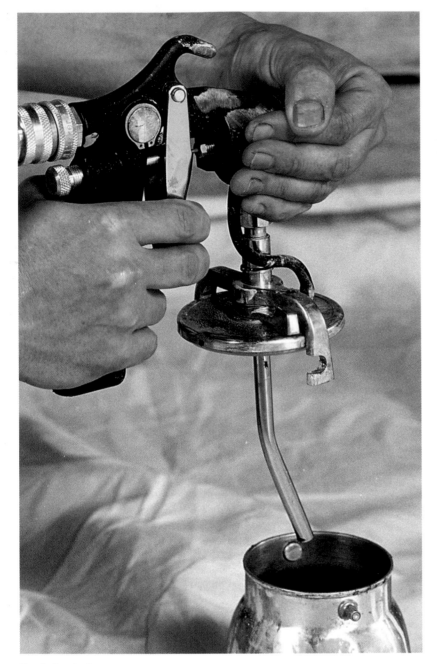

Back-flush the gun by holding your hand over the air cap and depressing the trigger.

Using a wrench, remove the fluid nozzle from the gun.

Cleaning and Maintaining the Gun

Unless you follow a systematic, diligent cleaning routine after using your gun, it will not operate properly the next time. After using the gun, remove it from the cup assembly, hold your hand over the air cap, and depress the trigger (shown above). This procedure "back-flushes" the gun, pushing the finish from inside the gun out into the cup. Pour the finish back into its container and then fill the cup halfway with solvent and spray it (you can spray it into a jar or can to retrieve it) to clean the inside of the gun, then repeat the back-flushing.

Remove the air cap assembly, and then use a wrench to remove the fluid nozzle from the gun (shown above). Remove the fluid needle and place all of the parts into a

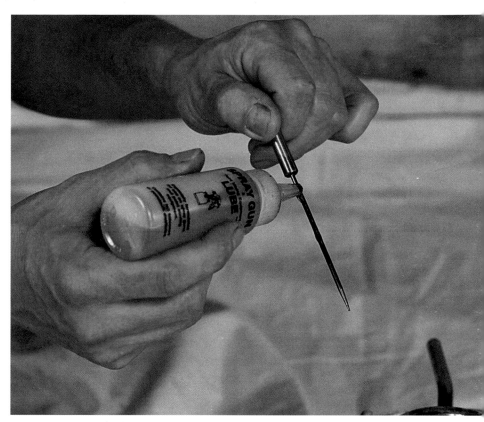

Lubricate the fluid needle before you put the gun back together.

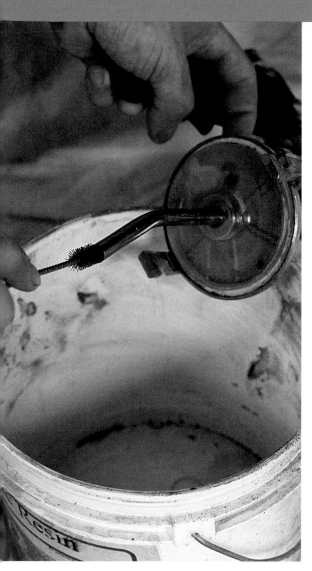

Clean the inside of the siphon tube with a wire brush.

jar of solvent. Check with the manufacturer to be sure that any plastic parts can tolerate the solvent you're using.

Using a small round wire brush, clean the inside of the siphon tube (shown above). Wipe the plastic gasket and the inside of the cup with solvent. After the parts you've soaked are clean, reinstall them in reverse order and place a few drops of spray-gun lube or petroleum jelly on the fluid needle and on all threaded parts like the fluid nozzle and air cap (shown above right).

If finish starts leaking out around the trigger, the packing nut may need to be tightened or replaced. If the gun sputters or doesn't spray a fine mist, clean the air intake hole and tube on siphon-feed guns. On pressure-feed guns, clean the nozzle and/or check valve that goes from the cup lid to the gun.

Parts wear periodically and many manufacturers sell "rebuild kits" to replace all the parts with the highest wear and tear at once. These include the packing nut and most gaskets and seals.

THE RIGHT STUFF

Hardware and paint stores carry countless varieties of finishing products. Consider the many types of varnishes, shellacs, and lacquers—both solvent based and water based—or the numerous varieties of oil finishes, Danish oils, and stains. Of course, there are related materials as well, like putties, waxes, and polishes. It's no wonder many people walk away confused. Fortunately, the products can be narrowed down into groups that work in similar ways. Once you know the general properties for each group, you'll be able to make better decisions about which materials to use for your project.

WOOD PUTTIES AND FILLERS

Cracks, splits, nail holes, knots, and other defects that can't be sanded or removed by steaming (see chapter 3, beginning on p. 64) have to be filled if you want to disguise them or you want a smooth finish. There are two ways to deal with these problems: fill in the area with wood or use some type of filler. I always try to fill the area with wood if it's possible. Wood provides a better-looking repair on long splits, cracks, and knots, and it is stronger and lasts longer than any type of putty. Also, a wood patch will change color at the same rate as the rest of the wood. Fillers don't change color the way that wood does, particularly unstained wood, so a visible patch will appear later.

These fillers should not be confused with paste wood filler, which is used to fill the pores of open-grained woods, knotholes, and dents. Products for filling holes and dents are known by a few names—wood filler, wood putty, and wood dough. The names are used interchangeably for the most part, although some types are generally associated with one term (I'll use the term wood putty, which is most commonly heard). Wood putty is available in five forms:

- Premixed and ready to use
- A powder that needs to be mixed with water before application
- A two-part product that is mixed right before application
- A filler that you make yourself from glue and sawdust
- Wax filler sticks

All forms of putty are based on the same general formulation of bulking agent, binder, and sometimes color. Ideally, putty should not shrink (or should shrink very little), should dry hard, and should be undetectable when finished. Unfortunately, ideal putties do not exist. Almost all putties shrink, and some tweaking of the putty is necessary to make it blend in with the wood after it has been finished. I have never found a putty that stained the same color as the wood with all types of stains.

Premixed Putties

All premixed putties contain a bulking agent, such as chalk or sawdust, in a binder, such as linseed oil, nitrocellulose lacquer, or water-based acrylic. The majority of these ready-to-use putties are water based or solvent based. You can buy putties precolored, or you can mix your own color. Precolored putties have an added pigment and are sold as a wood-tone color like maple or walnut. Color can be added to any putty with dry pigments or with a colorant compatible with the binder/carrier. Artist's colors, Japan colors, and UTCs (universal tinting colorants) can all be used to color putty. I prefer to use dry pigments because they do not affect the drying time of the putty and do not thin it. When you thin putty, it shrinks more as it dries.

Water-based putties are the most common type. They're easy to use and clean up with water. Some shrink more than others, but they are easy to sand when they're dry. Once dry or cured, they will not redissolve in the carrier (water).

Solvent-based putties dry extremely fast: You can't fuss with them too much after applying them. They dry out quickly in the can, but can be redissolved with acetone or lacquer thinner.

Putty Powders

These putties are sold as a powder that's mixed with water. The powders are plaster-like compounds that are usually mixed with sawdust. Putty powders have an indefinite shelf life in powdered form, but once mixed, they have to be used or discarded. They dry very hard. Although popular in the past, today they are being replaced by the premixed water-based putties.

Two-Part Fillers

Two-part fillers are either epoxy based or polyester based. These fillers are great for filling large cracks and knots in wood. They dry extremely fast, they do not shrink when dry, they can be used for structural repairs, and they sand very easily. They can be cut, drilled, and carved easily as well. Once cured, they do not soften or redissolve, which is a benefit when using finishing materials that would soften other putties.

Glue-and-Sawdust Fillers

Sawdust can be mixed with various glues to use as a filler. Any type of glue works—white or yellow glue, hide glue, or epoxy. Cyanoacrylate glue (also known by the brand name Super Glue) can be used, but it can't be mixed with the sawdust before application.

If you plan on staining the wood, use hide glue because it accepts stains well. Epoxy and PVA glues (white and yellow) do not accept stain well. Epoxy shrinks much less than PVA and hide glue, though, because it has no carrier to evaporate. Most epoxy does not sand well, but if you increase the resin to hardener ratio (more resin than hardener), it will dry harder and sand better. By using sawdust from the wood you're using, a better match is possible.

Wax Filler Sticks

Wax sticks are similar to crayons except they're a little softer. They are composed of wax, pigment, and sometimes a mineral oil to make the stick softer and easier to work with. While their most common use is repairing dings, dents, and other mishaps on finished wood, I find them the best for filling nail holes. They are sold in a wide variety of colors. Because they are typically used after stain or finish has been applied, you can find the color that is an exact match to the finished wood. The downside is that they don't dry hard.

STAINS

When you stain wood, you color it without obscuring the grain. This basic definition differentiates a stain from a paint, which colors wood and covers up the grain. There are two types of colorant used in stains— dyes and pigments—and three types of stains commonly used on wood—pigment

Paint and stains are formulated from the same product. Red paint (bottom) obscures and covers up wood grain. The same paint thinned with mineral spirits functions as a stain (top) because the grain is visible.

Pigment stains are made from pigment, a binder, and a carrier. They can be water based or solvent based, liquid or gel. Some pigment is visible on the bottom of the mixing stick.

based, dye based, or a combination of the two. The type of colorant used to make the stain has a big influence on how it works and the effect it creates on the wood.

Pigment Stains

Pigment stains are made by mixing a pigment, which is a dry, inert, colored powder, with a liquid vehicle. The vehicle is composed of a binder to make the pigment stick to the wood surface and a thinner or carrier that's compatible with the binder. Because pigments are inert, they do not dissolve in the vehicle.

Historically, pigments were simply powdered, colored products that were readily available—burnt charcoal, red and yellow fine clays, and sometimes pulverized colored rocks and stones. While some of these are still used, many pigments are now man-made, and a wood tone may contain several different pigment colors. The vehicles used in stains today may be oil based, water based, or solvent based. A

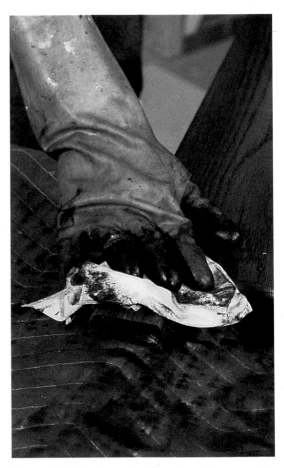

Pigment stains are wiped on, then the excess is wiped off. When used on open-pore woods, like the oak in this photo, the pores stain darker, adding contrast.

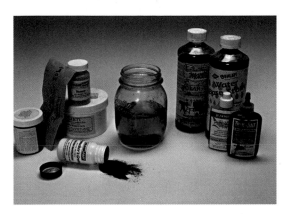

Dye stains are available as dry powders that you dissolve in the appropriate solvent. Premixed versions are also available as ready-to-use liquids or as concentrates.

Dyes are chemical powders that dissolve in their carrier. Here a water-soluble dye is being dissolved in a jar of hot water.

thickening agent may also be added to make the stain into a gel.

Despite the wide variety of pigments, they all color wood in the same way. Most pigment particles are large enough to see with the naked eye or with a magnifying glass. When a pigment stain is applied to the surface of wood and wiped off, the pigment collects in crevices, pores, and any cavity larger than the size of the pigment particles. Since the distribution and size of all these cavities is what determines the "character" of various woods, pigment stain accentuates the differences between woods.

What this means is that open-grained woods, like oak and mahogany, collect more pigment in the grain cavities and less in the denser flat grain between them. Soft and porous woods without large pores, like pine and poplar, stain evenly. Very dense woods, like maple, don't have many spaces for the pigment to lodge in, so the pigment stain will be much lighter.

Dye Stains

Dye-based stains color wood, too, but because dye is so physically and chemically different from pigment, it colors wood dif-

ferently. Dyes are colored powders, but unlike pigment, which is inert, dyes dissolve in their carrier. If you think of dye as colored table salt dissolved in water, you'll be on the right track. Because the color is dissolved into zillions of tiny colored particles, it's able to penetrate the entire wood surface very evenly and deeply. And because the particles are very small, they tend to transmit light, allowing grain and figure to show.

Dyes are available in different forms: premixed (either liquid or gel) or powdered, which has to be dissolved in the specified carrier (water, alcohol, or oil).

WORKING SMART

To prevent splotching on splotch-prone wood, spray on the stain and don't wipe it. It will lay on top of the wood, so it penetrates less but more evenly. Fast-drying stains like non-grain-raising or alcohol-soluble dyes work best. Water-based dyes can be used if you lightly mist them on.

Controlling Stain

A simple fact in finishing is that stains don't always color evenly when applied to certain woods. Problem woods are most softwoods like pine and fir and hardwoods like birch, cherry, and poplar. These woods have areas of different density and chemical makeup, and some stains penetrate those areas differently than the rest of the wood. The splotchy effect caused by this uneven penetration is called blotching. To make the wood stain evenly, you need to control the penetration of the stain. There are several ways to do this.

• **Switch to water-based stain** Oil- and solvent-soluble dye and pigment stains tend to splotch the worst. In some situations, switching to a different product, like a water-soluble dye, will create a less splotchy appearance.

• **Use gel stains** Both dye- and pigment-based gel stains stay near the surface, so they tend to color more uniformly.

• **Use washcoating** Washcoating is a thin coat of finish (like oil, shellac, or lacquer) or slow-evaporating solvent that keeps the stain at the surface. The latter is sold as stain controller or conditioner. The stain conditioner sold in paint stores is simple to make yourself. Mix 1 part boiled linseed oil (or an oil finish) with 9 parts mineral spirits. Apply this liberally to the surface of the wood, then apply the oil stain while the conditioner is still wet.

Of the above remedies, washcoating is the most foolproof method. But because woods vary so much in density and composition, you should get into the habit of practicing on offcuts from the project you'll be working on. A little bit of extra time experimenting will pay off when it comes time to finish the real thing.

Because dye particles are so small, they attach themselves to the wood at a molecular level and do not require a binder. One drawback to dyes is that they can only be used for interior applications, because they are not as lightfast (resistant to fading caused by exposure to light) as pigment stains.

Combination Stains

Manufacturers are well aware of the differences between pigment and dye. In an attempt to combine the effects of both, they make stains that contain both dye and pigment. These products combine the even coloration of a dye with the pore enhancement of pigment.

The effects of different stains are shown on the same wood. Clockwise from top left: unstained oak, pigment stain on oak, pigment/dye combination stain, dye stain.

Dyes vs. Pigments

DYE STAINS

- Achieve, bold, vivid colors without obscuring the grain
- Deposit color evenly over the wood surface
- Allow color to penetrate deeper into the wood surface than pigment stains

PIGMENT STAINS

- Accentuate surface texture on woods with distinct pores
- Are more lightfast than dye stains
- Dry hard and cannot be redissolved by a finish when oil is used as the binder

BLEACHES

Bleaches don't actually remove color or a stain—they change it so that it no longer appears colored. They work by altering the chemistry of the substance that's colored, either disrupting its molecular structure or converting it to a different substance that's colorless.

Bleaches have a number of finishing uses. They can lighten a wood's natural color, "remove" certain stains, and fix some problems that arise in the finishing process. There are three types of bleach that you can use, and it's important to select the correct one because not all bleaches will work in all situations.

Alkali/peroxide bleaches are commonly sold in paint and hardware stores as two-part liquids. These parts are denoted as A

Bleaches lighten the color of wood. Here, a two-part bleach is used to lighten the color of a cherry mirror.

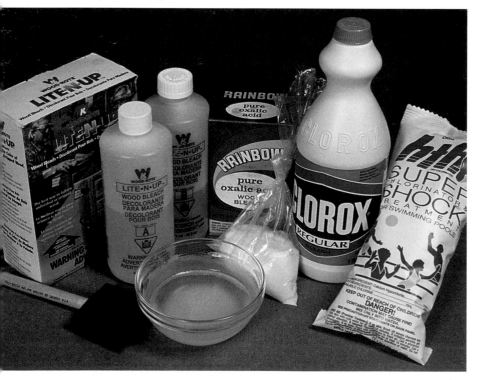

Three types of bleaches are used in finishing. From left to right: two-part bleaches, oxalic acid, and chlorine bleach (laundry bleach and swimming pool shock treatment).

and B, so the bleaches are also known as A/B bleaches. Two-part bleaches remove a wood's natural coloring and establish an even, off-white neutral base, which may be desirable in certain finishes. They can also be used to even out sapwood-heartwood differences. They tend to rob wood of its depth and luster, though, so they should be used with discretion.

Chlorine bleaches are used to "remove" dye stains and some other stains, like grape juice and tea, on bare wood. Chlorine is the active ingredient in laundry bleach. While laundry bleach can be used, it is weak so several applications may be necessary. A stronger and faster acting bleach can be made from swimming pool bleach.

Oxalic acid's greatest strength is its selectivity. It cleans up iron-based stains (like those that appear around nails), black water stains, and other mishaps without significantly altering the natural color of

WHICH BLEACH TO USE

NEED	BLEACH	HOW TO NEUTRALIZE AFTER USE
Lighten up or remove natural color of wood	Two-part bleach	Water then white vinegar (1 part vinegar to 2 parts water)
Remove dye stains	Chlorine bleach	2 to 3 applications of distilled water
Remove iron stains	Oxalic acid	2 applications of distilled water followed by baking soda dissolved in water*
Lighten up stripped wood	Oxalic acid	2 applications of distilled water followed by baking soda dissolved in water*
Remove water stains	Oxalic acid	2 applications of distilled water followed by baking soda dissolved in water*

*Dissolve 2 tablespoons of baking soda in a half pint of hot water.

WORKING SMART

Laundry bleach isn't very strong and loses its effectiveness sitting in a bottle, so several applications are often needed. Instead, try a small bag of shock treatment, which is used for swimming pools. Mix the bag's contents with water to create a concentrated bleach that works with fewer applications. The treatment can be purchased at a swimming-pool supply store.

the wood. Oxalic acid also mitigates the dark appearance of stripped and weathered wood, which is why you find it in deck cleaners and brighteners. Oxalic acid is usually purchased as a dry powder or crystals that are mixed with water and then applied to the wood.

The various effects of different bleaches are illustrated. From left: a two-part bleach lightens the dark color of walnut, oxalic acid removes a black water ring from oak, and chlorine bleach removes a dye stain.

Pros and Cons of Paste Wood Fillers

OIL-BASED FILLERS

Pros

- Can be used on bare wood and after a sealer coat
- Easy to apply and wipe off
- Wide availability

Cons

- Need a long time to dry
- Do not sand well
- Not compatible with some finishes

WATER-BASED FILLERS

Pros

- Can be sanded easily
- Can be top-coated after 24 hours
- Can be top-coated with any finish
- Can be stained after drying
- Easy to clean up

Cons

- Sometimes develops a chalky appearance
- Can't be used after sealer coat
- Tricky to use on large areas because it dries fast

PASTE WOOD FILLERS

All wood has a unique surface texture that is characteristic of its species. What determines this surface texture is the size and distribution of pores, which are the vessels that conduct sap when the tree is living. When wood is cut into lumber these vessels are cut at an angle, which creates open channels distributed across the surface of the wood. Wood with small, indistinct pores like maple and cherry are called close-grained. Other woods like oak, ash, mahogany, and walnut are called open-grained.

Some finishing treatments call for a glassy-smooth, uninterrupted surface appearance to the wood once the finish has been applied and dried. This is easy to achieve on close-grained woods because the finish can fill the small pores and and still flow out smoothly over the surface of the wood. On open-grained woods, a finish flows into the pores and dries to an exact duplicate of the surface texture of the wood. The result is called an open-pore finish.

Repeated applications of finish will eventually fill the pores of open-grained wood enough to get a flat surface when the finish is level-sanded. However, this process is time-consuming and ineffective in the long run, because most finishes shrink over time and the pore structure of the wood eventually reasserts itself. Instead, use a product called paste wood filler, which is somewhat like the filler used for holes and dents, but is modified so that it can fill all the tiny pore cavities on the wood surface. Actually, paste wood fillers don't completely fill the cavity of a wood pore—at best they bulk it up by about 75%. That fills the pores high enough, though, so that when several subsequent coats of finish are applied they can be level-sanded to a flat surface. Filling the pores in this manner creates a filled-pore, or "piano," finish.

Wood Pores

The pores of wood are straw-like vessels that conduct sap when the tree is alive. When cut into lumber, the pores are sliced open, creating an open cavity.

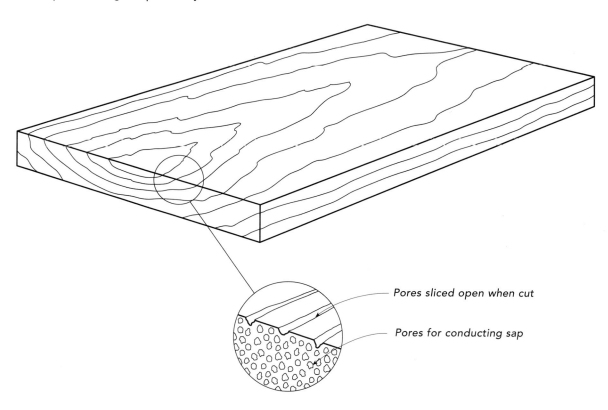

Pores sliced open when cut

Pores for conducting sap

Open-Pore Finish

On open-grained woods, finish will flow into the pores of the wood and follow their shape.

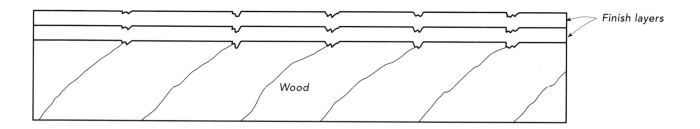

Finish layers

Wood

Paste wood fillers are available as water based (left) or oil based (right). They are either natural or colored.

Natural paste wood fillers dry to a color similar to or lighter than the natural color of the wood (right). Colored fillers dry to a darker color than the color of the wood (left).

Paste wood fillers offer some distinct advantages. The fillers:

• Partially fill the pores of open-grained woods with a nonshrinking material so that finishes can be built up quickly and efficiently.

• Act as a sealer when used on bare wood.

• Can be colored so that the wood and pores are stained at the same time.

• Can be used to add color just to the pores, creating contrast and dramatic effects.

The last point is an important creative advantage, because controlling the color of the pores can have a big influence on the way the finished wood surface appears.

There are two types of paste wood filler: oil based and water based. You can buy the filler as natural, which is the natural color of the ingredients used, or colored with pigment. Natural fillers dry to a putty color so they are best used on unstained or natural-colored woods. Colored fillers add color to the pores, highlighting them against the lighter flat grain in much the same way that a pigment stain does. All filler can be colored with the addition of colorants compatible with their binder.

Water-based fillers are best used on bare wood. Oil-based fillers can be used on bare wood or after a sealer coat—a technique that deposits the color of the paste wood filler just in the pores. This technique is useful in matching a finish (for more on this, see pp. 50-51). In spite of the advantages of water-based fillers, most professionals and large shops still use oil-based fillers because they are easier to use and control.

GLAZES AND TONERS

There's a myth that once a piece of wood has finish on it, you're stuck with the color of the wood. With the exception of making wood appear lighter, there's a great deal you can do to alter the finish without stripping it off the piece. You can change the tone (making it redder or greener), highlight the open grain, add texture, selectively apply color, or add distressing elements, just to name a few options. All of these techniques are done with products called glazes and toners.

Glazes

A glaze is a thin coat of color that is applied between coats of finish. It's usually pigment based. Glazes are similar to pigment stains—in fact pigment stains can be used as glazes—but generally products formulated as glazes dry more slowly and are thicker.

Glazes are always applied over a coat of finish either by spray, a brush, or a rag.

Glazes are pigmented stains that are applied over a finish. They add depth and richness to the piece. Here glaze is wiped on over a dyed and sealed maple top, then the excess wiped off, leaving a thin coat of color.

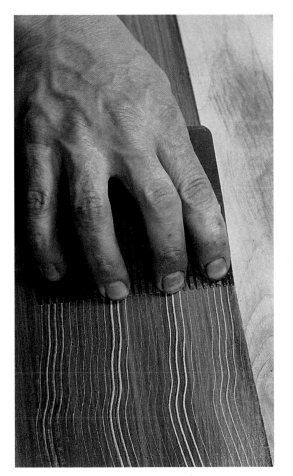

Manipulating glaze with a tool can produce creative effects. Here a graining comb is run across a brown glaze applied over an off-white base coat to simulate oak graining.

Glazes vs. Toners

GLAZES

- Alter the hue (make it redder or greener) or value (make it darker) of a finish
- Add richness and depth to wood
- Highlight pore structure (the same way pigment stains do, except after the wood is sealed)
- Highlight grain and selected areas
- Imitate wood grain or other effects

TONERS

- Alter the hue or value of a finish
- Add richness and depth to wood
- Add color to selected areas, for example to blend sapwood into heartwood or to shade edges darker

How Glaze Works

A glaze is applied over an existing finish. Because the finish acts as a sealer, you can wipe off the glaze once you've applied it without staining the wood.

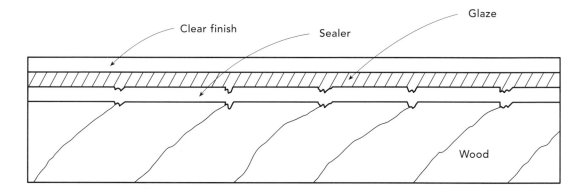

Once the glaze is applied, there are two options: wipe off the glaze, leaving a thin coat of glaze behind, or manipulate the glaze by hand with tools to create surface effects. The advantage to using a glaze is that the previous coat of finish acts as a barrier to prevent the glaze from staining the bare wood. This allows you to easily wipe off all the glaze if you don't like the way it looks or if you make a mistake.

You can buy glaze in a certain color, or you can make it from a premixed, un-colored base. You can also make your own glazes from various raw materials. Like most products, glazes are available in oil-based or water-based versions. Solvent-based glazes don't work because they would dissolve the finish they're applied over.

Toners

Toners are similar to glazes but differ in how they are applied. They are usually applied to the surface of a sealed finish with a spray gun, and they are not wiped off. When toners are applied over an entire surface, the process is generally referred to as toning;

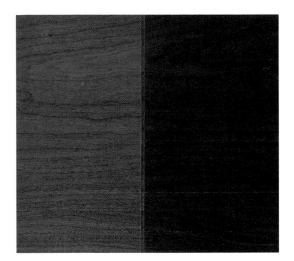

The hue of this light brown cherry panel (left) was changed to a rich reddish brown with a toner (right).

when a toner is applied to selected areas, such as edges, the process is called shading. Toner is applied with a spray gun, so very subtle effects can be accomplished.

A toner is made with either pigment or dye. The difference between the two types of toner is in the colorant used. A pigment-based toner tends to cover up and mask wood grain. A dye-based toner transmits light through it so it adds color without obscuring the grain.

Premixed toners are available, but most finishers choose to mix their own because it allows them to use the same finish they're using on the rest of the project to mix the toner. Premixed toners are available in easy-to-use aerosol form if you lack spray equipment.

FINISHES

The most basic purpose of a finish is to protect wood. If left in its natural state, wood gets dirty, stained, scratched, and dented, and it warps and twists from contact with moisture and heat. Finishes keep wood clean and prevent it from becoming

Choosing the Right Finish

Different finishes have varying degrees of protection, durability, ease of application, repairability, and aesthetics. There is no finish that excels in all of these categories (refer to the chart on pp. 60-61). For example, linseed oil is the easiest finish to apply, it looks good, and it repairs easily, but it is not durable. On the other hand, catalyzed lacquer looks good and is very protective, but it is hard to apply. When you choose a finish you should consider the following.

- How will the item be used? Will it be subjected to a lot of moisture, solvents, food, scrapes, and dents? Will it be primarily a display piece?
- What is your skill level and work area? Does the area stay clean and is it heated and dry?
- What do you want the wood to look like? Do you want a natural look or a thicker finish that accentuates depth?
- Will you be filling the pores?
- What color do you want the finish to impart to the wood? Do you want to alter the color of the wood? Is yellowing an issue? Do you want to minimize the color change of the wood as it ages?
- Will you rub out the finish to the sheen you like?
- Are you sensitive to certain solvents? Is flammability a problem? Are you concerned about the environmental impact of certain finishes?

45

Evaporative Finishes

The mix of resin in the carrier is like strands of cotton.

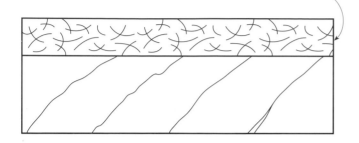

Successive coats of finish remelt the prior coat here.

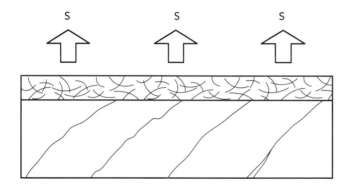

Then the packed strands form a dense clear film.

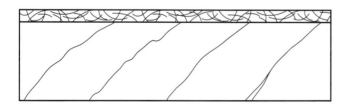

The solvent evaporates, leaving the packed strands together.

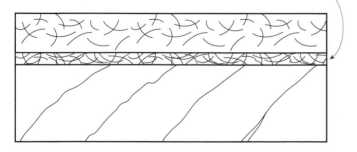

damaged. Natural wood also has a dry, matte appearance that downplays grain and figure. A clear finish applied to wood accentuates grain and figure and gives the surface depth and luster. So finishes not only protect wood, but they also beautify it. Finishes accomplish both of these tasks to varying degrees.

Keep in mind that finishes are generally divided into two distinctly different "types." Evaporative finishes cure to a hard finish by evaporation of the solvents in the finish. Some examples are shellac, lacquer, and water-based finishes. They are thermoplastic, meaning they can be softened by heat. These finishes share the common traits of being damaged by heat, solvents, and water. Reactive finishes cure by reacting with another component, either one outside the can (like air) or one that's added right before application. Some examples are oils, oil-based varnishes, catalyzed lacquers, and conversion varnishes. These finishes are thermosetting, so heat will not soften them. And because they do not dissolve in their original solvent, they are resistant to water and other solvents.

The hundreds of products sold as finishes can be grouped into more manageable categories, which have different general working qualities and degrees of protection.

True Oils

Oil is a general term in finishing, so right away we have to make a distinction between oils that dry (drying oils) and oils that do not dry (nondrying oils). When spread out and exposed to air, drying oils, like linseed oil, will dry to a solid. Nondrying oils, like mineral oil or baby oil, will not dry when spread out in a thin coat. Drying oils protect better than nondrying oils and should be used to finish wood.

The two drying oils most commonly used are linseed oil and tung oil. Throughout the ages, other drying oils have been used, but these are easily available and inexpensive. To distinguish these two products from other finishing products hyped as oil finishes, they are called true oils.

Both linseed and tung oils are penetrating finishes, which means they penetrate into the fibers of the wood and harden within the wood. These are the easiest finishes to apply—they are wiped on, allowed to penetrate the wood, and then the excess is wiped off with a rag. They cannot be built up to a hard, thick film like varnish or lacquer because the film dries too soft.

Linseed oil Linseed oil is derived from the flax plant. The oil is pressed from the plant in much the same way that olive oil is pressed. The remains of the pressing are used as cattle feed.

Linseed oil is available in several forms. In unrefined form, it is called raw linseed oil and is rarely used on wood because it dries very slowly. Our ancestors found that if the oil was boiled, the resulting product was thicker and dried more quickly. Boiled linseed oil made today uses a slightly different process: Chemicals are added to the raw oil to speed up its drying time and oxygen is bubbled through the oil. For wood-finishing purposes, boiled linseed oil should always be used.

Tung oil Tung oil is derived from the nut of the tung tree, which grows in Asia and South America. It is available in a pure, unrefined form or in a heat-treated form called polymerized tung oil. The heat-treating process makes the oil a bit more durable and speeds up the drying rate. It also minimizes the tendency of tung oil to

Reactive Finishes

A reactive finish is a mixture of resin, vehicle, and carrier.

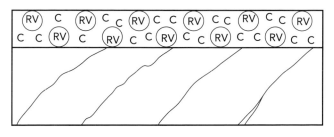

The first drying stage is when the carrier evaporates, leaving the still tacky resin/vehicle (RV).

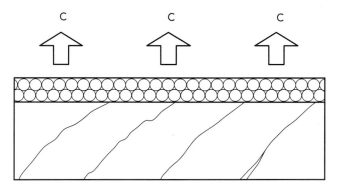

Oxygen from the air reacts with the resin/vehicle, forming a new compound—the dried finish. Think of the dried finish as a series of interconnected molecules.

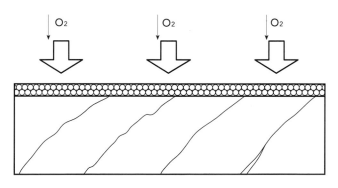

The dried finish is not dissoved by the solvent in the next coat.

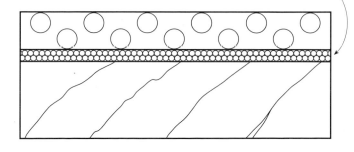

Solvents

The solvents used in finishes and finishing products can be divided into groups with common chemical characteristics. To alleviate some of the confusion, a distinction needs to be made between a true solvent and a thinner or diluent. A solvent is a liquid that dissolves or breaks up the resin in a finish, reducing it to a liquid state. A thinner or diluent is simply a liquid that reduces the viscosity of paint or varnish but is not a solvent for the resin. Let's look at nitrocellulose lacquer as an example. Its resin dissolves in butyl acetate and methyl ethyl ketone, but toluene and alcohol are added to the dissolved lacquer afterward as a thinner. These two thinners cannot dissolve the resin, but they are compatible with the mixture.

It's important that you have at least a basic working knowledge of how different solvents interact with the resins in finishes. These interactions determine which finishing products can be mixed together and which combinations should be avoided. Below are some common solvents and their characteristics.

Water is a very common and practical solvent. It's cheap, nonflammable, and nontoxic. Although it dissolves water-soluble dyes and many resins (such as gum arabic), these resins aren't used as finishes because the abundance of water in our everyday lives makes them impractical as finishes. Water is much more useful as a thinner.

Hydrocarbons (mineral spirits, naphtha, paint thinner, toluene) are both solvents and thinners. They have been the backbone of the paint industry for oils and oil-based finishes like varnish. They also dissolve waxes.

Alcohols (methanol, denatured alcohol) dissolve most natural plant and animal resins like shellac, rosin, copal, and sandarac.

Ketones (acetone, methyl ethyl ketone) are the solvents for lacquer resins.

Glycol ethers are unique in that they dissolve many natural and synthetic resins and are also capable of being mixed with water without separating. It is this ability that allows the formulation of water-based finishes. Glycol ethers evaporate slowly and are used as retarders to slow down the dry time of finishing materials so they handle and flow out better.

Blends, which are combinations of different solvents, serve many purposes. For example, brush cleaner is a mix of alcohol, toluene (hydrocarbon), and acetone. Putting solvents from the three different groups together ensures that the blend will clean most finishes from brushes. Lacquer thinner is a mix of methyl ethyl ketone, alcohol, and toluene. It will dissolve an evaporative finish but not a reactive one.

Solvents are grouped into families—alcohols, ketones, hydrocarbons, and glycol ether. Blends are products like lacquer thinner and brush and roller cleaner.

Two types of oil are commonly used for finishing. Tung oil (left) is lighter than linseed oil (right).

"frost," or dry to a whitish, matte appearance. Tung oil is slightly paler than linseed oil and has better moisture resistance, although neither oil when used as a finish has waterproof qualities comparable to more durable finishes like varnish.

Varnish

Varnish refers to finishes made from hard, durable synthetic resins that are modified with a drying oil. The resins have names like alkyd, phenolic, and urethane, and the oils are tung and linseed, as well as other semi-drying oils like safflower. Varnishes dry by the same process as true oils, but the incorporation of the resin makes the finishes more durable than oils. In fact, oil-based varnishes are the most durable finish that can be easily applied by the average finisher, surpassing most other finishes in resistance to water, heat, solvents, and chemicals.

There are two general groupings of varnishes: those based on a high percentage of oil in the finish (long oil varnishes) and those based on a low percentage of oil in the finish (short oil varnishes). Long oil varnishes are also known as marine varnishes, spar varnishes, or just plain exterior

varnishes. Short oil varnishes are for interior use and dry to a harder film. If the can says "interior only," it's a short oil varnish.

The type of resin used in the varnish determines the characteristics of the finish. Alkyd varnishes are the standard all-purpose interior varnish with good all-around protective qualities. Phenolic varnishes are used predominately for exterior varnishes and are usually made with tung oil. Urethane varnishes are generically referred to as polyurethane and have the best resistance to heat, solvents, and scratches.

Varnishes are typically applied with a brush, although very thin wiping varnishes and gel varnishes can be applied with a rag. Application of these products is very easy and straightforward, but they build more slowly than brushing varnishes.

Oil/Varnish Blends

Oil/varnish blends are products that are made from—you guessed it—oil with some varnish in it. The resulting mixture has

Long-oil varnish is known as spar, marine, or exterior varnish (left). Short-oil interior varnishes can be either liquids or gels (right).

Making a Match

Matching an existing finish brings together almost all of the materials we have discussed up to this point. (You'll see the techniques for applying the materials in chapter 4.) Matching a finish is not an "art," and respectable results can be achieved by beginners.

You don't need dozens of stain and glaze colors to match an existing finish. It's best if you use a minimum number of wood-tone colors (six is the most I've ever used). For dyes, the colors are a honey or amber color, a golden brown, a medium brown, a reddish brown, a dark brown, and a cordovan. You'll also need red, blue, yellow, green, and black.

For glazes, toners, and pigment stains, you should have comparable wood-tone colors to match the dye wood-tone colors, as well as pure concentrated pigment colors. These pure pigment colors can be oil based (for Japan colors) or water based (for universal tinting color) and include raw sienna, burst sienna, raw umber, burnt umber, Vandyke brown, and black.

They are used to "tweak" or modify the wood-tone colors, but can be diluted with thinner and used as stains. Optional concentrated pigment colors like white, red, yellow, and blue are helpful but not necessary.

Once you've chosen your wood-tone colors, it's time to make a stain board. You can make different boards for each type of wood, or you can glue different woods together and make one board. The board is stained with the wood-tone colors (both dye and pigment) and top-coated. This invaluable tool aids in identifying the base color, or undertone, of the finish that you are trying to duplicate.

Before you go into the matching process it's helpful to keep a few things in mind.

- Although many factory finishes are multistep procedures involving as many as six separate staining operations, most of these finishes can be matched fairly closely using dye stains, glazes, and toners.

- When you match a finish you have to do it under the correct lighting. Incandescent or fluorescent lighting will produce incorrect matches between the sample and the piece you are trying to match. It's best to match a finish under diffused natural daylight (not direct sunlight) or under special fluorescent bulbs that are daylight balanced.

- Always work from light to dark. You can always darken a color, but you must start over to lighten a color.

- If your sample is a flat or satin finish, squirt some mineral spirits onto the surface of the wood to simulate the effect of gloss. Most colors change slightly under different sheens.

There are five basic steps in matching a finish (see Colonial Cherry finish on pp. 222-224 as an example). First, you match the texture of the wood surface, then the overall undertone, the pore

some of the application ease of true oils but also some of the protective qualities of varnish. Danish oil, Nordic oils, and a host of the other finishes sold as oil finishes fall into this category. It's impossible to ascribe general protective qualities to these products because the amount of oil vs. varnish is not disclosed by manufacturers. However,

these blends do dry a bit harder than true oils, as well as build more quickly and require fewer applications.

Many finishers prefer to make their own blends. A basic recipe works on the rule of thirds: one-third varnish (pick your favorite), one-third oil (linseed or tung), and one-third mineral spirits. Because the color (for woods with distinguishable pores), the overall color, and finally the sheen. The difference between the undertone and the overall color is the hardest to explain because the impression to the casual observer is one color. However, considering and applying this one color as separate coloring operations—perhaps dyeing then glazing and toning—gives you more control over the matching process. As a side benefit, you'll get a finish that has more depth and luster.

Matching wood texture The texture of the wood surface plays an important part in the overall aesthetic impact. This is particularly true of old finishes prepared with edge tools like planes and scrapers. You can check for texture by looking at the surface in backlighting. A planed surface will show up as a scalloped surface. Also, pay attention to distressing marks. Are they filled with color? If so you'll have to distress before glazing. Also check for visible straight-line sanding scratches. A pigment will highlight these lines,

and if you can see them it means the manufacturer only sanded up to 150 grit or less, which you'll need to do to match the texture.

Matching undertone This step evens out tonal disparities and sapwood if done selectively or in several applications. On antiques, it simulates the natural patination on the surface of the wood (usually a yellow-gold color). The undertone is one of the hardest colors to "see" in a modern factory finish. To match it, you use one of the basic wood-tone colors in your palette, usually a dye-based stain. It should be the lightest color you see on the wood. Use the stain board to decide which one. It helps if you go a hair lighter and then adjust to the final color with glazes and toners.

Matching pore color On open-grained woods, the color of the pores has a tremendous impact on the overall color and appearance of the finish. You will have the most control over the pore color if you seal in the undertone color first, then apply an oil-based paste wood filler for filled-pore finishes.

To match pore color on open-pore finishes use a glaze.

Matching overall color After the paste wood filler is sealed, the color should only need small adjustments to get the final color. Using toners, you can "sneak" up on the final color, using either wood-tone colors or pure colors like red or green to adjust the final hue. To darken the color, use a dark brown toner. (Don't use black, as it cools the overall tone.) Green neutralizes a finish that's too red and vice versa. Shading with toner can also be used at this point to add extra color around edges and other decorative effects, as well as to touch up any areas. Antiquing such as specking, crayon distressing, and cowtailing is also done at this point.

Matching sheen After all the top coats are applied, rub out the finish to the desired sheen. Gloss finishes will make any color deeper and darker. As you rub the finish out to satin, you slightly lighten the color. A satin finish with flattening agents has the same effect.

oil increases the drying time, many finishers prefer to cut back on the amount of oil. The best all-around finish I've found is 1 cup of varnish, ⅓ cup of linseed oil, and 1 cup of naphtha (which dries more quickly than mineral spirits). You can always add Japan drier—an additive that speeds up the drying time.

Shellac
While most people think of shellac as a liquid you buy in a paint store, it's really a natural resin that's derived from the secretions of the lac bug, an insect that feeds off trees indigenous to India and Thailand. The secretions, in the form of cocoons, are gathered from the trees. They are refined into dry flakes that are dissolved in alcohol

There's an easy way to determine if an oil/varnish blend has a lot of oil in it. Pour some on a piece of glass or metal. If it wrinkles when it dries, it's mostly oil.

Oil/varnish blends are available under a variety of names like Danish oil, teak oil, and Nordic oil. They are blends of oil, varnish, and mineral spirits.

Shellac varies in color and wax content. From left: seedlac, dewaxed dark, #1 orange, and dewaxed pale. The dewaxed shellac solutions appear less cloudy.

to make the shellac solution you see in cans at the store.

Shellac is available in several forms. You can buy it premixed or you can buy it in flake form and mix it yourself with denatured alcohol. The premixed variety is available in orange (amber) and clear (which is shellac that's been bleached). Shellac flakes are available in a wider variety of color and wax content than the premixed variety, which always contain wax. Wax decreases the resistance of shellac to water and prevents some finishes from bonding to it.

All shellac naturally has a wax content. This wax is similar to beeswax and makes the shellac appear cloudy if you look at it in a jar. Removing the wax makes the solution clearer and also makes the shellac more resistant to water damage.

You can buy many different grades of dewaxed dry shellac, which is made by dissolving the shellac, then filtering out the wax through special filters. Why isn't dewaxed premixed shellac available?

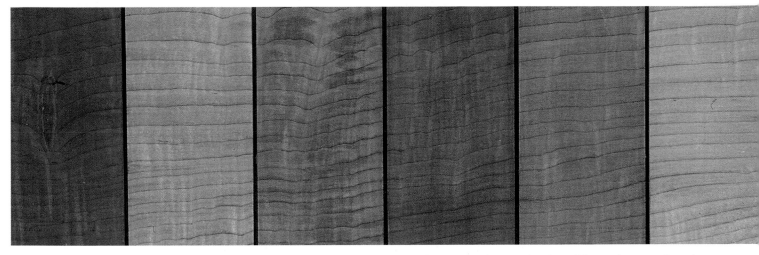

The various grades of shellac produce different colors on curly maple. From left: dark garnet, pale dewaxed, seedlac, buttonlac, #1 orange, and white (bleached).

Dewaxed shellac has a shorter shelf life than waxed shellac, so manufacturers would not be able to guarantee its performance.

Shellac comes in many different colors. Except for bleached shellac, the color is determined by environmental factors like time of year and climate. The most common type of shellac is #1 orange, which is the shellac used for the orange shellac you can purchase premixed. This color imparts a pleasant tone to pine. Other grades of shellac, like seedlac and buttonlac, are less refined and have a slightly different color.

When shellac is made from scratch, shellac flakes are mixed with alcohol in a ratio called a cut, which refers to the amount of shellac in pounds dissolved in a gallon of alcohol. For example, a 2-lb. cut would be 2 lbs. dissolved in 1 gallon of alcohol, and a 5-lb. cut would be 5 lbs. dissolved in 1 gallon. Premixed shellac is a 3-lb. cut, which is a bit thick for most finishing applications, so denatured alcohol is added to thin it. Shellac can be mixed to exactly the cut you want by factoring the ratio up or down.

The natural color of some shellac can be used to color woods like pine so no stain is required. Orange shellac was applied to the bottom of this pine board.

For accuracy, it's best to measure the alcohol for shellac in a measuring cup.

Use an inexpensive food scale to measure shellac. A postal scale can also be used.

The best alcohol to use for dissolving shellac is denatured alcohol, which can be purchased at any paint store. Buy a good grade—one that lists shellac reducer as one of its uses on the label. For accuracy, the alcohol should be measured with a liquid measuring cup. Though there are various ways to eyeball a given weight of shellac, it's best to weigh it on a scale. (A food-portion scale can be purchased at most department stores for about $10 to $15.) Mix the shellac and alcohol together in a glass or plastic jar that has a tight-fitting lid. Shake the solution periodically to prevent a large mass of partially dissolved

Shellac will clump at the bottom of the storage jar if not shaken periodically.

Lacquers are available in brushing and aerosol versions (left) or spray versions (right). The spray products come in a greater variety, such as vinyl sealer and CAB-acrylic.

shellac from forming at the bottom. If you place the jar near a source of heat or in the sun, the shellac will dissolve quicker. Once dissolved in alcohol, shellac begins a slow chemical process that eventually turns the hard resin into a gummy substance that won't dry. For this reason, you should try to mix up only what you'll use in a six-month period.

Lacquer

The term lacquer generally means a fast-drying, glossy, hard finish based upon flammable solvents. It is still considered by many professionals to be the best all-around finish for wood because it is fast-drying, imparts depth and richness, has moderate to excellent durability (depending on the type used), and rubs out well. There are several different types of lacquers with different performance characteristics:

- Nitrocellulose lacquers
- Acrylic modified lacquer (CAB-acrylic)
- Catalyzed lacquers

Nitrocellulose lacquers Nitrocellulose lacquers are the most common lacquer you will find, and if the label on the can simply says lacquer, it's almost certainly this type. These finishes are composed of an alkyd/nitrocellulose resin that is dissolved and then mixed with fast-evaporating solvents. Nitrocellulose lacquers have moderate water resistance but are sensitive to heat and certain solvents. The biggest drawback is their tendency to yellow over time, which looks bad on light-colored woods and white finishes.

Acrylic modified lacquers (CAB-acrylic) Acrylic modified lacquers are usually based on a mix of a nonyellowing cellulose resin called cellulose acetate butyrate (CAB) and acrylic. They have the general properties of nitrocellulose lacquers with the exception of being absolutely water-white, meaning they do not impart an amber shift when applied to light woods and do not yellow over time.

Why Finishes Yellow

Most finishing resins yellow over time because of exposure to light and air. Light—particularly in the ultraviolet region—breaks the electronic bonds that hold the finish molecule together, and, together with oxygen, forms new chemicals in the finish that are yellow colored.

Other factors such as high heat, moisture, and contact with rubber or plastic that contains sulfur may also have an effect. The rubber protective bumpers on the base of a vase may actually create yellow impressions in a clear lacquer finish.

To minimize yellowing, try to limit the amount of harsh sunlight on a piece and never leave plastic or rubber items like a vinyl tablecloth on finishes, especially nitrocellulose and CAB-acrylic lacquers, for extended periods of time.

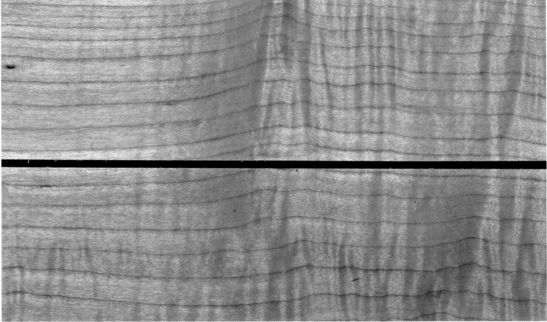

CAB-acrylic (top) lacks the amber effect of a conventional nitrocellulose lacquer (bottom), thereby preserving the creamy, white color. Also, it will not yellow over time.

Catalyzed lacquers and conversion varnishes
Catalyzed lacquers were developed to bridge the gap between the application characteristics of nitrocellulose lacquers and the performance and durability of varnish. These complex finishes are composed of urea/formaldehyde and an alkyd that has some nitrocellulose resin added to make it handle like normal lacquer. Catalyzed varnishes do not have nitrocellulose added. An acid catalyst is then added to initiate a reaction that forms a very tough, durable finish. They are reactive finishes.

Catalyzed lacquers are available in two versions. One is a two-part system that must be mixed in the proper ratio and then applied to the wood. These lacquers have a short pot life (the time in which it can be used). The second type, called precatalyzed lacquer, comes premixed, either by the manufacturer or at the store when you buy it.

Water-Based Finishes

Water-based finishes are based upon the same resins as the finishes we discussed previously—alkyd, acrylic, and urethane—but the flammable, polluting solvents have been partly replaced by water. The chemistry involved in this replacement is a little complex because none of these resins have a natural affinity for water. They must be chemically modified or "forced" to combine with water in a chemical mixture called an emulsion. Emulsions require the addition of chemicals called surfactants and special solvents generically called glycol ethers.

Water-based finishes based on an acrylic resin are sold as water-based lacquer, and finishes based on an acrylic/urethane mixture are sold as water-based polyurethane, "polycrylic," or some other acronym. "Hybrid" water-based finishes utilize conventional oil-modified varnish resins, like urethane, with water-based acrylics.

There are several things to keep in mind if you want to use water-based finishes. Because a large component of water-based finishes is water, you may be led into a false sense of security. But as anyone who has ever painted a closet with latex paint will attest, the other solvents in water-based products can make you feel dizzy and ill. You should always wear a spray mask rated for paints when spraying water-based finishes, and when brushing keep the room well-ventilated, just as you would for solvent finishes.

Something else to keep in mind is that a water-based finish tends to raise the grain. The simplest way to overcome grain raising is to use a sealer coat of dewaxed shellac, which not only prevents the next

coat of water-based finish from raising the grain but also adds a bit of amber color. You could also sponge the wood with distilled water to preraise the grain, or apply one or two light coats of sanding sealer, sanding between coats when dry.

Another thing to consider is that water-based finishes are optically neutral, meaning they don't add color. If you want to keep whites white or retain the creamy whiteness of maple, a water-based finish is the way to go (acrylics are best). On other woods like cherry and walnut, water-based finishes do not impart the warmth and depth that we normally associate with solvent- and oil-based finishes. Adding a bit of a compatible amber dye to the first coat will alleviate

---

Pros and Cons of Water-Based Finishes

PROS
- Nonflammable and less polluting
- Most are nonyellowing
- Fast-drying
- Can be sprayed and brushed
- Odor tends to be less harsh than solvent-based finishes
- Easy to clean up with water

CONS
- Water raises the grain
- Most don't impart depth and richness the way oils and solvent-based finishes do
- Finicky to apply in temperature and humidity extremes

FINISHING
FACT

FINISHING
FACT

To get solvent-
soluble resins
(oils) and water
to mix, chemists
add chemicals
called surfactants
to keep the nor-
mally ummixable
components
together. These
finishes always
have a milky
appearance, but
they are perfectly
clear when dry.

Water-based finishes are emulsions, so the finish appears milky in the can. However, these
finishes dry clear on wood.

this, as will staining the wood with a dilute
amber dye stain before finishing.

Using the correct tools is another consideration. Water reacts with metals, so
steel wool should never be used when
preparing wood or finishing. Also, natural-
bristle brushes absorb too much water and
become limp with water-based finishes, so
use a brush with synthetic bristle. Certain
sandpapers should be avoided if you sand
between coats. Check with the manufacturer, but as a rule, avoid stearated sandpaper. When using turbine-driven HVLP
spray equipment, the turbine should be of
adequate power to atomize water-based finishes (at least a three-stage turbine).

Paint

Paint is actually a clear finish with pigment
added. Paint can be based on just about
any resin, but the most common are oil,
water, and lacquer. Oil-based paint is made
from linseed or safflower oil, alkyd, and
mineral spirits. Water-based paint is made
from acrylic and vinyl resins, glycol ethers,
and water. Lacquer-based paint contains
nitrocellulose resin and lacquer thinner. A
less-common paint, milk paint (made from
water, lime, and casein), can also be used
for an interesting, old-fashioned effect.

Paint can be used as a finish for an
entire piece, but sometimes the best

The various woods on the bottom were finished with a water-based lacquer. The same woods on the top were finished with a solvent-based nitrocellulose lacquer. Note the deeper color and warmth of the top. Woods from left to right are white oak, curly maple, cherry, and mahogany.

effects are created when paint is used as a contrasting design element, like a border (see Lightly Distressed Paint finish on pp. 206-207) or a piece with painted legs and a clear finished top (see Antique Pine finish on pp. 203-205). Whichever paint you use, apply the same general application rules you use for clear finish.

WAXES AND POLISHES

The products used to care for furniture are a bigger business than the finishes themselves. Waxes and polishes for wood furniture are sold in every supermarket and drugstore in this country. How many of these same stores also sell furniture finishes? This competition for consumer dollars has given rise to some strong promises about what these products can do.

In spite of claims to the contrary, waxes and furniture polishes do little to protect wood. What they do is clean dirt, help remove dust, and help change surface appearance and tactile quality. They provide a small amount of resistance to scratches and scrapes, but they certainly do not "feed" or "nourish" the wood (or the finish) or provide any long-term protection the way that finishes do. They also cannot revive or improve the durability of a badly

CHOOSING THE RIGHT FINISH

CONSIDERATION	FINISHES FOR BRUSHING
Heat	Oil-based polyurethane
Water	Oil-based polyurethane, oil-based varnish (phenolic)
Scratching (wear)	Oil-based polyurethane
Solvents	Oil-based polyurethane, oil-based varnish (alkyd and phenolic)
Rubbing qualities	Lacquer, shellac
Yellowing	Water-based lacquer, water-based polyurethane
Film depth and clarity	Lacquer, shellac, oil-based varnish (alkyd and phenolic)
Dusty environment	Lacquer, shellac
Cold environment	Lacquer, shellac
Safety/fire issues	Water-based lacquer, water-based polyurethane
Health	Shellac, water-based lacquer, water-based polyurethane
Food contact	Shellac
Repairability	Lacquer, shellac

*Additives may need to be added to the finish   **As long as film is not built up significantly

deteriorated finish. The major difference between waxes and polishes is that a coat of wax leaves a thin film of solid wax on the surface, while most polishes leave a liquid film that eventually evaporates.

Waxes

Wax has been used on furniture since recorded history began. It's been used as a finish on bare wood, as well as a finishing touch over a finish. Because all waxes are solids at room temperature, a solvent is added to dissolve the wax to make it easier to apply to the wood. The solvent evaporates, and the solid wax remains as a thin film on the surface of the wood. The solvent is usually mineral spirits, though some wax manufacturers use turpentine, which adds its characteristic scent. Some formulations use toluene, a faster-evaporating solvent.

FINISHES FOR WIPING	FINISHES FOR SPRAYING
Oil-based polyurethane	Conversion varnish, catalyzed/ precatalyzed lacquer
Oil-based polyurethane, oil-based varnish (phenolic)	Conversion varnish, catalyzed/ precatalyzed lacquer
Oil-based polyurethane	Conversion varnish
Oil-based polyurethane, oil-based varnish (alkyd and phenolic)	Conversion varnish, catalyzed/ precatalyzed lacquer
Shellac	Lacquer, shellac, catalyzed/ precatalyzed lacquer
Water-based lacquer and polyurethane***	Conversion varnish, CAB-acrylic
Oil-based varnish (alkyd and phenolic)	Lacquer, shellac, catalyzed/ precatalyzed lacquer
Shellac	Lacquer, shellac, catalyzed/ precatalyzed lacquer
Shellac	Lacquer, shellac, catalyzed/ precatalyzed lacquer*
True oils	Water-based lacquer, water-based polyurethane
True oils	Water-based lacquer, water-based polyurethane
True oils	Shellac
Oil finishes**	Lacquer, shellac

***When only several coats are used, as it becomes hard to wipe evenly

The solvent used in waxes has an effect on the wax, but only on how fast it evaporates as you're applying it. Slow-evaporating mineral spirits allow plenty of time to apply the wax and then to wipe it off evenly. Fast-evaporating thinners, like toluene, may cause the wax to dry before you come back to wipe it. Most waxes have the solvent listed on the label, but if not, you can identify them by their characteristic smell. Toluene smells like lacquer thinner. Turpentine has a characteristic pine odor, while mineral spirits has a petroleum-like odor.

Although generically called paste wax, there are three types of waxes used in wood care. The traditional wax is beeswax, but carnauba and paraffin waxes are used by manufacturers, typically in combination with one of the other waxes.

Beeswax is the natural by-product of bees. It is rarely used by itself in a furniture paste wax. Although it has a pleasant satin

Waxes are clear or colored pastes that are applied with steel wool or cotton cloths.

you use to seal the tops of jams and jellies. It is softer than both carnauba and beeswax and is used in combination with the other two to make them easier to apply and to lower the cost.

Waxes are sold either as natural (also called clear) or colored. Natural reflects the color of the ingredients, which in most cases are taupe or off-white. Colored waxes are made by adding pigments or oil-soluble dyes to the wax while it's being made. Colored waxes stain the color of raw wood if applied directly. If applied to finished surfaces, they do not change the overall color, but they can be used to mimic age and to add contrast by highlighting the pores of open-pore finishes. In fact, the best use of colored wax is on a dark, open-pore finish. When a natural wax is used on that type of finish, the light-colored wax shows in the pores where it's trapped, creating an unappealing look.

Polishes

Polishes are very different from waxes. They are liquids and contain very little to no wax or oils. Whereas wax leaves a thin film on the surface, polishes almost always evaporate completely. This means that polishes do not protect as well as a wax. But in spite of this, polishes are useful for routine cleaning and dust removal, as well as temporary surface improvement. There are two general categories of polishes: those based on petroleum solvents and those that are an emulsion of water and petroleum solvents.

The solvents used in polishes are distilled from petroleum and consequently have a somewhat "oily" feel and an objec-

sheen, I find pure beeswax somewhat difficult to apply, and it's expensive.

Carnauba wax is a natural product harvested from the leaves of trees in South America. It is harder and glossier than beeswax. Pure carnauba is very hard to apply, so it is rarely used on its own, except by wood turners who hold a cake of the pure wax against an object while it's turning on the lathe.

Paraffin is a petroleum product, and most manufacturers use the same stuff that

Polishes are liquids that are best used for cleaning and for temporary surface improvement. They may contain a fragrance or a color for masking scratches.

tionable odor. The odor can be removed by chemical means, but instead a fragrance is usually added to disguise the smell of the solvent and add a pleasant scent.

Petroleum-based polishes are simply slow-evaporating mineral spirit-type solvents. These products are good for general cleaning of oil-soluble grime and dirt (like fingerprints) and leave a temporary luster and shine on a finished surface. Most products contain no wax or oil. For example, lemon oil is actually mineral spirits with an oil-soluble fragrance and dye added to it to imitate the smell and color of a lemon.

Emulsion polishes clean more effectively than petroleum-based polishes because they clean both water- and oil-soluble dirt and grime (water-soluble grime is usually from food spills). These polishes are white or off-white and are sometimes called creams. Like petroleum polish, emulsion polish typically does not have wax or oil in it.

Polishes are available in pump, aerosol, or liquid form. You can get the same results by wiping an old finish with mineral spirits. In fact, mineral spirits or paint thinner makes a good furniture cleaner and is used by most refinishers and restoration shops.

SURFACE PREPARATION

Surface preparation is essential for a quality finish, but it can be overdone. For surface preparation to be successful, it has to be done efficiently, and the best way is a three-stage approach: remove the marks from rough milling, smooth the wood, and correct defects and blemishes like dents, knots, and cracks. The first two stages are completed with planes, scrapers, or abrasives, while the third stage requires various fillers. When you proceed in an orderly manner, you'll get better results, and surface preparation will become a more enjoyable part of finishing.

USING PLANES AND SCRAPERS

Planes are very efficient at removing milling and machining marks, as well as smoothing the wood. Generally, a long-soled plane such as a jointer or jack plane is used first, followed by shorter-soled smoothing planes for final smoothing.

Scrapers are easier for beginners to use. Start with a cabinet scraper to remove machining marks and level the surface, then follow with a handheld scraper. Both tools are used in much the same way. Holding the workpiece firmly, push the scraper away from you while exerting downward pressure. When sharp, the tool produces fine shavings; when dull, it produces dust and needs to be resharpened.

SANDING

Sanding is unquestionably one of the most popular ways to smooth wood for finishing. It can be done by hand or with large, powerful machines (like belt sanders). In the middle range is a plethora of random orbit machines, palm sanders, and profile sanders. While sanding is generally viewed as a necessary evil, it can go a lot easier if you proceed in a logical and orderly method.

Prior to sanding, you should remove dried glue with a scraper, as sandpaper will quickly gum up with glue and wear out prematurely. Wood can be smoothed with abrasives ranging from 80 to 220 grit. You should always start with the lowest abrasive grit capable of removing the defects from the surface. Once the initial leveling is done, successive grits simply remove the scratches from the previous grits and replace them with smaller scratches.

Sanding will proceed easily if you plan ahead. Use sharp cutting tools during the machining and shaping process. Burning

from dull router bits or sawblades is very hard to remove. Try and glue up large panels as flat as you can. Finally, use sharp abrasives. Using worn or dull sandpaper is counterproductive and will usually cause other problems.

Hand-Sanding

Sanding by hand seems almost an anachronism in today's high-tech world of power tools. But if you are finishing small items or just one project, there's no need to run off and purchase a power sander. Sanding by hand can be efficient. Because you have more control over the sanding tool, you can sand in the direction of the grain throughout the process. Most power sanders, on the other hand, put deep cross-grain scratches in the wood, which then have to be sanded with another finer grit to remove them. Also, hand-sanding allows you to use coarser initial grits like 60 or 80 to remove machining marks. Power sanders shouldn't be used with anything lower than 100 grit.

When you begin, start with 60- or 80-grit sandpaper, then move to the next grit. Do not jump grits (such as from 60 to 120). Make sure all the sanding marks from the previous grit are removed with the next grit. To check for scratches, backlight the surface by putting a lamp behind it or wipe it with mineral spirits (see Checking Surface Preparation on p. 71 for more on this).

Sand at a slight bias to the grain—about 5 to 8 degrees. This angle cuts the wood fibers best. Remove dust from the wood surface and the paper periodically to prevent the paper from loading and cutting less efficiently.

If your goal is to flatten the wood, you need to back up the sandpaper with some rubber, hard cork, or a wood block to give the sandpaper some support. Round over

Hand-Sanding

1 Tear a large sheet of sandpaper into small sections by placing it over a sharp edge. The coarse grits tear more easily if you roll the paper back and forth across the edge first.

Wrap the sandpaper around a block and sand at a slight bias to the grain (approximately 5 to 8 degrees). Move the sandpaper from one edge to the next, maintaining even downward pressure (about 10 lb. to 15 lb.) on the block. If you're unsure of the amount of pressure you're applying, press down on a bathroom scale with your hand to check.

Sand flat edges with the block. When sanding edges, move to a fresh part of the sandpaper because the sandpaper loads up quickly.

Sand round or curved edges "shoeshine" style by rolling the sandpaper back and forth. Don't use a block because it will put flats on the curved areas and distort the profile. For complicated moldings and other profiles, back up the sandpaper with your fingers or use small rubber blocks manufactured in convex and concave profiles.

Break all the sharp edges with fine sandpaper. This also makes the edge safer.

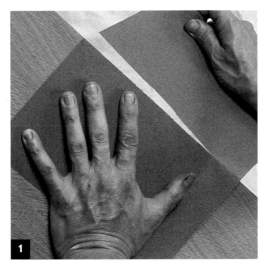

Belt Sanding

1 To flatten a large panel, use 100-grit sandpaper and start the belt sander at a 30- to 45-degree angle. Move it slowly across the board, maintaining only enough downward pressure on the sander to keep it flat. The larger and heavier (4-in. x 24-in.) sanders are easier to keep flat.

2 Switch to the opposite angle and repeat. This cross-hatching technique flattens the panel by removing high spots.

3 Finally, sand with the grain. You need to make four or five passes to remove all the cross-grain scratches. Wipe the piece with naphtha or mineral spirits to highlight errant scratches you might have missed. Then switch to 120-grit sandpaper and continue sanding with the grain. When you progress to this grit, you may want to switch to a random-orbit or orbital-pad sander.

the sharp edges of a wood block where they contact the paper so they don't break through the paper.

Machine Sanding

Power sanders are the most efficient tool for preparing large panels and larger projects. Three types of sanders fall into this category: belt sanders, random-orbit sanders, and orbital-pad sanders. The techniques differ for each type because they remove wood differently.

Belt sanders are the most difficult tool to master, but they are worth the time to learn. They remove wood the fastest and most efficiently, and they can do it with the grain, avoiding cross-grain scratches.

Random-orbit sanders are the best for beginners because they are easy to use. These sanders work in a circular motion to remove stock quickly. The pad is mounted on a mechanical device called an eccentric, which applies opposing scratches that nullify the scratches left by the circular motion. The sanders are available in right-angle and palm styles. The right-angle versions are a little more aggressive, while the palm style is a little easier to control.

Orbital-pad sanders use an oscillating jitterbug-type motion that produces small curlicue type scratches. These sanders are similar to random-orbit sanders but remove stock less efficiently. They are good for use in tight corners and edges and come in several pad sizes.

Regardless of the type of power sander you use, start with the lowest grit that's capable of removing the machining marks on the wood. If you are removing saw marks or planer chatter, start with 100 grit. I don't recommend lower grits because they leave scratches that are hard to remove. You can skip grits as you get into higher numbers. For example, you can go from

Using Random-Orbit and Orbital-Pad Sanders

1 Sandpaper is attached with either PSA (pressure-sensitive adhesive) or a hook-and-loop (Velcro-type) system. The hook-and-loop system allows for easy removal and reattachment of the paper, which is impossible with PSA. The best random-orbit sanders have holes punched in the pad and paper and can be hooked up to a shop vacuum for efficient dust removal.

2 Start the sander with the machine on the surface. If you bring the running machine down on the work, it may gouge it. To do the smoothing, use the same cross-hatching technique as with belt sanding. It ensures the entire board is worked evenly and no areas are missed with any of the grits.

3 Use a random-orbit sander on narrow surfaces as long as they are flat and no less than half the width of the sanding pad. Slightly concave and convex surfaces can be done as well, but you must use a foam pad from the manufacturer.

4 Use an orbital-pad sander on narrow edges. Keep the sander moving constantly to avoid sanding flats on rounded edges.

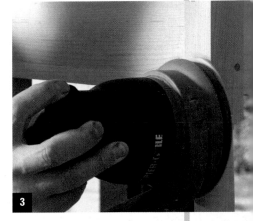

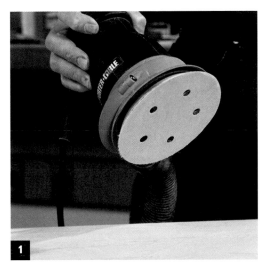

120 to 180 (skipping 150) or from 150 to 220 (skipping 180). Change grits as soon as the paper becomes dull. You can always tell when this happens because the machine starts to slide rather than "bite." Use aluminum oxide or silicon-carbide paper, preferably stearated because it lasts longer.

Keep the machine moving and don't sand in one spot too long, or it will leave a depression that may not be visible until a finish is applied. Always hand-sand with the grain to remove all remaining circular scratches.

Tight Corners and Complex Profiles
One reality of surface preparation is that you will have tight corners, complicated profiles, and other areas impossible to reach

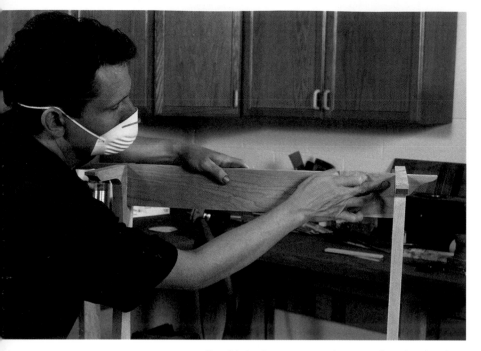

Sand into the corner using your hand to back up the sandpaper. Fold the sheet of sandpaper into thirds but make sure that the abrasive does not touch itself.

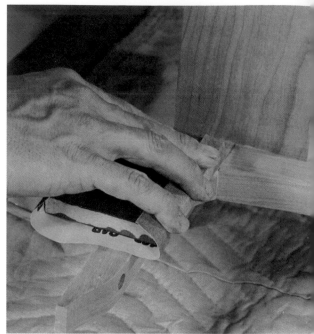

When two pieces of wood are glued with the grain at right angles, divide the sanding so that you sand each piece with the grain. At 220 grit you can sand in any direction, because the scratches are too small to be seen.

with a power sander. While there are machines capable of sanding these areas, they can be pricey, and it's not always economical to buy a machine for every situation. I prefer to simply switch to hand-sanding techniques for these areas.

Right-angle corners I work right up to the edges of a right-angle corner with a machine, then switch to hand-sanding to finish it off. Make sure you use the same grit paper that was in the machine. It's best to lightly sand, or feather, back into the area that you machine-sanded so you don't create a depression. As an alternative to sandpaper, you can use a hand scraper. Starting at the intersection of the two boards, pull the scraper away from the corner.

Complicated profiles There are several ways to handle complicated profiles, round and turned items, and moldings.

The first option is to use your hand to back the paper and then sand each facet of the profile separately. For example, the concave, convex, and flat areas would be sanded one at a time. Tight concave curves are best done with this technique so your hand cushions the paper and the piece. You can also try cushioned sanding blocks, which are sold in different grits on ¼-in.-thick cushioned pads, which you can cut to smaller sizes as needed.

Small, rubber profile blocks that back up the paper can be used to sand the whole profile if the block shape matches the profile shape. These blocks also work if you break the profile down into separate parts.

Another option is to rub a piece of Styrofoam along the profile until it "cuts" a matching profile. Then simply put a piece of sandpaper over the block.

You can make a copy of the profile with automotive two-part filler. Using wax paper as a release and modeling clay as two dams, you can make an exact hard profile. Pour the filler between the dams spaced approximately 3 in. apart.

If you need to smooth carvings, don't use sandpaper. The only tools for this job are very fine synthetic steel wool or cushioned sanding blocks.

CHECKING SURFACE PREPARATION

It's important that you check the surface after preparing it but before applying a stain or finish. This way you will avoid surprises and the potential task of stripping off the finish and starting over. The easiest way to do this is to wipe down the wood with mineral spirits or naphtha (naphtha evaporates faster). The solvent wets the wood, so any errant defects, glue spots, or sanding scratches will be noticeable. Distilled water can also be used, but it raises the wood's grain, so you would need to resand the surface.

You may encounter a variety of problems as this stage, but most can be fixed. Low spots are areas that were too low for the sandpaper to reach. If they are deep, the only remedy is to go back and relevel the whole area. Do not try to sand out a deep low spot by sanding just in that area because you'll create a depression that will be noticeable after the finish is applied. If the low spot isn't too deep, you can feather-sand it level with the rest of the surface.

Sanding scratches are visible scratches left over from lower grits. To fix them, resand with the lowest grit capable of

Wiping the wood with mineral spirits is the best way to check surface preparation. It highlights machining defects, as well as low spots, glue spots, and scratches from low grits.

removing the scratches. Feather-sand back into the rest of the surface to avoid creating a low spot. You can also use a scraper to remove the scratches, then follow up with the last grit of sandpaper you used initially.

Remove glue spots with a sharp chisel or scraper, then sand the area with the last grit you used initially.

Once you're satisfied that the surface is properly prepared, you must remove all the dust and debris that has collected on the surface, particularly in the pores. Planed and scraped surfaces are usually ready to finish and don't require this step.

The best method for removing debris is to vacuum the surface with a soft brush attachment, but there are other ways. You

When applying putty with a large putty knife use just the corner of the knife to work the putty into the defect so the putty doesn't get into the pores.

One method that doesn't work very well is a tack cloth. Although this is effective at removing dust from the surface, it can't clean the wood's pores and may interfere with some water-based finishes.

CORRECTING DEFECTS AND BLEMISHES

Defects, such as knots, cracks, and splits, are natural problems in the wood. Blemishes are things like dents, scratches, and gouges, which arise during surface preparation. How you correct defects and blemishes depends upon a number of factors, but the main one is the severity of the damage.

Gouges and other small defects can be repaired with wood putty. Wood putty is available in a wide variety of forms. All types are applied in the same way, but the technique differs for close-grained woods and open-grained woods. Knots and large cracks require a different treatment because there is more space to fill.

Deep dents usually need to be steamed out (see the photos on p. 75). Most light scratches and shallow dents can be sanded out during the surface-preparation process. If you get a chip or tear when routing or during surface preparation, immediately glue in the piece and let it dry before you do any further preparation. If you can't find the piece, glue on a piece of new wood cut from the same board.

can wash the surface with naphtha, mineral spirits, or alcohol. Or brush it off with a brush. On open-grained woods, whisk the dust off with just the tip of the brush. The final option is to blow the surface with compressed air. This is a good method, but unfortunately it blows dust into the air, which will settle back into slow-drying finishes like varnish.

Gouges and Small Defects

To apply putty, put some on the tip of a small screwdriver, piece of wood, or putty knife and push it into the defect (see the photo above). Leave the putty in a little mound or dome because it shrinks when it dries.

After the putty dries, level it with a piece of fine sandpaper backed up with a small piece of wood (the putty should powder when you sand it). Be sure to sand it up to the last grit that you used on the wood. Sanding putty on open-grained woods is especially tricky. Any putty that gets into the open pores is impossible to remove and will be visible under most finishes. As a precaution, apply some clear packing tape over the defect. Cut a mask around the defect with a sharp X-Acto knife and remove the tape from over the defect. Add the filler to the defect and let it dry. Then level-sand it to the tape, remove the tape, and lightly sand it level with the wood.

When you apply finish or stain to the wood, it may not match the surrounding wood, in spite of the manufacturer's claims. To test the effect on the putty, fill a sample defect on a piece of scrap and stain it. If the filled area doesn't match the stain, you can refine the match (see the photos at right). Generally, there are two guidelines to follow.

For a natural finish (no stain), use glue and sawdust as the filler. My first choice is five-minute, two-part epoxy because it dries very clear and fast. Also, it does not shrink and is not softened by finishing products.

For stained finishes, use a water-based filler. You will either get lucky and the filler will match, or it will dry lighter and you'll need to fine-tune it with touch-up techniques. You can always add color to the filler before applying it to tweak it, but you'll need to see if the color is right by applying it to a scrap first.

Knots and Large Cracks

The best solution to knots and large cracks is to fit in a piece of wood, but this technique rarely creates an invisible repair. My technique for filling knots and large cracks

Fine-Tuning Filler Color

1 The cherry-colored pigment stain left this water-based filler lighter than the rest of the wood. To correct this mismatch, try dry pigment powder mixed with dewaxed pale shellac.

2 Paint the grain lines first. While it's certainly possible to paint the grain lines later, you get better results painting them first because you can refine the shape of the lines with the next step. Using the sharp point of a red-sable artist's brush, paint in the grain lines with a color like burnt umber or Vandyke brown. Black can be mixed in to darken either color.

3 Paint in the background with a lighter color. You can "thin" the grain lines by painting the lighter color over the edges. Remember, wood is not opaque so don't use too much pigment. Also, avoid trying to get the color right all at once. Use light washes of color and look at the touch-up from different angles to ensure you're getting the color.

uses two-part epoxy or two-part polyester putty. Most water- and solvent-based putties shrink over time and aren't as strong as epoxy or polyester. They are also softened by most finishes.

You can color the epoxy or polyester filler with sawdust or dry pigment powders, depending on the effect you want. When you add sawdust from the wood, you're working on, it will dry to the same color of the surrounding wood and blend in. When you add a colored powder you can create contrast with the surrounding wood, adding a nice decorative touch. For example, cracks in cherry can be filled with epoxy tinted with black pigment. Or a dark wood like walnut could have some gold-colored pigment added. When finished, the cracks stand out and add a decorative effect.

When filling large knots and cracks (wider than ⅛ in.), it's best to glue in slivers of wood along with the epoxy to bulk

Filling Knots and Large Cracks

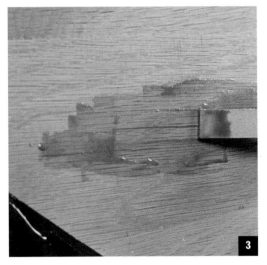

1 To make the crack in this oak blend in with the surrounding wood, use five-minute epoxy mixed with some sawdust collected during sanding. To make the crack contrast with the wood, use a powdered pigment instead. The technique is the same for both options.

2 With a small piece of wood, push the sawdust mixture down into the crack. Put tape on the other side of the board to cover the crack and prevent the mixture from going through. You can also force the epoxy into the crack by holding a hair dryer or heat gun to it. Whichever method you choose, wait overnight for the glue to dry.

3 As the glue dries, it may shrink down into the crack, requiring a second application.

4 When the glue is fully cured and hardened (overnight is best), you can scrape or sand off the excess.

up the void. Cut off some slivers from a short piece of the same species and glue them into the knot or crack with the epoxy. You may want to tape off the other side of the knot to prevent epoxy from coming through. When the epoxy is dry, cut off the ends of the slivers with a saw and then sand the area flush.

Dents

Dents are formed when the fibers of the wood are compressed. Dents should not be confused with gouges, where wood fibers are cut, shredded, or missing. Dents can happen during the assembly and gluing process, so it's always a good idea to use a carpeted or protected surface during assembly and pads to protect the wood from clamps.

Because wood absorbs water easily, reintroducing water and heat generally swells the wood to make it level. If you get to the dent quickly, you can almost always steam it out (see the photos at right). Even very deep dents will swell back to almost a level surface, and the rest of the depression can be removed by scraping and fine sanding. Very minor dings can be swelled by placing a drop or two of distilled water on the depression. Always use distilled water on bare wood. Tap water contains iron salts that react with tannin in the wood and create dark spots.

Older dents may not steam out because the cells of the wood tend to retain their shape. These dents can be fixed with the colored epoxy or polyester technique used for knots and cracks. The color can be fine-tuned with shellac and pigment if necessary.

Dents that occur during finishing are difficult to repair invisibly. But if they do happen and you can't start over, I suggest

Steaming Dents

1 Pour some distilled water in and around the dent. (Tap water can create dark spots and should not be used.)

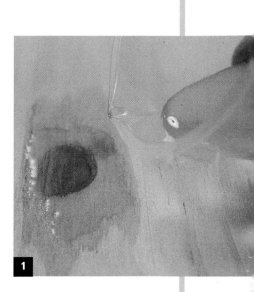

2 Place a piece of cotton or another absorbent natural fabric over the dent. Touch the tip of an iron set on high to the dented area and hold it for 10 to 15 seconds. Switch to a wet part of the fabric and repeat for as long as it takes to swell the dent. Examine the dent when dry and repeat steps 1 and 2 if necessary.

3 A little sanding is almost always necessary after steaming. Feather-sand the area around the dented area so that a depression doesn't show when a finish is applied.

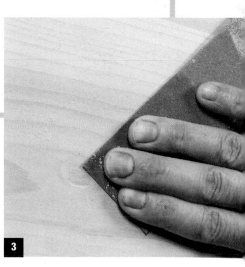

Dents vs. Gouges

Dent
In a dent, the wood cells are compressed and flattened. When heat and moisture are added, though, the cells return to their original shape.

Gouge
In a gouge, cellular material is torn away and must be replaced.

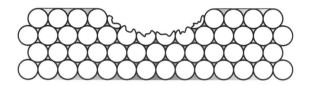

WORKING SMART

Choose cyano-acrylate glue with water-thin viscosity to fill scratches and cracks. It wicks into a small crack by capillary action and fills it better. Be aware, though, that you cannot add colorants to this type of glue.

---

using colored wax sticks. If the dent is on a noncritical surface like a side, it will rarely be visible. Unfortunately, tops and other critical surfaces need more work. They should be repaired by scraping off the finish (this is easier than stripping it) and then sanding or steaming out the dent.

If you don't remove all of the dents before finishing, you will have several problems. First, the compressed fibers may take a stain or finish differently than the wood around it, appearing darker or lighter. Second, the depression will be visible if the piece is viewed in backlighting.

Scratches and Small Cracks

Cross-grain scratches should always be sanded out. These scratches look magnified because they expose end grain, and end grain always finishes darker than face or side grain. You should also try to sand out deep scratches parallel to the grain whenever possible. Although these scratches will still be visible after finishing if not com-

pletely removed, they will be less noticeable than cross-grain scratches. On critical surfaces like tops you should try to fill them (follow the technique below).

Small cracks are usually from defects that occur while the tree is alive or while it's dried into lumber. They can be found in the middle of boards or at the ends. They are usually parallel to the grain and can be quickly and efficiently repaired using cyanoacrylate glue (commonly known as Super Glue) and sawdust (see the photos on the facing page). While it's possible to use epoxy, I find the consistency of cyanoacrylate is better suited for this purpose. Deep scratches that can't be sanded out can also be repaired using this method.

An alternative method is to fill small cracks and scratches with wood putty. I find the water-based putties to be the most effective. You can color the putty while it's in paste form, or touch it up later with pigment and shellac (see p. 73).

Filling Scratches and Small Cracks

1 To fill a small crack like the drying crack shown here, squeeze some cyanoacrylate glue into the crack.

2 Immediately start to sand the area with 150-grit or 180-grit sandpaper. The sanding works up some sawdust, which mixes with the glue and dries to an almost invisible repair. You may need a second application.

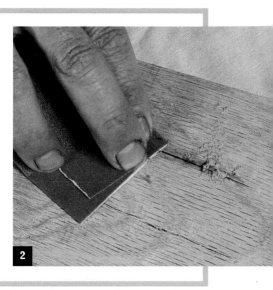

TROUBLESHOOTING SURFACE PREPARATION

PROBLEM	CAUSE	REMEDY
Dark repeating lines across surface of board perpendicular to grain	Planer or jointer chatter; dull planer or jointer knives	Use a coarser abrasive to start or spend more time with initial grit
Darker areas on non-splotch-prone woods	Dull sandpaper	Use fresh sandpaper
Wood feels fuzzy after sanding	Wood not completely dry*	Let wood dry; apply dilute glue; shellac before final sanding**
Dark circular scratches after sanding	Initial grit scratches not removed with grit change; initial grit used was too low	Strip and resand
Surface feels gritty or rough after finish is applied	Sanding debris not removed	Sand finish level
Scalloped or uneven surface is visible in backlighting	Power sander platen worn or uneven; incorrect belt-sanding or handsanding technique; surface not sanded level after cabinet scraping	Strip and resand
Pigment stain won't take	Wood sanded at a grit too high	Resand, dropping down several grits
Small cuts in surface	Scraper nicks	Sand after scraping
Flat spots on curved area	Hard backing used on sandpaper	Use a cushioned abrasive or foam pad
Putty shrinks under finish	Solvents in the finish softened the putty	Switch to a different putty; use epoxy/polyester putties
Putty stains a different color than the wood	Putty absorbs stain differently than wood	Touch up with pigment/shellac

*Some woods, including pine, firs, and some mahoganies, may be naturally fuzzy, even when dry.
**Dilute glue is 1 part white or hide glue to 15 parts water. Dilute shellac is a ½- to 1-lb. cut.

COLORING THE WOOD

Learning to apply stains effectively is at the foundation of wood finishing. Although arguments can be made for the aesthetics of natural wood, the reality is that stains add color, contrast, depth, and richness to wood. They can be used for subtle grain enhancement or for startling creative effects. They also solve problems, like adding color to otherwise uninteresting woods, evening out tonal variations, and blending different types of wood together. You also need to know the basics of removing color by using bleach. Like staining, removing color can add a decorative effect or solve problems.

WORKING SMART

The final color of a stained piece of wood is the sum of the wood's natural color plus the color of the stain. Most store samples are done on pine, oak, or maple. If you're using mahogany or walnut, the stain will look different.

PREPARING TO STAIN

Try to stain the wood as quickly as you can after preparing the surface so that dirt, debris, and oil from your hands don't get onto the surface and there's less chance of dents and dings. The surface of the wood should always be sanded and cleaned before you stain it. All glue, sanding debris, and dust should be removed from the wood. You may choose to stain before gluing up, in which case you should mask off all gluing areas from stains with a binder (like pigment stains). Make sure that your work area is also clean, and find a place with plenty of light.

Stain can be applied by hand with various applicators or by spraying. Rags should be clean and absorbent natural fiber like cotton. Old T-shirts are best. Heavy-duty paper towels are fine, and both natural and synthetic brushes can be used. Synthetic pad-type applicators can be used with any stain, but foam brushes will not work with some solvent-based stains. Spray equipment should be set for medium to light viscosity, and thick pigment stains should be thinned with the appropriate carrier.

Pigment stains should be stirred or shaken well before use to mix the pigment that tends to settle to the bottom. Dye stains can be used without stirring, but if you mix the dye from a powder, you should make sure it's fully dissolved. It's also a good idea to strain dyes before using them. If you have several cans or jars of the same color stain, mix them together in case the stain from one batch is different than the next. If you mix a custom stain, always make more than you think you'll need, and be sure to write down the mix ratios.

Regardless of the stain you use, you'll need plenty of solvent for the stain and clean rags handy. Solvent can lighten up a

stain while it's still wet, and clean rags catch drips and blot up excess stain. Keep sandpaper and a scraper easily accessible in case you run into a spot of dried glue.

Before you start, practice on sample cutoffs from your project. Use at least a 4-in. by 5-in. piece so that you have a good idea of what the stain will look like on a larger piece. Apply the stain in the same way you plan to stain your project. I once got a different color on a piece of oak because I wiped the stain on the sample and sprayed it on the project. Apply the same finish you plan to use so you can visualize the final color. Stained woods change color and deepen as the finish is applied.

PIGMENT STAINS

Pigment stains accentuate the surface texture of some woods. They add contrast and richness to woods with large, open pores like oak and ash, darkening and therefore accentuating the pores.

To create this effect, pigment stains are applied to the wood and then the excess is wiped off. While there are variations in the amount of stain you leave on the surface, the best, cleanest effects are obtained when you wipe the surface clean. The type of carrier and resin that is used will have an effect on the application.

Oil-based stains have a long open time, which means they allow you plenty of time to wipe off the excess, but they take a long time to dry before you can apply a finish.

Varnish-based stains are composed of pigment mixed in varnish. They have less open time and are generally used for a one-step application of color and finish.

Fast-dry oil/varnish blends stains dry rapidly and you must work quickly to get the excess off. They can be top-coated in an hour or less.

Water-soluble stains also dry rapidly so you must work quickly. They can be top-coated quickly after the dye is applied, but they raise the grain of the wood. Before application, raise the grain with distilled water and then resand with the last grit you used.

Pigment stains that dry to a hard film, such as oil stains and oil/varnish blends, are good choices when you will be brushing or wiping on a top coat. These binders will not redissolve or soften when clear finishes are applied.

Pigment stains are much more lightfast than dye stains. The iron oxide pigment in wood stains is one of the most fade-proof colors. Pigment stains should be used where lightfastness is an issue or where strong sunlight is present for long periods.

Applying Pigment Stains

It helps if you can take the project apart before applying pigment stains. Remove doors and hardware and mentally break down large pieces into more manageable areas so that you have plenty of time to wipe off the excess stain. If the excess stain starts to get tacky, use some solvent for the stain to wipe off the excess. (To determine the solvent, look on the can and see what is used to thin or clean the stain.) You may need to restain because the solvent will lighten up the surface.

Otherwise the application is pretty simple. Using a brush, rag, or spray gun, apply the stain in any direction. A brush helps for getting the stain into crevices, moldings, and complex profiles. For over-head staining—like on crown molding—a gel stain works best. Leave the stain for a minute or two, then wipe off the excess with a clean rag. You can wipe it off in any direction, but to be safe, make a last swipe or two with the grain of the wood. A spray gun will not get into right angles

Applying Pigment Stains

1 Apply a pigment stain by brushing or wiping the stain on the wood in any direction. Here I use a stiff-bristle brush to work the stain into the groove of the molded edge of the door panel.

2 Use a clean rag or paper towel to remove the excess stain. To get stain out of crevices, use the tip of the cloth or a clean brush. If the stain is still wet and you want to change the color, wipe on a different color stain immediately.

3 Here I apply a redder shade of cherry stain before the brown cherry stain has a chance to dry.

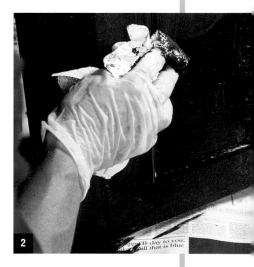

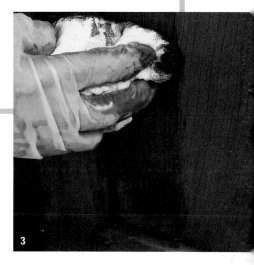

WORKING SMART

If pigment stain doesn't get the wood dark enough, try changing to a combination pigment/dye stain or just a dye. Or sand to a lower grit, like 120. Letting the pigment stain sit longer does not make it darker, and if you apply several coats of it, you'll "muddy" the grain of the wood.

and crevices, so it's best to brush those areas first, then spray.

To get stain out of crevices, whisk a dry brush back and forth to pick up excess stain.

Liming, Pickling, and Whitewashing

The process of applying a white-colored pigment stain to wood is known by several different names—liming, pickling, and whitewashing. The pigment stain is the same for all, but the techniques are different, and different looks are created.

Liming puts white color just in the pores of the wood. The stain is applied over sealed wood so that the color stays only in the pores when the excess is wiped off.

Pickling accomplishes the same look as liming, but the color may be off-white and the stain is applied over partially sealed wood so that some color stays on the surface.

In whitewashing, the white stain is applied over bare wood, which results in an even white-colored film over the entire surface and in the pores. The technique can be done by hand on woods that take

stain evenly, but on denser and harder woods like maple, the stain may need to be sprayed. (See Whitewash finish on pp. 210-212.)

If you can't find a white-colored stain, just thin some oil- or water-soluble white paint by diluting 1 part paint with 2 parts thinner, adjusting the ratio for different intensities.

DYE STAINS

Dye stains are not as easy to find as pigment stains, so don't be surprised if your local paint or hardware store doesn't have them. Available as a powder or premixed and soluble in various solvents, dye stains are the only way to achieve bold, dark colors on wood without painting it. Because the coloring particle is small, dyed wood absorbs and transmits light, letting subtle figure and grain show through. (Pigment stains, on the other hand, absorb and reflect light.)

Powdered dye stains should be dissolved in the solvent specified by the manufacturer. For water-soluble dyes, hot tap

Applying Water-Soluble Dyes by Hand

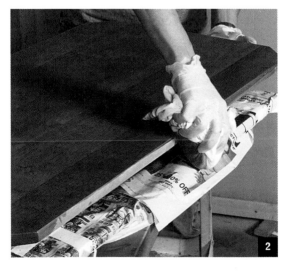

1 With a cloth pad or a sponge, apply the dye over the entire surface as quickly as you can. Apply the dye in any direction.

2 Apply dye to the edges last. Note how the panel is raised off the table with wooden cleats so the edge is easily accessible.

water can be used, but for light colors you may want to switch to distilled water to avoid a tannin-iron reaction, which causes small, gray spots. After the dye dissolves, it's best to strain it to make sure that any undissolved particles are removed. Dyes should be stored in glass or plastic jars. Stored in a cool, dry place away from direct sunlight, they should remain usable for many years.

Premixed dyes are either ready to use or should be thinned down with solvent. Make sure the solvent is compatible with the dye.

Applying by Hand

Both water- and solvent-soluble dyes can be applied by hand. However, the techniques vary slightly.

Water-soluble dyes should be applied with a rag, sponge, or synthetic-bristle brush. I prefer using sponges and rags because they drip less than brushes. It's a good idea to preraise the grain of the wood first. To do this, sponge the wood with dis-

tilled water. After the wood has dried, resand the grain with the last grit you used. Regardless of the applicator, saturate the wood quickly with the dye, wiping it on in any direction. Apply it quickly, then blot off the excess. Because wood accepts water so easily, it makes little difference in color if you let the dye sit or apply more dye. For woods like oak, where the grain is almost always raised during staining despite pre-raising, I sand the wood with a piece of synthetic steel wool while the dye is still wet. The dye dries in as little as several hours if the weather is warm and dry, but to be on the safe side, I usually wait overnight before applying a finish.

Solvent-soluble dyes (alcohol, non-grain-raising [NGR], and oil based) dry quickly, especially the alcohol types, so a technique adjustment is required with these dyes. I pour the dye into a shallow pan and dip the bottom of a wadded-up cotton cloth into the dye. I lightly pad on the dye with the slightly dampened cloth, working quickly to avoid lap marks.

> **WORKING SMART**
>
> To minimize grain raising and speed up the drying time of water-soluble dyes, mix the dye with water to dissolve the dye, then thin it with alcohol.

Applying Alcohol-Soluble Dyes by Hand

1 Pour dye into a shallow pan. Wad up a clean cloth into a pad and dip just the bottom of it into the dye. Scrape the pad over the edge to remove any excess dye.

2 Wipe on the dye, working quickly to avoid lap marks. If the dye is drying too quickly, you can add a retarder like a glycol ether or lacquer thinner to the dye. Water can be used but will raise the grain of the wood.

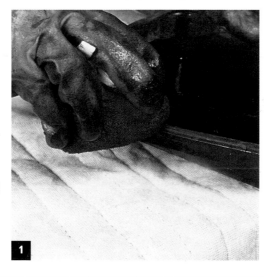

1

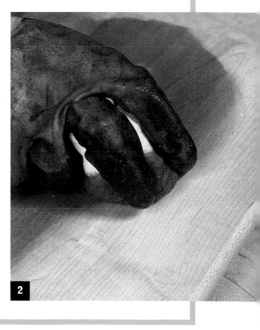

2

Spraying Water-Soluble Dyes

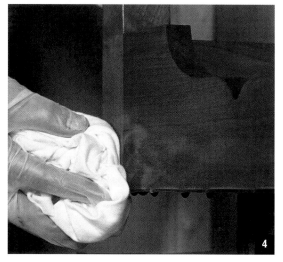

1 A small inexpensive gun works well for spraying this coffee table.

2 Lift the piece off the work surface with blocks, then start spraying the dye anywhere on the piece.

3 Spray the dye until the wood is saturated and appears wet. Make sure you spray the insides of the piece, too.

4 Use a clean cloth to blot any drips that collect at the bottom of the piece.

Because the dye dries quickly, you can slowly work up to the color that you want with multiple coats.

You can top-coat solvent-soluble dyes within an hour or so if you spray the top coat, but if you plan to apply the dye by hand, let it dry overnight. Because dyes have no binder, they can easily be pulled up if you brush or wipe on a top coat with the same solvent base as the dye. To minimize this problem, I make a thin sealer coat

of the top coat finish. Once the dye is completely dry, I brush or wipe on the sealer quickly and thinly to seal in the dye.

Spraying

Spraying dyes is the quickest application method. Water-soluble dyes are nonflammable, so you can spray them just about anywhere that's convenient. Solvent-based dyes should be sprayed outdoors or in a spray booth. While spraying speeds things up quite a bit, there is one problem with it: The vortex created by the spray gun prevents dye from getting into right angles, corners, or crevices of moldings. You should sponge or wipe these areas first, then blend them in with the dye from the spray gun.

Water-soluble dyes In preparation, dissolve the dye and then strain it through a fine mesh filter or a coffee filter. Set the spray gun up for fine viscosity liquids or the smallest aperture nozzle for your gun. Water is difficult to atomize, so it's not uncommon to get what appears to be a mist of large droplets when you spray. This mist shouldn't keep the dye from drying evenly.

Spraying water-soluble dye couldn't be easier. Set up the gun for a medium fluid delivery and a medium fan pattern. Spray the wood as evenly as possible to get it wet, blotting up puddles with a cloth. If drips land in the middle of an unstained area, spray over them immediately with dye or they may be noticeable when they dry. You can wipe the wood when it's wet, or leave it alone. It won't make much difference because water-soluble dyes penetrate the wood very quickly so there's not much to wipe off.

When you are finished spraying, clean the gun by running denatured alcohol through it. Do not use water, because it may corrode parts on inexpensive guns.

Solvent-soluble dyes Spraying solvent-soluble dyes (alcohol, NGR, and oil) is a bit trickier than spraying water-soluble dyes and requires more patience. The setup for the gun is the same, though. Use a small aperture nozzle and set the fluid control setting to the halfway point—not a fine, dry mist and not too heavy. The concentration of the dye should not be too strong.

Spraying Solvent-Soluble Dyes

1 Whether you use a small pressurized canister or a spray rig, the process for spraying solvent dyes is the same: Start with one light coat, let it dry, then apply a few more light coats.

2 Apply more light coats as desired, gradually working up to the intensity that you want.

3 Move around the piece. Avoid spraying too long in one spot because it will saturate the wood, causing the stain to bleed or dry unevenly. If this happens, wipe or blot the excess dye immediately.

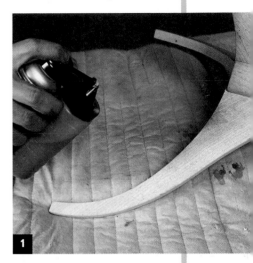
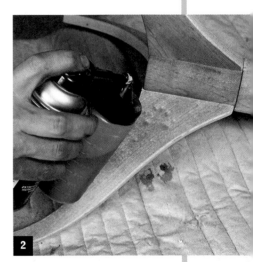
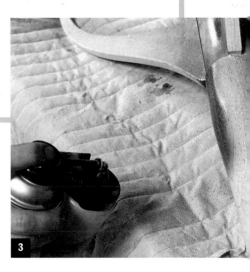

This cherry panel was stained on the bottom right with a pigment stain. You can see that the stain penetrates differently on the heartwood and sapwood. The bottom left side was dyed using a spray gun. The top is unstained.

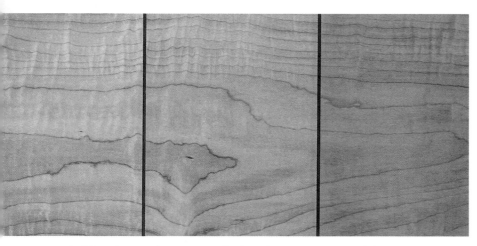

A dilute brown dye stain applied to the center panel of this curly maple provides some extra grain enhancement. A darker yellow-brown dye stain applied to the right panel mimics an aged appearance. The left side is natural.

It's best to work up to the color that you want in dilute, thin coats rather than apply one heavy coat. As when you apply solvent-soluble dye by hand, it's best not to saturate the wood with dye or it may dry streaky or uneven.

Spray the inside of the piece first, then move to the outside. Keep the gun moving and spray even coats. Do not let the dye puddle or get too wet. Because the dye dries quickly, it's hard to visualize the intensity of the dye color. You may want to stop periodically to check your progress and gauge the color. You can stop and wipe the dye with naphtha or mineral spirits to see if the color and intensity are correct. (Wiping with these materials removes less dye than wiping with alcohol.)

Whether or not you wipe the dye after spraying is up to you. I like to wipe it because it makes the dye penetrate more and gives more richness and depth. It's also a way to get the dye into corners and crevices. But not wiping has its advantages. It alleviates uneven penetration, or splotching, and provides a more uniform color to the piece. You see this look on many factory-finished items like furniture and kitchen cabinets. And, of course, not wiping saves time.

Using Dyes Effectively

Dyes not only provide deep, bold coloration, but they can also cause some common finishing problems. To use dyes effectively you'll need to deal with problems including difficulties matching sapwood to heartwood, warming up cool-toned woods, "kicking out" figure, and mimicking an aged appearance to the wood.

To match heartwood to sapwood, it's best to use a sprayer. If you don't have one, you can apply the dye with a small pad or sponge. You can use either a water- or solvent-soluble dye, but a 50/50 mix of water/alcohol to a water-soluble dye works best. Because sapwood is a different density than heartwood, it may dye differently. If you want to bring up the sapwood to the color of the heartwood, sponge the heartwood area with distilled water. This wets the wood and shows the approximate color of the finished wood so you can see what color you need to match for the sapwood. It also prevents any errant sprayed dye from absorbing into the heartwood.

It's best to "sneak up" on the color with several dye colors rather than try to hit it in one shot. To preview your match, let the dye dry, then wipe it with naphtha or mineral spirits. This action will approximate the color of the wood when it has a finish on it, but won't dissolve the dye.

To warm up a cool wood like poplar or kiln-dried walnut, use an amber-colored dye. You can buy it under a variety of names, but if you can't find the right color, try this recipe for a nice caramel color: 10 parts yellow dye, 1 part red dye, 1 part black dye (by weight). I typically dilute 1 teaspoon of this mixture with 1 pint of water, but you can experiment with different ratios to get the effect you like.

You may also want to "kick out" figure, or "pop" the grain in figured woods. To do this, first dilute a brown dye until it's the color of strong tea. Saturate the wood with this dye and then let it dry. Sand the wood with the last grit you used on the piece.

Mimicking an aged appearance is also an option. As wood is exposed to light and air over time, the surface changes color. Generally light woods develop a yellow/brown appearance, while most dark woods develop an orange-brown color. Matching this color is the first step in

Different application techniques result in different effects. From left to right: white stain applied to bare wood, white stain applied to sealed wood, and sprayed white stain.

antique reproductions, and it's generally done with a dye. You may use either a water- or alcohol-soluble dye stain, but I like water-soluble stains the best. I typically start with a stock amber, golden brown, or orange-brown color (depending on the type of wood) and tweak it with primary colors like red or black until it's the color that I want.

CHANGING COLOR

At some point you will run into an age old finishing problem: The color of the stain on the wood is not what you want. Sometimes you can fix the problem easily by darkening or lightening the stain. Dye stains respond to these changes better than pigment stains do. Other times you need to know a bit about color theory so you can correct the problem without stripping or sanding and starting over.

Modifying Pigment Stains

As long as the stain hasn't dried, you can modify the color. To lighten the stain, wipe it with the thinner applicable for the stain.

Pigment stains (left) accentuate the surface texture better than dye stains (right).

The left side of this walnut board was dyed with an orange-brown dye to warm it up. The right side is unstained.

You can use synthetic steel wool and thinner if thinner alone doesn't get it as light as you want. To darken the stain or change the hue, apply a darker or different color stain while the first one is still wet.

If the stain has dried and it's not the color you want, your options for modifying the color are limited. For a lighter stain, your only option is to remove the existing stain with stripper. Lacquer thinner also works as long as the stain hasn't cured for more than several days. For a darker color or different color, you need to wipe on a different color stain. You can do this only for stains that have a binder that does not redissolve in its carrier like oil, oil/varnish blends, and water-soluble stains. Another option is to use a glaze or toner after the stain is sealed. (For more on this, see chapter 6.)

Modifying Dye Stains

It's easy to modify the color and intensity of a dye. Because a dye contains no binder, you can modify it while the dye is still wet or after it has dried. Making modifications once the dye is dry gives you greater control over the final color, and you can adjust it any time before the top coats are applied.

To make the dye darker, you'll need a stronger concentration of dye powder to solvent. You can also put dark brown or black dye into the dye solution or wipe it on the wood. Dark brown is preferable because many black dyes have a bluish undertone, which will throw off the color. To make the dye lighter, simply wipe the wood with the solvent for the dye, or add solvent to the dye solution before applying it.

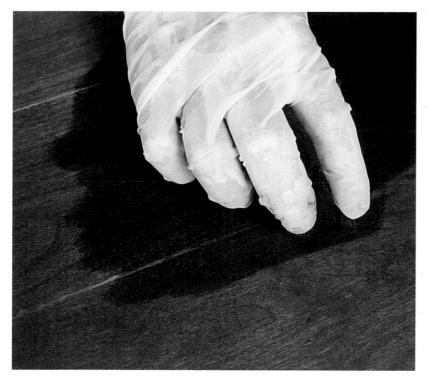

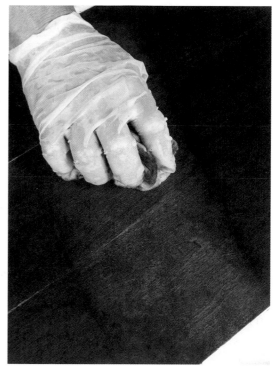

To darken a stain, apply a dark brown stain. Black stain would cool the color too much because it has a bluish undertone.

To lighten a stain, wipe it with the solvent for the stain. Be sure to wipe pigment stains before they start to dry.

You may change the color before application by adding another color to the dye. Or you can wipe a different color dye over the dyed wood.

Correcting Color

Most of the time you will apply color theory when tweaking or changing standard wood-tone colors. This sounds intimidating but it's not—you only have to know a few basic principles.

The colors you'll use for corrections appear on a basic color wheel, which is a circle divided into six segments. The primary colors are red, yellow, and blue; they can't be mixed from other colors. Between red and yellow is orange, between yellow and blue is green, and between blue and red is purple. These three colors are called secondary colors because each is mixed (or made) from two primary colors.

You can manipulate wood-tone colors by using the primary and secondary colors of the color wheel. Obviously if you want something redder, just add red. But what if something is too red? How do you neutralize the red without darkening the color? That's when you look at the color wheel. The opposite of red is green. Adding green to red neutralizes the redness and brings the overall color toward a medium brown. Adding blue has the same effect on orange, and purple neutralizes yellow.

Of the three primary colors, yellow is the most luminous. Add yellow when you want to brighten up a brown color. Black decreases brightness, so add it when you want to tone down a color. White pigments can be added to wood-tone colors to create chalky pastels.

You can also think of colors as cool or warm. Cool colors have a dominant blue or

Basic Color Theory

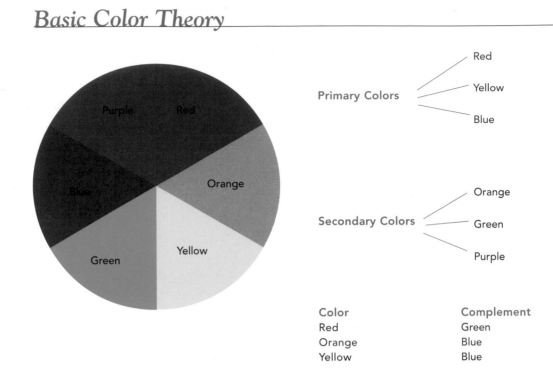

Primary Colors
- Red
- Yellow
- Blue

Secondary Colors
- Orange
- Green
- Purple

Color	Complement
Red	Green
Orange	Blue
Yellow	Blue

This mahogany board was modified several times. First it was stained with a dark brown dye stain (left). Then it was wiped with water to lighten it (second from left). Then a dark red dye was applied (third from left). Finally, a dilute green dye was applied to neutralize the red (right).

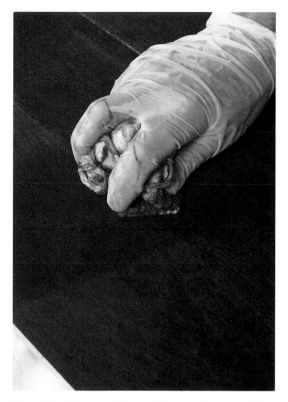

To make a brown stain redder, apply pure red stain. For a more subtle red, use a diluted red.

To neutralize red, apply its complementary color—green—over it.

green undertone. Warm colors have a red or orange undertone. To warm up a cool wood-tone color, apply red or orange over it. Those colors correct the problem much more quickly than several coats of a warm brown color. The opposite look is just as easy. Apply a blue or green color over a warm brown to cool the color.

Using these methods will allow you to tweak the color of the wood while the stain is still on the wood, but remember that the color of a finish may shift the color of a stain. Orange shellac will obviously add an orange color. Many varnishes have an amber color that will warm up the overall color. The important thing to remember is that you can continue to manipulate the color as you finish. With glazing and toning, you can arrive at the perfect color every time (see chapter 6).

BLEACHING

The flip side of staining is bleaching, or removing color. While it may seem strange to talk about bleach and staining together, there are situations where you need to remove the color from wood. The most common situations occur when:

- The natural color of the wood is too dark
- The color of the wood needs to be evened out to a neutral white color
- Dye needs to be removed from the wood
- The wood has iron or other stains that need to be removed.

The real trick in using bleaches is to use the correct bleach for the job. Bleaches work by a chemical reaction between the

Bleaching with Oxalic Acid

1 To remove the stain on this cherry mirror (caused by letting a piece of wet steel wool rest overnight on it), mix a solution of oxalic acid. Fill a glass or plastic container with hot water and add the dry oxalic acid crystals until no more dissolves.

2 Brush or wipe this solution liberally on both the stained area and the rest of the wood.

3 After the bleach dries and the stain is removed, wash the dry crystals off the wood and neutralize it with vinegar. Then resand the wood.

bleach and the color on the wood. The reactions differ from bleach to bleach, so one bleach will work in some situations and not in others. There are three types of bleaches used in wood finishing: oxalic acid, two-part (also called A/B) bleach, and chlorine bleach.

Oxalic acid removes iron stains like black water rings. It may also remove some other stains caused by certain inks as well as some pigment stains.

Two-part bleach removes the natural color of wood and bleaches it white or off-white. This bleach is used to lighten dark woods like walnut or to change maple and birch to a bone-white color. Two-part bleach can also be used to bleach woods with heartwood and sapwood to an even base color so that stains color evenly.

Chlorine bleach removes dye stains and some food stains like grape juice. A laundry bleach like Clorox can be used, but it's pretty weak. A faster-acting bleach can be made from swimming pool bleach.

Most bleaches are hazardous to use, so you need to take some precautions. Oxalic acid is poisonous. The sodium hydroxide in two-part bleach is a strong caustic and can burn your skin and blind you. Chlorine bleach can cause severe eye problems. Always wear gloves, a dust mask, and safety glasses when mixing dry bleach powders. Also, never apply one type of bleach over another (except the components of two-part bleach) without washing the wood first with plenty of distilled water.

Using Oxalic Acid

Oxalic acid is sold in dry crystal form in paint and hardware stores. It is sometimes called wood bleach, so check the label; oxalic acid should be the only ingredient. Oxalic acid is unique in that it removes a

Bleaching with Two-Part Bleach

1 Just before application, mix the two parts of the bleach in a glass or plastic dish. Apply the solution to the wood immediately.

2 Use a synthetic-bristle brush or rag to apply the bleach.

gray or black stain formed by water or alkalis that come into contact with wood. However, you must keep two things in mind when using oxalic acid.

- It works only on bare wood. If you have a finish on the surface, it must be removed and the wood must be sanded lightly so that the oxalic acid can penetrate.

- It does not remove the natural color of wood, although it may lighten it because it's cleaning the wood. When you apply oxalic acid, apply it to the whole surface so that you get a consistent color.

In a plastic or glass container, add the dry oxalic acid crystals to hot tap water until no more acid dissolves. While the solution is still hot, brush it onto the entire surface of the wood. Wet the surface well and let it dry overnight. A second application may be needed on stubborn stains.

When the stain is gone or lightened enough, clean the surface of the wood several times with clean distilled water to remove the acid that crystallizes on the surface. Never sand or blow off the dry crystals. Neutralize the surface by wiping it with a solution of distilled water and borax or sodium bicarbonate (baking soda) and let it dry. When it's dry, resand the wood.

Using Two-Part Bleach

Two-part bleach is sold as two containers (usually labeled A and B) in one box. Part A is sodium hydroxide and Part B is hydrogen peroxide. When the two parts are mixed, either right before application or on the wood, a powerful oxidizing reaction takes place that's effective in removing the natural color of wood.

To use this bleach, apply Part A to the wood and, while it's still wet, apply Part B. Part A may darken the wood, but Part B will reverse the effect. It's possible to mix the two parts before application, but then

> **WORKING SMART**
>
> If you want to get rid of a stain but don't know what caused it, try oxalic acid first. If that doesn't work, try chlorine bleach but make sure you remove the oxalic acid bleach with plenty of water first. If the chlorine bleach doesn't work, then try two-part bleach.

Bleaching with Chlorine Bleach

1 For a fast-acting chlorine bleach use swimming pool bleach dissolved in hot water. Add the powder until no more dissolves and wait for a few minutes until it starts foaming.

2 Using a synthetic-bristle brush, a rag, or a sponge, apply the bleach liberally to the entire surface of the wood. If the bleach doesn't lighten the dyed wood enough, apply a second application to further lighten it. The bleaching action continues even though the wood appears dry, so wait overnight before applying the second coat.

3 When the wood is dry and you have the lightness you want, wash the wood with several wipes of distilled water and then resand.

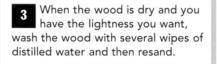

you must apply it immediately after mixing, and any unused bleach has to be discarded. Always use the freshest product you can; hydrogen peroxide loses its effectiveness when stored for long periods of time.

Brush or wipe the two parts on with a rag. Never exceed two applications, and do not flood the surface. Too much bleach may cause a greenish tinge on some woods, such as walnut, that's hard to get rid of. (You have to neutralize such a tinge with red dye.)

Typically the bleaching process takes a while, so it's best to wait overnight to gauge the results. After the surface of the wood is dry, neutralize the bleach with a solution of 1 part white vinegar to 1 part distilled water.

If two applications of bleach don't lighten the wood enough, neutralize the surface and apply some oxalic acid. Resand the wood to the required smoothness.

Using Chlorine Bleach

Chlorine is a strong oxidizer that will remove most aniline dye stains (it is ineffective on pigment stains). You can use laundry bleach, but several applications may be necessary. I prefer to make a stronger bleach from shock treatment for swimming pools. It's sold in small packets. Make sure the active ingredient listed is calcium hypochlorite.

If you use pool bleach, make a solution by dissolving 1 tablespoon of the dry powder in 1 cup of hot water. Wait several minutes until the mixture starts to bubble and then apply it to the entire surface of the wood. The bleach starts to lighten the dye immediately, but it may take several applications and overnight drying to gauge the full effect. Some dyes may only lighten, in which case you will have to restain to a uniform color. Because this bleach is only effective on the dye, it rarely lightens the wood. Chlorine laundry bleach can be used in the same way, but several applications are necessary.

The dried bleach recrystallizes on the surface of the wood if you use the pool bleach treatment, so you'll need to rinse it off with clean, distilled water.

COLORING PROBLEMS AND THEIR SOLUTIONS

The reality of coloring wood is that problems arise. Because wood is not a consistent and homogenous material, stains can penetrate unevenly, causing splotching. Sometimes there are wild tonal variations in the wood that need to be evened out to achieve a consistent color. When different types of woods, solid and plywood for example, are used in the same piece they can stain differently. Plywood may contain stress cracks from the manufacturing process that are too deep to sand out. And end grain can stain darker than face grain, resulting in an inconsistent and unattractive appearance.

To solve these problems you have to understand that the culprit is not the stain. The fault lies in the wood's density and surface texture and the way it's reacting to the stain. A pigment stain will accentuate surface texture, as the pigment lodges in pores, sanding scratches, and any cavity larger than the size of the pigment particle. Dyes color deeply and evenly and do not accentuate surface texture.

Knowing the basic difference between pigment and dye is essential in solving staining problems. Remember that pigment stains accentuate surface texture and dyes do not.

Wood Imperfections
Every effort should be made during surface preparation to eliminate wood imperfections like small cracks, splits in veneer, and deep sanding scratches. However, some-

Stress cracks formed during the veneer-slicing process are not visible with a dye stain (left). They are exaggerated when a pigment stain is applied (right).

times the problems can't be fixed and must be dealt with at this stage. For example, small stress cracks that are formed in veneer during its manufacture are impossible to remove during surface preparation but can be masked at the coloring stage.

Dealing with these problems is quite simple. A pigment stain will accentuate the imperfections, so you should use a dye stain. Another less effective way to deal with the problem is to spray on pigment stain but not wipe it. When you spray pigment stain, it tends to sit on top of the wood, whereas when you wipe it you force it into the defective areas.

Matching Veneer and Solid Wood
When veneer and solid wood are used in the same piece of wood it's likely that they will stain differently. To avoid this problem you can do one of two things.

Finishing Cherry

Cherry is one of our premier native hardwoods. Freshly sanded, it's a pinkish salmon color, but eventually it mellows to a deep reddish brown. In an effort to speed up the natural darkening process, finishers often apply a stain, but the results are disappointing.

The problem with finishing cherry is threefold. First, the density changes abruptly over the area of the wood because resins surface during kiln-drying. Second, cherry exhibits wide tonal variations—even within boards from the same tree—that cause color variations when a stain is applied. Third, cherry typically contains a large amount of sapwood, which affects the look of the finish.

Three finishing approaches work well with cherry. The first method darkens the wood slightly and removes the pinkish color. Over the next year or so, the wood will mature to a deep reddish brown if it's exposed to plenty of light. The second method darkens the wood more than the first method. The third method uses dye to equalize sapwood and heartwood and to even out tonal variations, dark reddish-brown pigment stain to bring out the reddish color and to delineate pore structure, and dye toners to tweak the color. It is used for pieces with a lot of sapwood and boards with different colors.

METHOD 1

1. Sand the wood to 180 or 220 grit and remove the sanding dust.
2. Flood the surface with boiled linseed oil or an oil/varnish blend. Let it dry at least overnight.
3. Pad, brush, or spray on a dark garnet-colored shellac. Several coats should be sufficient. When dry, wax with dark paste wax.

METHOD 2

1. Sand the wood to 180 or 220 grit and remove the sanding dust.
2. Apply a 2-lb. cut of shellac to the wood. Wait 30 minutes, then lightly scuff-sand the wood with 320-grit sandpaper.

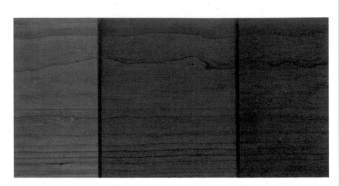

To equalize the differences in cherry, a yellow-amber dye stain was applied to the left side, then a dark brown pigment stain was applied to accentuate textural and tonal differences (center). The same board was then finished with clear lacquer (right).

3. Apply a gel stain. Let the wood dry overnight.
4. Apply several coats of the finish of your choice.

METHOD 3

1. Sand the wood to 180 or 220 grit and remove the sanding dust.
2. Dye the wood with a water- or alcohol-soluble honey-amber dye. You can use a premixed dye or make one in the ratio (by weight) of 15 parts yellow, 1 part red, and 1 part black. I dilute this two or three times the manufacturer's recommended concentration. If you use a water-soluble dye, preraise the grain to minimize raised grain after the dye is applied. Let the wood dry overnight.
3. Pad, brush, or spray on a 2-lb. cut of shellac as a sealer. Apply one thin coat—just enough to seal the dye. When the shellac is dry, scuff-sand the surface lightly with 320-grit sandpaper to remove raised grain.
4. Apply a dark reddish-brown pigment stain and wipe off the excess. If you want a browner, less red color, use a dark brown stain. Let the stain dry according to the manufacturer's instructions.
5. When the stain has dried and the color is right, apply a clear finish. For further coloring you can spray dark brown or dark red toners. After toning, apply clear top coats to protect the toner color.

This kitchen cabinet door was made from a cherry plywood center panel and a solid cherry frame. The door was dyed, sealed (top left), and then glazed (top right) to make the color more uniform. The bottom is unfinished.

To make maple black, use a dye stain. It results in a bold black and lets figure show through (top right). Pigment stain doesn't stain dark enough (bottom left). Repeated applications of pigment stain result in a painted appearance (bottom right). The top left is natural maple.

The first option is to dye the entire piece a light undertone color with a dye stain. After the finish is sealed, you can refine the color by selective application of a glazing stain. Or you can double-glaze, meaning you apply glaze to just the lighter areas, seal it, and then glaze the entire piece. (See chapter 6 for more on glazing.)

The second option is to seal the wood with sealer or thinned finish, then spray a toner over the entire piece to establish a uniform color. Dyes or pigmented toners can be used.

Bold, Dark Colors on Dense Woods

Some hard, dense woods like maple, birch, and ash will not stain an even dark color with a pigment stain. On maple, there just aren't enough crevices for the pigment particles to lodge in. On birch and ash, the pore structure makes it difficult to get even

coloration because the pores accept more pigment than the flat grain.

To get any dense wood a dark, bold, even color, use a dye stain. Dyes color evenly and don't accentuate pore structure and surface texture.

End Grain

End grain stains darker than face grain and side grain. This is most noticeable with pigment stains. You can't completely prevent the problem, but you can mitigate it by using a dye stain. However, using some dyes on certain woods can also cause problems.

The best solution is to apply a dilute coat of shellac to the end grain before applying the stain. This minimizes stain penetration into the porous end grain, resulting in a more even color. You can substitute a finish for the shellac as long as it's thinned. For example, use thinned lacquer for lacquer fin-

The end grain on this oak board was coated with a 1-lb. cut of shellac (left) before a pigment stain was applied. The right portion of the end grain was untreated.

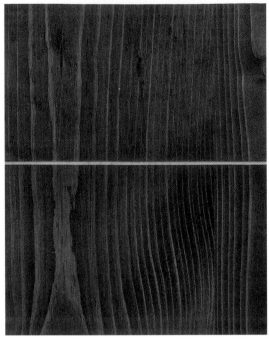

A gel stain was applied to the bottom half of this pine board, minimizing the splotching evident on the top, where a liquid pigment stain was applied.

WORKING SMART

Almost any thinned finish can be used to control penetration of a stain into wood. You can use shellac, sanding sealer, or just thinned finish. Another option is to saturate the wood with the solvent for the stain that you'll be using and then immediately apply the stain.

---

ishes. Make sure the finish doesn't contain a solvent that's the same as the stain, or it will redissolve it and be ineffective.

Splotching

When the surface of wood accepts stain unevenly, an unattractive appearance called splotching may result. Splotching is most commonly caused by areas of different densities in the wood and by swirling grain patterns. These conditions allow the stain to penetrate more in certain areas and less in others. Most softwoods like pines and firs, as well as hardwoods like birch, cherry, and poplar, are prone to splotching.

There are four techniques that you can use to solve splotching problems:

- Use a gel stain
- Washcoat the surface of the wood with thinned finish
- Use a water-soluble dye stain
- Spray the stain

Any of these options or a combination of them will work on even the most splotch-prone woods. Here's an overview of the techniques.

Gel stains Gel stains are normal stains (either dye or pigment) that are thickened by the manufacturer to a gel-like consistency. Because of their thick consistency, they penetrate more evenly and therefore minimize or eliminate splotching. These stains are very effective on softwoods like pine. They work on other woods as well, but they are not always completely successful. I suggest that you practice on a piece of scrap to see if the color is what you want.

Washcoating Washcoating is nothing more than partially sealing the surface of the wood by applying a thinned finish or slow-evaporating solvent to the wood. When

A washcoat of mineral spirits was applied to the top half of this board before a liquid pigment satin was applied. It minimizes splotching but stains lighter.

Causes of Splotching

Alternating swirly grain pattern cause a ripple pattern across the face of the board.

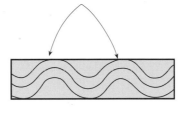

Resin deposits at surface cause uneven, darker stain penetration.

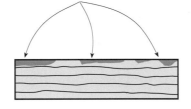

Areas burnished with dull sandpaper stain lighter.

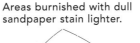

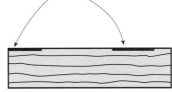

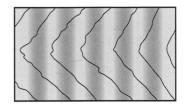

the surface is partially sealed, the stain applied over it tends to sit on the top, penetrating less and therefore reducing splotching.

There are two types of washcoats: slow-evaporating solvents and thinned finishes. Slow-evaporating solvents like mineral spirits are absorbed into areas that tend to soak up the most stain. By "preloading" these areas with solvent, the stain that's applied over them will be absorbed less, creating a more even stain. Commercial "stain conditioners" are slow-evaporating solvents. It's important to remember that mineral spirits products work only on oil-based stains. Use water for water-soluble stains. To apply a stain controller or slow-evaporating solvent, flood the surface with the solvent and then, before the solvent dries, apply the stain. It's important not to

let the solvent evaporate, or the stain can cause splotching.

A thinned finish partially seals off the surface so a stain appears more even when applied over it. To apply a thinned finish use the following guidelines:

- For shellac, use a 1-lb. cut. Brush or wipe on the shellac quickly, saturating the wood. Wipe off the excess quickly. Sand with 320-grit sandpaper when dry and then apply stain. Shellac is compatible with any stain.

This cherry board was sprayed with the same color NGR dye stain. The left side was the wiped with a cloth while the right side was not. The right side appears more uniform and less splotchy.

- Thin lacquer by adding 1 part lacquer (sanding sealer can be used) to 3 parts lacquer thinner. Brush, spray, or wipe it on the wood, then wipe off the excess. Allow it to dry for 30 minutes, then lightly sand with 320-grit paper and apply the stain. The wet wood will telegraph a splotchy appearance. Most oil-based stains can be applied over a lacquer washcoat except fast-drying stains, which may redissolve the lacquer binder.
- For oil, mix 1 part boiled linseed oil with 6 parts mineral spirits. Flood the mixture on the surface of the wood. You can either apply the stain while it's still wet or after it has dried for a day. This technique works for oil-based stains.

Apply a water-soluble dye stain Dyes, particularly water-soluble types, tend to color more evenly than pigment stains because they penetrate the wood surface more evenly regardless of density. Dyes are particularly effective on pine and poplar, but dark dyes can splotch cherry. You may want to switch to one of the different techniques for this wood. Applying a water-soluble dye over a washcoat of shellac works particularly well on cherry, but you'll have to spray the top coats because the dye will come off easily with brushing or wiping.

Spray the stain If you spray a stain and do not wipe it, it colors more evenly because it sits on the surface of the wood and doesn't sink into crevices. Most commercial finishers avoid splotching with this technique. To do it, set up the gun with a medium-wide fan pattern and cut back on the fluid control so that a small amount of dye is released. (See techniques for applying alcohol dyes on pp. 83-84.) Gradually work up to the color that you want and then let the dye dry without wiping it. If you wipe, it will splotch. Work color into corners the gun can't reach with a small brush or cloth folded so that it has a sharp, pointy corner.

TROUBLESHOOTING STAIN AND BLEACH PROBLEMS

PROBLEM	CAUSE	SOLUTION
Stain is too light	You sanded the wood too much (past 220 grit) Hardwoods don't stain dark with pigment stains Pigment stain not stirred	Sand to a lesser grit Switch to a dye stain Stir the stain
Stain is too dark	The sample you saw was on a hardwood and you're using a softwood; stain too concentrated	Thin stain
Stain doesn't look like the sample	You're using a different wood than the sample	Switch to a different stain
Stain won't dry	Oil-based stains can take a long time to cure, especially at low temperatures Manufacturer switched to a different resin	Raise temperature Wait longer for stain to cure
Finish pulls up stain	Stain isn't dry enough Solvent for the finish is the same as the stain	Wait longer for stain to cure Use a different top coat, stain or spray top coat
Stain is splotchy	Wood is not sanded with fresh sandpaper Wood has uneven density or swirling	Use a stain conditioner, gel stain, or washcoat Spray stain
Stain doesn't color pores	Water-soluble dyes don't color pores on open-grained woods	Apply a pigment satin over dye, or glaze, or use a paste wood filler
Solvent dye streaks around pores and bleeds in figured areas	Alcohol is evaporating too fast	Add a retarder to the dye (glycol ether or lacquer retarder)
Bleach doesn't work	Wrong bleach for the job Bleach is too old	Use the correct bleach Use fresh bleach
Bleach leaves greenish tinge	Too many applications of two-part bleach	Color out green selectively with red dye
Surface feels rough	Grain raised Residual powder on surface	Resand wood Wash off with distilled water
Finish turns white	Residual bleach left on surface	Strip and sand; neutralize bleach and wash with distilled water
Oxalic acid won't remove black ring	Ring is caused by ink	Sand out or replace wood

FILLING PORES

A filled-pore surface that's as smooth as glass adds a refined, elegant look to furniture. You can create this look on woods with large, open pores by filling the pores with paste wood filler. Paste wood fillers do more than just make the surface level. Colored fillers can blend in with the rest of the wood or contrast with it. If you're looking for a natural, unsophisticated look, don't fill the pores. But if you want a more refined look, try these techniques for a beautiful finish.

OIL-BASED FILLERS

Oil-based fillers are the oldest type of paste wood filler. They offer many creative options and are easy to use and apply. I find them easier to control than water-based fillers, especially in subtle coloring situations like matching a finish.

In an oil-based filler, the binder—either a true oil or oil-based varnish—determines its handling characteristics and the drying time needed before it can be top-coated. You can tell what type the binder is by the drying instructions on the can. Fillers with a true oil binder require days to dry, while those with varnish binders can dry much faster and be top-coated in as little as four hours.

You can apply oil-based fillers one of two ways. The first is to apply the filler to bare wood. The filler can be a natural color to blend in with the wood's natural color or it can be colored. You can add a compatible stain or concentrated colors like artist's pigments or Japan colors to the filler. With this technique the filler colors both the pores and the surrounding wood.

The second method is to stain the wood the desired color first (or leave it unstained) then seal it with finish before applying the filler. This method puts the filler only in the pores and gives you more control over the final color of the wood. I recommend this method when matching color.

Regardless of the method you choose for applying fillers, you will find that some are not ready to use. They may need to be thinned, or they may require additional stain or color.

Mixing Oil-Based Fillers

The consistency of oil-based fillers varies among manufacturers. Some companies make thick pastes that need thinning, while others provide a ready-to-use product. For the best results, the paste wood filler should be the consistency of heavy cream. If it's not, add mineral spirits or naphtha.

To color oil-based paste wood fillers, use artist's colors, UTCs (universal tinting colors), or Japan colors.

Using Oil-Based Fillers

1 After cleaning the pores of dust and sanding debris, use a stiff-bristle brush to apply the filler to the surface of the wood, working it into the grain.

2 With a rubber squeegee or a piece of cardboard, scrape the excess filler off the edge into a pan. Scrape with the grain of the wood.

3 As the edge of the scraper loads up, scrape the excess filler off the edge into the pan.

Wait for the carrier to "flash" off, which is signaled by a hazy look to the filler. (The time this takes depends on the evaporation rate of the carrier, the thinner you've added, and the temperature and humidity.) Then wipe the excess filler off the surface with a piece of burlap.

5 Wipe across the grain or in a figure-eight pattern. You can use the squeegee on legs and aprons as long as they're flat.

Use a small corner of the burlap to remove excess filler from complex areas like this beaded edge.

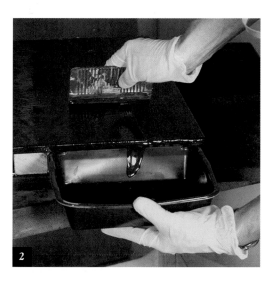

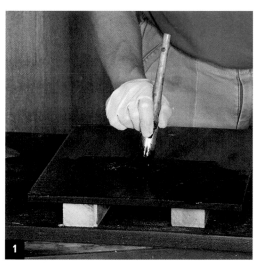

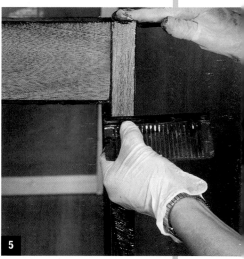

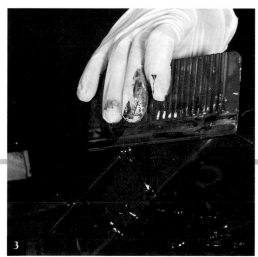

Naphtha makes the filler dry faster, so if you need a little extra time to apply and wipe off the filler, use mineral spirits. Stir the filler thoroughly because the bulking agent and pigment will settle to the bottom of the container.

To fill pores and color bare wood at the same time you have several options. You can mix an oil-based stain (either dye or pigment) with the filler before application. Because the stain will thin the filler, you may want to adjust your thinning ratio to allow for this. Beyond stain you can use just about any colorant that's compatible with the filler: dry pigment powder, artist's oil colors, UTCs, or Japan colors. Simply add the color to the filler and stir it. When using thick, pasty colors like artist's oil colors, I find that mixing the color with a bit of mineral spirits or naphtha first helps.

I think the best way to add color is with a concentrated pigment color. Concentrated pigment colors do not change the consistency of the filler, and they are available in a wide range of colors.

Applying Oil-Based Fillers

The effect of the filler is determined by what it's applied on: bare wood (it colors pores and the wood) or sealed wood (it colors only the pores). You can use any sealer to seal the wood before filler application. A thin sealer coat partially seals the wood and allows some of the color from the filler to stay on the surface. A thick sealer coat completely seals off the wood surface and puts the filler only in the pores.

To prepare for applying the filler, first lightly scuff-sand the sealer with 320-grit sandpaper to provide a smooth surface for the filler. You need to scuff-sand only those places where you'll be applying filler. Typically only flat visible parts of the furniture like tops and drawer fronts are filled.

However, you can apply filler to all surfaces like legs, aprons, and sides if you want to increase the aesthetic appeal of the piece.

Once you've applied and prepared the sealer, the application steps are the same for both bare wood and sealed wood. Before applying the filler make sure the pores are free of sawdust or other dirt. While it's possible to spray filler, I find hand application easier. Use a stiff-bristle brush to apply the filler over the entire surface you want to fill. Work the filler into the surface of the wood and then immediately scrape off the excess filler (in the direction of the grain) with a rubber squeegee, credit card, or piece of cardboard. I find rubber squeegees work best. Scrape the filler off the edge of the surface into a shallow pan (see photo 2 on p. 105). Clean the excess filler off the edge of the squeegee periodically with a clean rag.

After the filler hazes, or loses most of its carrier, wipe any remaining filler off the surface of the wood with a piece of burlap or cheesecloth. Wad up the burlap and wipe the surface across (perpendicular to) the grain. If you wipe with the grain, you may pull the filler out of the pores.

When you've removed all of the excess filler from the surface, finish up by wiping the surface in a figure-eight pattern. Then inspect the surface in backlighting; any remaining filler will be noticeable. If the filler has set, it will be hard to remove with the dry burlap, so you may have to use a rag moistened with naphtha or mineral spirits instead.

When you're satisfied with the wiping step, let the filler cure for a day, then inspect the surface. If you're still satisfied with the look, allow the filler to continue curing for the time recommended on the label. I like to let fast-drying varnish-based fillers cure for at least one day after applying the filler; I let slower fillers cure for at least three days. If the weather is cold or damp, extend the drying time. On woods with very large pores like oak, you may have to apply another coat of filler to get a smooth look. After the final filling, let the filler cure according to the directions.

After the filler has cured, sand it lightly with 320-grit sandpaper in the direction of the grain. Sand very lightly, just enough to remove any bumps or other problems. Most oil-based fillers do not cure hard because of their large oil content, so the paper will load and gum up quickly, requiring frequent changes. Once you've sanded, wipe the surface with a tack cloth or clean cloth.

Oil-based paste wood fillers will take most oil- and solvent-based finishes as a top coat. Water-based finishes perform better if a coat of dewaxed shellac is applied over the filler to prevent adhesion problems. Hand-applied solvent lacquers also benefit from a sealer coat of shellac because the solvents in the lacquer can soften the dried filler and wrinkle it. If you're spraying the lacquer, mist the first several coats on lightly and let them dry before applying full, wet coats.

WATER-BASED FILLERS

Water-based fillers are based upon the same general formula as oil-based fillers, but water is the carrier and a water-compatible resin like acrylic is the binder. This combination has several effects:

- Water-based fillers dry very fast so it's almost impossible to apply the filler and wipe it off cleanly. These fillers also raise the grain.
- Water-based fillers stick to sealer coats so it's impossible to apply them over sealed wood and then remove them without removing the sealer.

To color water-based paste wood fillers, use UTCs or artist's acrylic colors.

- When water-based fillers dry, they look chalky. They deepen when a finish or stain is applied over them.
- Unlike oil-based fillers, water-based fillers can be stained after they dry with certain solvent-based stains.
- Water-based fillers are easy to sand because they powder easily.
- Water-based fillers can be top-coated with any finish without adhesion problems.
- Water-based fillers are easy to clean up.
- Water-based filler are nonflammable.

Using Water-Based Fillers

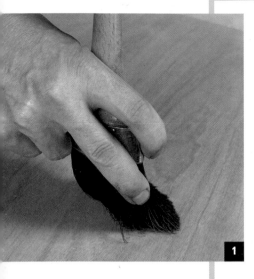

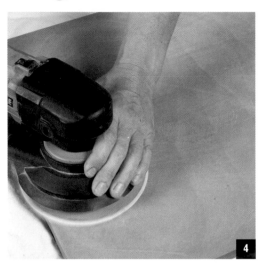

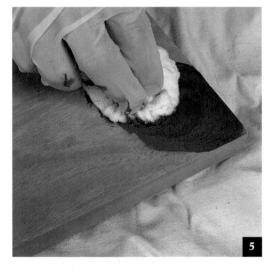

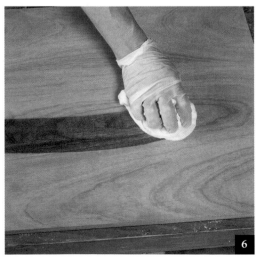

1 Clean the pores with a stiff-bristle brush, vacuum, or compressed air.

2 Using a synthetic-bristle brush, apply the filler liberally all over the surface of the wood, working as quickly as possible.

3 With a squeegee or a piece of cardboard, scrape the excess filler off into a pan as quickly as you can. It's fine if you can't remove all the filler or remove it cleanly.

4 After the filler has dried (usually three hours), sand it level with the surface of the wood starting with 150- or 180-grit paper. It should powder easily. If it doesn't, let it dry longer. Keep the sander as flat as you can and watch the edges. You can always hand-sand instead.

5 If you missed a spot or sanded through the filler, apply more filler to the area with a clean rag.

6 Water-based fillers can be stained after they dry but before they fully cure with certain solvent stains. Here a light, amber-colored alcohol dye is applied over a natural-colored filler. This technique stains the wood filler slightly darker than the wood color. Use a dark-colored filler for a better contrast.

When you prepare a water-based filler, be sure to stir it thoroughly. Most water-based fillers are thick and can be thinned to a more workable consistency with small amounts of water (but no more than 10% of the total mixture). Aim for about the consistency of thick latex paint. As with oil-based fillers, you can buy the filler in natural, which will dry to off-white, or colored. Several formulations are available in a transparent gel that dries water-clear. You can add water-compatible colorants such as dry pigment powder, UTCs, or artist's acrylic colors.

Because of its fast drying time, water-based filler is best applied directly to bare wood. The fast drying time also means you can work only on small areas at a time before the filler starts to set.

Before you start you'll need lots of clean rags and some clean water nearby. Make sure the pores are free of sanding dust. Using a synthetic-bristle brush, apply the filler liberally to the surface of the wood and then immediately wipe off the the excess with a squeegee, credit card, or piece of cardboard (it's not necessary to scrape it in the direction of the grain). Then wipe as much of the filler off with a clean rag. If you have a large, dried clump, moisten the rag with water before wiping. Let the filler dry for at least three hours (check the label on your can of filler for a more exact time). Hot, damp weather will extend the drying time.

To see if the filler is ready to sand, do a sanding test. If the filler powders easily, it's ready. If it gums up, it needs more drying time. When it's ready for sanding, you'll need 150- or 180-grit sandpaper. You can use an electric palm sander, but be sure to hold it as flat as you can (see photo 4 on the facing page). If you're nervous about

using a power sander, hand-sand the filler. Periodically wipe off the excess dust.

You're finished sanding when you can see clean grain, but there's still filler in the pores. You may find it difficult to see this stage. To help, you can wipe the surface lightly with a water-dampened rag to get rid of all the sanding dust. Inspect the surface in backlighting. If you sanded through the filler into open grain or missed a spot, apply more filler with a small cloth and then resand when dry.

When the surface is filled to your liking you have the option of staining the wood and the filler. However, you have to do it before the filler has fully cured (within a day), and you can only use certain stains. Any stain based upon alcohol or glycol ether works fine, but oil-based and straight water-soluble dye stains will not. A water-soluble dye with some alcohol in it works, though. Commercial water-based pigment stains usually contain enough glycol ether to work as well. If you wipe on the stain, work quickly and avoid overworking the surface because the solvents will soften the filler in the pores and lift it out.

WORKING SMART

Paste wood fillers shrink as they dry, so it's normal for pores to become visible again once the filler has cured. To make the surface glass smooth again, apply several coats of clear finish and then sand the finish level. Apply another coat or two before final rub out.

Water-based fillers dry to a chalky appearance (right), but darken when a dye and/or finish is applied (left).

Changing the color of a paste wood filler has a large effect on the visual impact of the wood. A filler the same color as the wood downplays the pores (far right). The same colored filler was tinted with burnt umber to make the pores more visible (second from right). Then black was added to make the pores very prominent (second from left). Because black "cools" the overall color, red was added to warm up the filler, which also warms up the overall effect (far left).

GETTING THE COLOR RIGHT

To achieve certain effects you need to use the proper color filler (natural or colored). You can buy colored fillers or you can color them yourself. Keep in mind when you choose your filler color that the different types of filler (oil- and water-based) lend themselves better to certain effects than others.

Tweaking Fillers

You can adjust the color of a filler by adding a colorant compatible with the filler. Whatever change you make will have an impact on the overall color of the wood. Even a slight change in the color of the filler can have a dramatic impact. Following are the various types of colorants and what type of filler they can be used with.

- Dry pigment powders can be added to either oil- or water-based filler.
- Metallic flakes and powders and pearlescent flakes can be added to either oil- or water-based filler.
- UTCs are compatible with both oil- and water-based fillers.
- Japan colors should be used only with oil-based fillers.
- Artist's oil colors, oil-based stains, and paint work only with oil-based fillers.
- Artist's acrylic colors, water-based stains, and latex paint can be added to water-based fillers.
- Water-soluble dyes are used with water-based filler.
- Oil-soluble dyes are used with oil-based filler.

To make any filler darker add black, Vandyke brown, raw umber, or burnt umber. Adding black usually cools the

TROUBLESHOOTING PASTE WOOD FILLERS

PROBLEM	CAUSE	REMEDY
Pores visible after applying finish	More than one application of filler needed Low-solid finishes may telegraph pore outline	Apply second coat of filler Sand back finish after applying several coats*
Whitish or gray spots	Oil-based filler not dry	Let filler dry longer; seal filler with shellac before applying finish
Small air bubbles in pores	Filler not dry	Wait for filler to dry (need to strip)
Surface wrinkled	Solvents in the lacquer softened the oil-based filler	Apply lighter coats of lacquer or seal filler with shellac
Smudges or "ghosts" visible under finish	Residual filler wasn't removed from surface	Remove finish, sand, and start over

*Usually solvent lacquer

overall color, so you would probably have to add some red to counteract it. To lighten a wood-tone filler, use raw sienna or golden ochre. Using white creates an opaque pastel color that may not look natural.

To cool down a wood-tone color slightly, add raw umber. This pigment has a greenish undertone that neutralizes warm colors. To warm up a wood-tone color, add just a bit of orange or red.

Coloring with Oil-Based Fillers

To blend in the pores so they match the rest of the wood on light, unstained woods like ash and oak, apply a natural filler to the bare wood. To make the pores the same color as the rest of the wood on darker woods like walnut, seal the wood, then apply a filler the same color as the natural color of the wood.

For a contrast between filler and wood color, seal the wood before applying filler. (You can stain the wood before sealing it or leave it unstained.) Apply a colored filler that contrasts with the wood (either lighter or darker).

You may also color the pores and the surrounding wood at the same time by applying the filler to bare wood. (See pp. 104 and 106 for options.)

Coloring with Water-Based Fillers

To blend the pores into the surrounding wood, apply a natural filler to light-colored woods or a filler colored to match on darker-colored woods. Because natural water-based fillers dry to a chalky off-white color, they may have to be tinted to match before application. Transparent fillers work well on all types of wood because they have no color.

To make the pores contrast darker than the color of the wood, apply a dark brown filler and sand off the excess when dry. Then apply a solvent-based stain (alcohol or glycol ether) to color the wood. The stain will deepen the color of the filler even more. To make the pores lighter, use a natural filler or one tinted lighter than the color of the wood.

6

GLAZING, TONING, AND SHADING

When most people think of coloring wood, the first technique that comes to mind is staining. But other techniques add color after the initial staining and preliminary sealing of the wood surface. Glazing, toning, and shading not only add color, but they also produce a variety of creative and textural effects. They add depth to the wood, adjust color, correct mistakes, and emphasize grain. They also simulate age and create grain on otherwise uninteresting woods. Glazing, toning, and shading make the difference between a good finish and a spectacular finish.

WORKING SMART

If a product you're using as a glaze is drying too fast, you can slow it down by adding a retarder. Add mineral spirits to oil-based products and water to water-based glazes.

GLAZING BASICS

Glazes are applied over sealed wood and then wiped with various tools to create different effects. Glazing is only done between coats of hard, film-forming finishes like lacquer, varnish, and shellac. You cannot glaze between coats of an oil finish or an oil/varnish blend. Like stains, glazes are composed of pigment, binder, and carrier, and they can be oil based or water based.

You don't want the glaze to dissolve the sealer coat over which it is applied. Most glazes are oil or water based and won't dissolve the finishes addressed in this book. Oil-based glazes are generally used for solvent lacquers, shellac, and varnish. Water-based glazes are used with any finish.

Several products are typically used as glazes (also known as glazing mediums):

- A premixed, clear- or neutral-colored glaze that is tinted with pigment by the user (neutral is actually an off-white color in the can, but the white disappears once pigment is added)
- A ready-to-use premixed, colored glaze
- Liquid wood stains (excluding lacquer and alcohol-based stains, as well as other fast-drying stains)
- Gel stains
- Concentrated pigment colorants like Japan colors or UTCs that are thinned

You can apply a glaze with a number of methods. Brushes are my favorite, but rags and sponges may be needed to achieve certain effects. If you spray the glaze you will need to thin it to a sprayable viscosity.

Applying Glazes

Glazes are either wiped cleanly off the surface, leaving a thin film of color on the wood surface and in the pores, or they are manipulated with tools or applicators to create special effects.

The technique you choose determines the type of glaze you should use. Premixed glazes are formulated in a thick, gel-like consistency and have a long open time. That means they stay wet much longer than a conventional wood stain and stay in recesses fairly well. They are also easy to texture when doing techniques like graining. Wood stains and thinned concentrated colors generally have a shorter open time, so they are hard to handle if you plan on applying complicated graining or other decorative effects. Their thin consistency also makes them hard to handle on overhead or vertical surfaces.

Simply wiping the surface clean after glazing can create several effects, depending in large part on the color of the glaze and the type of wood. One effect is enhanced grain. The wood is sealed, wiped with a tinted glaze, and then wiped clean. The glaze puts color only in the grain, adding contrast. All of the glazing products work with this technique.

Another wiping technique adds overall color and depth or changes the color. To do this, apply colored glaze over partially sealed wood or sealer that has been sanded with 180- or 220-grit sandpaper. Then wipe off the glaze evenly. Any glaze can be used for this technique, but the premixed glazes offer more open time on large areas.

To soften a bright dye stain, apply a premixed clear- or neutral-colored glaze over the entire surface and wipe off the excess.

For more decorative effects you'll need to manipulate the glaze once it's applied. To do **strike-outs and graining,** apply colored glaze over the entire surface, then, before it sets up, selectively remove the glaze. The best glazes for these effects are

Wiping the Glaze

1 Apply a dark oil glaze (in this case liquid) over stained and sealed wood to give it more depth and to highlight the grain. Start by brushing the glaze on with a bristle brush. Apply it in any direction you want.

2 Work on manageable sections at one time. For pieces like this top, you can raise it up on cleats so you can reach the edges.

3 With fast-drying glazes, you often have to break down your project into even smaller sections like one side of a base or top. In small sections you'll have time to go back and wipe the glaze before it has dried.

4 Wipe off the glaze. Use a clean cotton cloth and turn it frequently to expose clean cloth. Notice the glaze has accentuated the grain and left a little color on the surface.

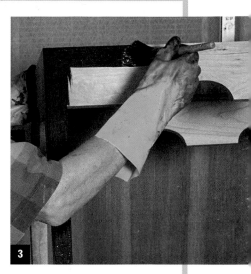

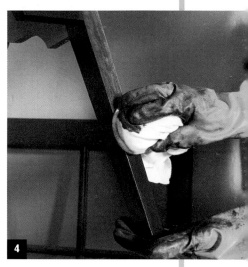

thick, premixed types. Gel stains can be used for graining as long as they have enough open time.

For **highlighting,** selectively apply thin glazes with a soft brush. The best glazes to use are thinned Japan colors or UTCs. Liquid and gel stains can also be used as long as they are not fast-drying.

To get an **antique look,** apply a glaze over marks made in the wood that simulate wear and tear. Leave the glaze in corners, crevices, and moldings to mimic the buildup of waxes and dirt. Any glaze can be used for this effect, but liquid stains don't build up well in corners because they aren't thick enough.

The drying time the glaze needs before top-coating depends on the type of glaze, the top coat, and how you are applying it. If you are applying a top coat by hand, allow the glaze to dry long enough so that the friction from the top coat applicator doesn't pull up the glaze. To see if it's dry, lightly wipe your finger or a dry cloth

DECORATIVE FILLED PORES

Glazing to put color only in the pores creates dramatic effects on some woods. Ash, oak, and pecan have large open pores that form dome-like cathedral shapes on the face grain. When these pores are filled with a glaze that's colored to contrast with the rest of the wood, the result can be quite striking.

To achieve this effect, the wood is either dye-stained, bleached, or left natural. It is then given one coat of finish to seal in the color and to keep the glaze only in the pores. The glaze is then brushed on and wiped off, so it's left only in the pores. (The wood shown below is plain-sawn ash.)

Amber dye/purple glaze (left); purple dye/beige glaze (right).

Blue dye/gold glaze (left); bleached raw umber glaze (right).

across the surface in an inconspicuous area. If the glaze is dry, you shouldn't get any glaze on your finger or the cloth. Drying times vary depending on the type of glaze and environmental conditions.

If you are spraying solvent lacquer over an oil-based glaze, you can spray the lacquer as soon as it hazes. That time allows the solvents from the lacquer to "tie" the glaze to the previous coat of lacquer. Once these glazes start to dry, they can wrinkle from the action of the solvents on the partially cured binder. To avoid this, lightly mist the first several coats of lacquer and allow them to dry before applying full, wet coats.

A nice feature of glazing is that you can remove most or all of the glaze if you make a mistake or are not satisfied with the color. To remove a glaze, wipe it with thin-

ner before the glaze has cured. Use mineral spirits for oil-based glaze and water for water-based glazes. Oil-based glaze can be removed completely as long as the surface it was applied to was completely sealed, but water-based glaze tends to soften most finishes slightly so they are hard to completely remove. Do not use strong solvents like toluene or lacquer thinner to remove an oil glaze.

Striking-Out

Striking-out creates a dramatic contrast by selectively removing glaze from certain areas so they are lighter when the top coats are applied. It is usually done on ring-porous woods like ash, pecan, and oak to highlight the areas between the dark pores. It can also be used on moldings and carved areas to give them more depth. The effect

Striking-Out

Apply the glaze color over the entire surface of the wood. Spraying is the best application method, but you can use a brush instead. First, brush on the glaze, then wipe or brush it lightly with a soft cloth or dry brush to even it out. Make sure the sealer coat has been sanded to give it some tooth.

As soon as the glaze starts to dull or haze, you can strike out. Use a clean piece of cotton cloth or paper towel and follow the grain pattern. One technique is to increase the pressure to remove more glaze around swirly knots.

A steel wool pad produces a more diffused effect. Start with a small piece of 0000 steel wool.

4 To accentuate moldings, wipe the glaze off the high parts.

After wiping, you can soften the harsh, wiped edges by brushing the strike-outs lightly with a dry, soft brush. Working with a light touch will feather the strike-outs into the rest of the glaze. This cannot be done while the glaze is wet.

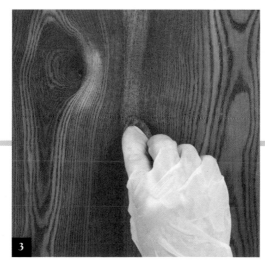

WORKING SMART

It's difficult to reproduce grain realistically unless you study real wood grain. When graining, it helps to have several pieces of wood nearby with different grain patterns so that you have an idea of what looks real.

can range from garish to subtle, depending on the color of the glaze, how dark it is, and how much pressure is used when wiping it.

It doesn't matter whether or not you stain the wood before you strike out, but you must seal the wood. Once the sealer is dry it should be sanded to provide a smooth surface and some "tooth" for the glaze. You can use 320- or 220-grit sandpaper; the lower grit allows more of the glaze to "take" on the sealed surface.

Spraying on the glaze produces a more uniform application, but you can also apply the glaze with a brush. If brushing, wipe it lightly with a soft cloth to even it out. Then before the glaze starts to set, selectively wipe off the glaze in certain areas with a small piece of clean, dry cloth or a small pad of extra fine (000 or 0000) steel wool. On ring-porous woods, follow the cathedral-like, long, dome-shaped areas defined by the pore structure. Change to a fresh part of the wiping applicator after each wipe to reduce the risk of smudging. The effect is determined by the type of applicator and pressure you use.

You also have the option of wiping the glaze completely off in selected areas. With a cloth rag or a piece of paper towel, wipe the glaze hard enough to remove it. If not enough glaze comes off, moisten the cloth or towel with some solvent (mineral spirits for oil based; water for water based). This look is a litle harser than the subdued, softer effect of partially removing the glaze.

Graining

Graining is a decorative effect that can make a plain wood look like a more expensive one or make metal or fiberglass doors look like real wood. The technique may seem a little intimidating, but it's really quite easy, and the basics can be learned quickly.

For this technique you'll need a curved rubber grainer, which is made of molded rubber with semicircular ridges mounted on a curved handle. When dragged across a glazed surface and rocked, the ridges scrape away some of the glaze, leaving the remaining glaze in realistic wood-grain patterns. You can purchase the tool (and the brushes you'll need) at just about any paint or hardware store.

The first step is to apply the base coat color. You can purchase off-white- or tan-colored base coats at most paint stores or purchase tinting base and make your own. Latex (water-based) or oil-based paints both work. The base color should be the lightest color that you see in the wood that you are trying to produce. Most graining effects utilize a light, tan-colored base coat. Apply the base coat, allow it to dry, and then sand it with 220-grit sandpaper to smooth it. Remove all the sanding dust.

For the glazing step, you can choose between premixed glaze, a thick wood stain, or a gel stain. Do not use a stain that's too thin because they have a tendency to run on vertical surfaces and flow together on horizontal ones. You can use a dark-colored glaze for striking patterns that contrast heavily with the base coat color, or try a glaze that's just slightly darker than the base coat for a more subdued effect. Apply the glaze with a brush. You can brush in any direction because brush marks and uneven application will be removed with the next step.

Before the glaze starts to set, take the graining tool and scrape it down the surface of the wood hard enough so that you expose the painted base coat (usually very light pressure is needed). Because the face of the graining tool is curved, it must be gently rocked as you push or pull it across the surface in order to produce wavy grain

Graining

1 Paint the base coat color with an opaque paint. Use a yellowish off-white for oak, a reddish-yellow for mahogany, or a light brown or tan for walnut. The base color should be the lightest background color that you can see in the real wood.

After the base coat has dried, sand it with 220-grit sandpaper and apply the darker graining color. The color can be dark for striking contrast or closer to the base coat color for a more subdued, natural effect.

Pull or push the graining tool across the surface, rocking it up and down to produce different effects. If you don't like the results, you can redo the base coat several times before you have to apply more glaze. You can apply the glaze just to the area that you want to redo.

Overlap the graining strokes by about ½ in. to blend them in with the previous strokes. Or tape out the area that you're not working on to get a sharp, defined edge that simulates individual glued-up boards.

When the glaze has dulled or hazed, but before it starts to dry, you can soften it and blend light or dark areas with a clean, dry bristle brush. Natural-hair brushes are best.

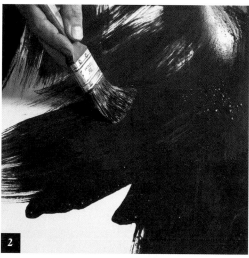

119

WORKING SMART

To double-grain, seal one graining effect with finish, scuff-sand, then grain again using another technique. Use different colors to build up realistic-looking wood with depth.

lines. Make sure you take the tool from one edge to the other each time. Overlap each pass to make sure there are no dark, ungrained areas between passes.

One of the effects of this technique is to create the look of several boards glued together to make a wider board. To create this effect, vary your rocking technique to produce different grain patterns. Changing the rocking speed produces different grain effects, or you may prefer to produce

straight grain by not rocking the graining tool at all. Short, quick rocks produce abrupt, short grain change. Slowly pulling and rocking gently produces gradual grain shifts. Positioning the face of the curved rubber differently in relation to the board will also produce different grain patterns. If you don't like the pattern you created, just go over it again with the tool.

Before the glaze sets you can soften the graining and blend light and dark areas by

Highlighting

1 To draw fine grain lines, wipe enough glaze off the brush so that you create fine lines when you brush it across a piece of white paper.

2 "Draw" fine lines across the surface of the sealed wood. You can create various widths by the way you hold the brush.

3 To selectively apply glaze, use the chiseled edge of the brush and work dark glaze into the deep parts of moldings or crevices.

4 Use just the tip of a dry brush to feather dark glaze into the rest of the surface. Do this after the glaze has dulled but before it dries hard.

brushing lightly with a dry brush. Use the very tip of a large, clean bristle brush to whisk the surface lightly. It's best to whisk in the direction of the grain.

Highlighting

Highlighting is a technique that applies glaze selectively to certain parts of the wood. Also known as dry-brushing, highlighting can be used to create a variety of effects. It adds dark color to accentuate depth on moldings and carvings; it creates fine grain lines and texture on plain edges or moldings; and it blends in lighter areas to darker areas (like sapwood to heartwood).

You'll need a fine-bristled brush and colorants like Japan colors or UTCs to do the job. A small artist's brush can be used for fine, detailed application, but a larger brush should be used on larger areas.

Prepare the glaze by thinning the concentrated colorant to the intensity that you want. (Thin Japan colors with mineral spirits, UTCs with water.) A 50/50 mix is fine for dark grain lines and for accentuating carvings and moldings. For blending light/dark areas, though, you'll need more thinner. Mix the colorant and thinner on a piece of glass to help you visualize the intensity of color and how it will look on the wood.

To create fine lines or texture, use an artist's brush or a small bristle brush. Dab the tip of the brush into the thinned colorant, then brush it across a piece of paper or test piece of wood until you see fine, delicate lines. Then apply the color to the surface of the wood. A light touch creates fine grain lines, while a whisking motion in different directions creates patterns of texture. You can leave the lines as is or soften them by whisking a dry brush across the surface.

To accentuate carvings, moldings, and crevices, use a small, square-tipped artist's brush (sold in art-supply stores under the name golden nylon, which is a fine, soft synthetic bristle.) Jab the tip of the brush into the thinned color and apply the color to the wood in the areas you've selected. The sharp, square tip of an artist's brush allows you to be exact in your placement. After the carrier flashes and the glaze looks dull, you can soften it or blend it in by whisking the tip of a large, dry natural-bristle brush over the area. Clean the tip of the brush frequently with a clean cloth.

To blend light areas, dab the tip of a large brush into the thinned colorant. Put the color onto the light areas by stabbing just the tip of the brush lightly onto the area that you want to darken. Hold the brush at a 90-degree angle. As soon as you're finished, you can feather the color into the darker areas by whisking a dry brush over it. You can also leave it as is.

As with any glazing technique, if you make a mistake you can start over by wiping off the glaze before it dries with a solvent-dampened rag.

Striation

Striation is a method of reproducing straight or slightly wavy grain lines in quarter-sawn or riftsawn wood. The effect can be a subdued grain effect as in mahogany or a more pronounced oak pattern. The wide variety of tools available means you can achieve almost any look. Here's a look at some of the tools and their effects.

- Dry brushes held perpendicular to the face of the wood and lightly dragged will produce softer, nondescript lines.
- Paper towels, burlap, and rags dragged through the glaze will produce a variety of grain patterns.

121

Striation

1 Apply a darker glaze over the base coat color with a brush. Brush it on in any direction.

2 To reproduce fine, soft grain lines, hold a large-bristle brush perpendicular to the surface and drag it lightly from one end to the other. Wipe the bristle with a clean rag and overlap the first two passes slightly to blend them together. The mottled pattern in the photo is done by lightly moving the brush from side to side as you drag it.

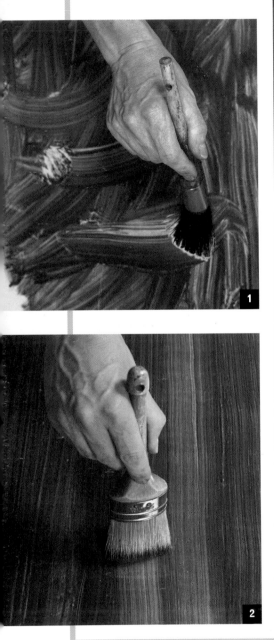

3 To produce a ribbon pattern, use a piece of paper towel, burlap, or any rough-textured cloth. Hold it with the tips of your fingers spaced evenly apart. Pull the towel through the glaze.

4 To use a graining comb, hold it in your hand so that you exert equal pressure across the width. Pull it lightly through the wet glaze.

5 To soften the graining, brush it lightly with a dry brush in the direction of the grain.

- Graining combs are thin pieces of flexible steel that come in various widths, teeth spacing, and teeth width. They can be used to reproduce quartersawn oak patterns.

To begin, paint the wood with a base coat color. You may use any color, but for most woods tan works well. For light oak use an off-white opaque base with a touch of yellow, and for mahogany mix raw sienna and burnt sienna into an off-white base. After the base coat is dry, sand it with 220-grit sandpaper and remove the sanding dust.

The glaze color should be darker than the base coat. Try mixing raw sienna, burnt umber, or Vandyke brown into a clear or neutral base. Apply the glaze with a brush, then drag your chosen tool through the glaze before it sets up. A large, soft-bristle brush dragged lightly through the wet glaze will produce a soft grainy pattern. You can make straight or slightly wavy lines. If you move the brush from side to side slightly, you will produce a mottled, ripple pattern similar to curl or ripple figure. Do not stop the brush at all; use a smooth, consistent motion from one edge to the other.

To use a paper towel or a cloth, hold it with your fingers and drag it through the wet glaze. You can do this in straight or wavy lines to reproduces the light/dark patterns found in ribbon mahogany.

When dragging a graining comb through the wet glaze, do not stop once you start and keep the lines as straight as possible.

Antiquing

Antiquing involves a series of techniques designed to simulate the wear and tear that naturally occurs over time on a piece of fur-

niture. During the course of normal use, furniture is subjected to dents, small scratches, dirt buildup, and chipping and flaking of paint and finish. When this wear and tear happens gradually and the piece is otherwise well cared for, it develops a pleasant surface quality and appearance called patina. When dents, dirt, wax buildup, and other marks are added deliberately, the process is called antiquing or distressing.

Antiquing new furniture falls into two categories. One option is to paint marks on the finish to simulate (but not actually cause) physical damage. These marks are layered between coats of finish. The second option is to actually damage the wood surface or finish to mimic wear and tear.

Faking the damage Several techniques—specking, cowtailing, and crayon distressing—are routinely used by factories to mimic wear and tear. These effects do not damage the surface of the wood and can be used on anything from the most elegant, filled-pore, lacquered mahogany to plain open-pore oak finished with wiping var-

To get the feel for specking, practice on a piece of white cardboard. When the specks are the right size, you can move on to a piece of furniture.

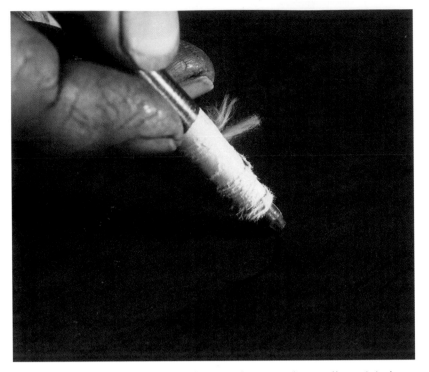

Use a china marker to make small semicircles or ellipses that simulate dents and small gouges. You can remove the marks with mineral spirits if you want to redo them.

nish. The techniques are easy to do, and the only mistake you can make is to get carried away, which results in a contrived look.

All the techniques explained here are done after staining and sealing. Whether you do them before glazing and other coloring or after is up to you. Doing them before subdues the effect. Once you've finished with any of these techniques, you should seal them with clear coats of finish.

Specking is the look of a fine spray of small brown specks or dots on a sealed surface. The look mimics the small brown dots that are left behind by house flies, which is why the techniqe is also known as fly-specking.

The specking can be created with thinned Japan colors or UTCs, as well as with gel stains and liquids stains (both pigment and dye). You'll get the best results with thinned glaze. And as a bonus, like other glazing techniques, if you make a mistake, you can remove the glaze specks. On most wood finishes, a brown or dark brown glaze is used, but you can use any color.

Dip the bristle of a toothbrush into your chosen colorant and run your thumb across the tip of the bristle to spatter a fine series of dots across the surface of the wood. Practice on a piece of wood or cardboard to get the pattern right. Small, fine dots will barely be visible but will add a subtle elegance; large, dark specks tend to look contrived.

Cowtailing involves whisking small swirls or dark marks on the surface with a stiff-bristle brush. Cowtailing is similar to highlighting except that the brush used is different. I like to use a large, oval natural-bristle brush. Soak it in hot water for several minutes or until it becomes limp, then twirl it between your palms to spin out the water and to fan out the bristle. Stick the brush in a jar or can (handle down) so that it dries with the bristle upright, maintaining the fan shape of the bristle. Once it's dry, dab the brush into thinned colorant and wipe the excess color on a piece of paper or scrap wood until only fine, thin lines appear. Then lightly flick the brush in a quick circle motion on the wood to produce tight swirls of fine lines.

Crayon distressing requires a china marker, which is a wax pencil used to make small half or quarter circles on the sealed surface of the wood. The dark brown or black markers are available at craft stores or art-supply stores.

Causing physical damage Antiquing can also involve minor physical damage to the surface of the wood or the finish. The effect is more realistic than faking the damage, but the challenge is in using restraint and care to avoid a contrived look. You have hundreds of options to choose from, including whipping the wood with chains and pouring a bucketful of nails and screws over the bare wood. I prefer a more restrained approach so that minor damage to the surface looks more like wear and tear than disfigurement. Here are some ideas:

- Bounce the tips of keys on a large key ring lightly on the surface of the wood to simulate the minor dents and dings that occur on areas of heavy use, like tops, drawer knobs, and edges.

- Use an ice pick or small finishing nail to produce a very convincing worm hole. You can also use a small drill bit chucked in a drill.

- Drag a thick piece of nylon string along an edge to chip off paint and clear finishes.

- Pull a thicker piece of rope shoe-shine style across edges of moldings to burnish them.

- Dab wax between coats of paint. The wax will make the top coat flake off.

- Cut sandpaper through sharp edges to simulate wearing away the finish and stain.

- Use a stiff wire brush to make small scratches on the wood or the finish.

- Run a brick along molded edges to grind them down.

The real trick is to create the damage the way it would happen naturally. Consequently, it's best to distress the wood after the stain and sealer coats have been applied, then wipe a glaze over the entire piece before it's wiped clean. The glaze will stay in your distressing marks, accentuating them. The marks will look more realistic because normal wear and tear is usually

Lightly drop a key ring full of keys to simulate small dents and dings. Hold the keys several inches off the surface and let them drop under their own weight.

Wear away the finish and stain from sharp edges with 100-grit sandpaper. Just sand in areas of heavy use, not over all the edges.

filled in with layers of dirt, oils, and wax over time. Beginners tend to overdo distressing their first time. Practice restraint and do a little bit at a time.

Making a Glaze

Most glazes that are sold in paint and home centers are clear or off-white liquids that you'll need to tint to the color you want. The colorant you use must be compatible with the solvents in the glaze (oil or water).

For oil- and water-based glazes, you can use dry pigment powders, which are available through art-supply stores or specialty suppliers. For oil-based glaze, you can use artist's oil colors, oil paint, Japan colors, or UTCs. For water-based glazes, you can use artist's acrylics, water-based paint (latex), or UTCs.

UTCs, Japan colors, and artist's colors are all concentrated pigments. You need very little of them to tint a glaze. About

Making a Glaze

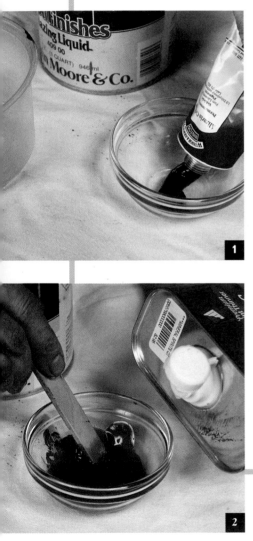

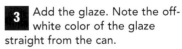

1 To make a glaze using concentrated tints like artist's colors, Japan colors, or UTCs, place some of the tint in a dish or can.

2 Add a bit of mineral spirits to the oil-based tints or add water to water-based tints. This makes thick colorants like artist's colors easier to disperse into the glaze.

3 Add the glaze. Note the off-white color of the glaze straight from the can.

4 Stir thoroughly until the glaze is well mixed.

1 teaspoon per cup is all that's needed for dark colors, and less for a light-colored glaze. To test the intensity, smear some of the mixed glaze on a piece of glass to see how dark it is. While paint can also be used to tint glaze, most paint contains white and can appear opaque or cloudy.

TONING AND SHADING

Toners and shaders refer to the same product, toner, but I like to treat them separately because toning and shading are different techniques. Both techniques use the same material: a pigment or dye mixed into clear finish that is sprayed onto the surface of the wood. Toners and shaders are not applied by hand because hand application would leave noticeable lap marks and ridges.

Toning is the process of applying a transparent colorant over the entire surface of the wood. The technique can correct, adjust, and even out the color. **Shading** selectively applies color to certain parts of the wood. Shaders are typically used to match sapwood to heartwood, cover up repairs or mistakes, or highlight certain areas of the wood with color. Both techniques are done after the wood is sealed, representing the last coloring step in a multicolored finish sequence.

You can purchase toners premixed and in small aerosol cans or larger containers, or you can make them yourself. They are easy to make from stain and a compatible finish. Because most professional finishers have these ingredients on hand, they usually make the toner from scratch.

Pigment-based toners consist of pigment and finish. The concentration of pigment has to be low enough that the wood grain can still be seen. To make a pigment toner, add a compatible stain or concentrated pigments such as Japan colors or UTCs to the finish. Most oil-based colors

and small amounts of UTCs can be added to both varnish and solvent lacquer. UTCs and water-based stains can be added to water-based finishes. For some lacquers, particularly specialty lacquers like catalyzed lacquers, you should check with the manufacturer for a compatible colorant. Pigment-based toners tend to mask wood grain, which is helpful in certain situations such as disguising repairs or hiding wood grain.

Dye-based toners are made by adding dye to finish. Either dry dye powders or liquid dyes can be used, but the powders should be dissolved before they are added to the finish. Oil-soluble dyes are used for varnish and lacquer; alcohol-soluble dyes can be used with shellac and with most lacquers; and water-soluble dyes can be used with water-based finishes. NGR (non-

WORKING SMART

If you have trouble finding concentrated colors, buy some liquid pigment stain the color that you want the glaze to be. Let the stain sit for a couple of days. Spoon up the settled pigment from the bottom of the can and use it to tint your glaze.

A pigment-based toner (right) can obscure wood grain, while a dye-based toner (left) lets grain and figure show through.

grain-raising) dyes and concentrated dye liquids can be added to most finishes, but you should test for compatibility first by adding a bit of the dissolved dye to the finish. If it gels, turns cloudy, or separates, it's not compatible. Dye-based toners allow the wood grain to show, even when dark colors are used, so use them when you want the grain to show.

Toning

The best use of toning is to change the overall color once it has been stained and sealed. It can be used to darken a color that's too light and correct a color that's the wrong hue. In some cases it can be used on splotchy and otherwise hard-to-stain woods as the entire coloring operation to achieve an even color.

You must apply toners with a spray gun. You can use any type of spray gun, but make sure you can adjust it for a fine, wide, even spray. Most quality guns can be adjusted for toning; avoid the less expen-

A combination of toning and shading adds richness, depth, and dynamics to this cherry panel (left). It was toned with a reddish dye, then shaded with a dark brown. The right is untreated.

sive guns that lack a fan-width control knob on the gun.

Set the gun for the correct viscosity and fill it with toner. Then, using a piece of wood or white cardboard as a practice panel, adjust the gun's fan-width control for a wide pattern and the fluid delivery knob for a fine mist. Adjust the gun so that you have an even pattern with no darker areas in the center of the pattern or at the edges. Once you have it set, hold the gun approximately 8 in. to 10 in. from the surface and begin spraying. Move the gun evenly across the surface and try not to overlap too much or you'll see lines. It's best to use thin toners and work up slowly to the color you want with multiple coats.

Shading

Shading selectively applies a toner. Because of the need for precise application of the toner, the best guns for shading are small touch-up guns that can be easily adjusted to a fine, small spray pattern. A large gun can be used as long as it can be adjusted to a emit a fine, small spray. It should have both fluid-delivery and fan-width control knobs.

To shade, pour some toner into the gun's cup and turn both the fluid-delivery

Shading is easier with a small touch-up gun. Here it's used to blend the sapwood into the heartwood on the leg of a cherry table.

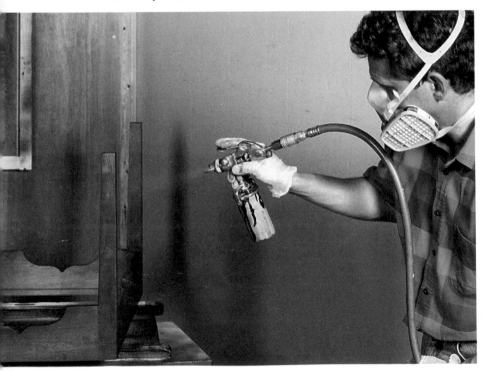

TROUBLESHOOTING GLAZING, TONING, AND SHADING

PROBLEM	CAUSE	REMEDY
Glazes		
Glaze color isn't what you want	Wrong color used (too light or too dark)	Wipe glaze off with thinner and reapply
Glaze doesn't feel dry	Glaze is long-oil based and may not dry hard*; cool temperature	Let glaze dry longer
Glaze wrinkles when lacquer is sprayed	Solvents are attacking partially cured binder	Strip top coat; spray lacquer within dry time of glaze or mist on first lacquer coats*
Finish applied over glaze won't dry or takes a long time	Glaze not dry enough when finish was applied	Let finish dry longer
Glaze lifts under lacquer	Glaze coating window was missed	Strip and refinish; apply lacquer finish within specified window or mist on first coats
Glaze turns white in some areas and pores	Carrier not evaporated	Wait 1 to 2 hours then spray light coat of highly thinned lacquer
Toners		
Grain muddy or hard to see	Pigment toners mask grain	Switch to dye-based toner
Toner too dark	Too much colorant added Gun set up for high fluid delivery	Strip and redo Work up to color in light coats and low fluid rate

*Glazes made for solvent lacquers are usually sprayed before they start to cure. These products are long-oil glazes and may take a longer time to dry before they can be top-coated with other finishes. Also, they do not dry as hard as liquid and gel wood stains.

and fan-width controls clockwise to close them. Using a piece of white cardboard or wood as a test piece, adjust the fluid control until a fine spray pattern is visible, and adjust the fan width until you get about a 1-in.- to 2-in.-wide pattern. Work the area that you want to shade slowly in light passes until you get the intensity that you want.

You can feather a shader into the rest of the piece by increasing the fan width and the distance from the gun to the workpiece. Feathering is effective when you want to blend in a repair or make the color of sapwood closer to heartwood.

The left side of this cherry board was shaded with a dark brown dye toner. Note how the right side lacks the dramatic visual impact of the left.

APPLYING FINISHES

Wood finishes vary in appearance, protection, and durability. While these qualities influence the type of finish you choose, you need to decide the best way to apply your chosen finish. Because finishes vary dramatically in viscosity, film build, and dry time, application methods differ from one finish to another. Low-tech applicators like rags or paper towels are easy to use, while spraying takes skill, practice, and an investment in equipment. However, applying finishes is a lesson in trade-offs. Some easy techniques create finishes with poor durabilty. You'll need to decide what's most important to you.

FINISH BASICS

Finishes are applied in various ways: wiped on with a rag or cloth, brushed on, rolled on with a roller or pad, or sprayed on. Some finishes like shellac can be applied by any method, but most lend themselves best to one application method. Finishes have three characteristics that affect the way you apply them and what they look like: dry time, viscosity, and build.

The single most important aspect that affects the application method is **dry time.** If you want to wipe on the finish, then wipe it off, it has to have a slower drying time. Slow-drying oil and oil/varnish blends can be wiped on and then smoothed out or wiped off evenly with the applicator before the finish starts to tack up and dry. Most varnishes have some time after application when they can be smoothed out. Fast-drying lacquer and shellac are less forgiving and cannot be wiped once they're applied.

Dry time also affects the time it takes to apply the complete finish. Multiple coats of fast-drying evaporative finishes can be applied in a single day, but slow-drying reactive finishes like oils and varnishes may need several days between coats to dry.

Viscosity is the second factor. Thick finishes are hard to wipe or brush and must be thinned for application. Some finishes, like lacquer and varnish, can be thinned quite a lot, while others, like water-based finish, can be thinned only slightly.

Finish build is the third consideration. Finishes with a high content of resin (called a high solids content) require fewer applications to form a durable film than finishes with a low solids content.

Viscosity and build affect the aesthetic qualities of the finish. Thin applications of oil and oil/varnish blends result in a natural appearance. However, varnishes, shellac, and lacquers can be applied in thin, low-solids coats to imitate an oil finish (with much better resistance to heat and water). Thick, high-solids finishes can create a "plastic" look that's durable, but the look detracts from the natural beauty of the wood.

OIL FINISHES

Oil finishes fall into one of two categories: pure oil like linseed or tung, or oils fortified with a hard resin like phenolic or alkyd and thinned with mineral spirits. Both types are applied in the same general way (except for the situation noted below to correct bleeding). Oil finishes are applied in very thin coats, and there is a limit to the number of applications. Thin coats dry quicker than thick coats, but because oil does not dry hard, once you reach a certain point, further coats build a soft, gummy film on the surface.

Before application, the wood should be sanded to at least 220 grit. You can sand up to 400 grit, but beyond that you may affect the oil's ability to penetrate the wood. A 400-grit surface appears shinier or a bit glossier than a 220-grit surface. Clean the wood of all sanding dust and debris by vacuuming it or wiping it with a cloth moistened with naphtha or mineral spirits.

The first coat of oil gets flooded onto the surface of the wood. Allow the oil to sit on the wood for 30 minutes to an hour. Pure oils can be left on the surface for as long as an hour, but oil/varnish blends may have to be removed after about 10 minutes because they can tack up and become sticky if allowed to sit too long. As dry spots appear, replenish them with more oil. After the waiting time is up, remove the excess oil so it doesn't tack up. If you don't remove the oil soon enough, it won't wipe easily and you'll need to moisten a rag with mineral spirits or naphtha to remove it cleanly.

Applying Oil Finish

1 Apply the oil with a rag or brush. Figured and more porous areas will absorb the most oil, creating dry spots. Replenish these areas with oil. Do not allow the oil to stand long enough to get tacky.

2 Wipe the excess oil off with a clean, dry rag. Be sure to wipe crevices and corners.

3 After the first coat is dry, you can apply more oil and wet-sand with fine sandpaper. Use 400-grit paper and sand with the grain. This will create an oil/sawdust slurry that partially fills the pores and creates silky-smooth surfaces.

4 Wet-sand rounded edges and moldings by holding a small piece of paper with your fingers to back it up.

5 After you've applied all coats of oil, apply a paste wax with a piece of 0000 steel wool.

6 After the wax hazes but before it gets hard, buff it with a clean, dry cloth.

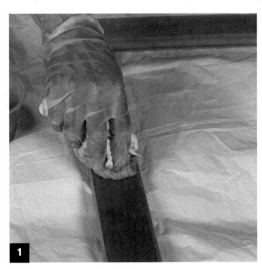

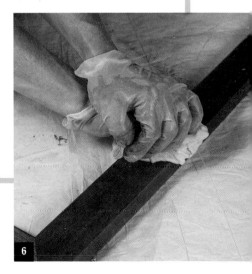

The Truth about Oil Finishes

Oil finishes are the finish of choice for beginners and for those who want an easy, uncomplicated finish. There is a lot of marketing hype about their protective and maintenance qualities. Oil finishes are easy to apply and make the wood look attractive, but they also have some potential problems that you need to consider.

Rags used to apply oil finishes that are not disposed of properly can ignite and start a fire. All rags used for oil finishes have the potential to start a fire by spontaneous combustion. As the oil on the rag cures, it absorbs oxygen from the air. The reaction that follows, which converts the liquid oil to a semi-solid, creates heat as a by-product. If the rag is spread out, the heat is dissipated harmlessly. However, if the rag is balled or wadded up, the heat is not as easily dissipated. The reaction feeds off the heat, and the rag gets increasingly hotter until it ignites. All rags used to apply oil finishes should be disposed of properly. The best way is to soak them in water and then drape them over the side of a workbench to dry. Do not throw them in the trash.

Oil finishes are not protective. Even though oil finishes are touted as protective, they are not for two reasons. First, oils are inherently weak finishes against water, heat, and solvents. Second, they cannot be built up to a hard film to protect the wood. They are mostly penetrating finishes, so they are not left on the surface for protection, leaving the wood vulnerable to scratches. Trying to build up an oil finish by applying more coats is futile. Built-up oil dries soft and gummy and will provide no scratch resistance. A coat of wax helps to deflect possible scratches, but only slightly.

Even oil finishes to which resin has been added do not provide significant protective qualities. The resin makes the oil build faster, meaning that it takes less time to create an attractive, deeper finish than pure oil, but only marginally more durable.

Oil finishes require maintenance. An oil finish looks great for a while, but after a year or so, the surface begins to oxidize from exposure to light and air and begins to look dry. The only thing to do at this point is to apply more oil.

Oil finishes yellow. Linseed oil finishes yellow considerably after about a year, despite the amber color they have when applied. The yellowing is rarely a problem on dark woods, but on light woods like maple or birch it can be unattractive. Most oil/varnish blends contain linseed oil so they yellow some. Tung oil yellows much less.

Oil finishes don't prevent stain or glaze from being rubbed off. Oil finishes are not the best choice for use over stained wood and cannot be used with glazes because they don't provide enough protection for the stain or glaze to keep it from being rubbed or scratched off. Areas of frequent contact with hands like chair arms or drawers will easily wear through and show bare wood quickly.

The best use of oil finishes is when you want a natural-looking finish. Oils deepen the color of wood, and accentuate figure and provide contrast. They can be used in conjunction with harder finishes like shellac, lacquer, and varnish to "pop" grain and figure and to seal the wood. The harder top coat provides the necessary scratch, water, solvent, and heat resistance.

Oil/varnish blends thinned with mineral spirits present problems on open-pore woods if you flood the surface. The pores will continue to "bleed" oil after the excess finish is wiped off. If the bleeding oil dries on the surface, it forms scabs of gummy finish that are hard to remove with a dry cloth. Moistening the cloth with some lacquer thinner is the best way to remove the scabs, but in severe cases stripping may work better.

You can avoid this problem by not flooding the surface in the first place. Instead, apply the first coat or two thinly and allow them to dry. Once the pores are sealed, they won't bleed. If you do flood the surface, you'll need to keep wiping it to prevent bleeding. Check the surface every hour or so and wipe off any oil. It may take several days for the oil that's trapped deep in the pores to dry.

When the first coat is dry you can either smooth the surface with fine sandpaper and apply more finish, or wet-sand the next coats as you apply them. The two options have different looks. Not wet-sanded, the pores will remain distinct and open. Wet-sanding allows you to partially fill the pores of large-pored woods, which results in a smoother-looking surface.

As you apply more finish, you increase the depth and luster of the wood. The number of coats you apply is up to you. Three coats is a minimum, and more than six to eight coats doesn't make an impact because they are being applied to completely sealed wood, so no finish penetrates. Oil/varnish blends build quicker than pure oil finishes. Whichever product you use, when the last application has dried for a week, you can apply a coat of wax for more protection and to bring up the sheen.

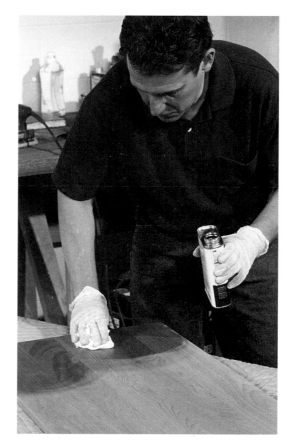

Oil finishes are the first finish most beginners choose. They are easy to apply and look great, particularly on wood like cherry.

VARNISH

Brushing is the most efficient method of applying varnish because you can apply it thick. Two coats of a brushed varnish provide as durable a finish as six or seven coats of lacquer or shellac. Because varnishes remain tacky for an extended period, dust and other particles in the air can fall to the finish and become embedded. When the varnish cures hard, these form "pimples" in the surface of the dry film.

Wiping varnish is a less efficient method of application (less varnish is applied), but it results in a smoother finish and less problems with dust. Because the finish is applied thinned (wiping varnishes are about half the solids content of brushing varnish) and the finish application is less thick, the finish dries much quicker.

WORKING SMART

Plan your varnishing so that you do it at the end of the day. That way the dust you kick up in the air by walking around the finishing area all day won't settle into the finish.

Brushing Varnish on a Flat Top

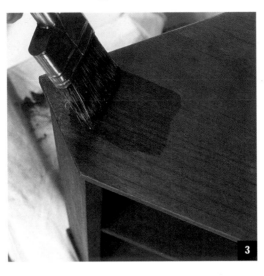

1 Pour the varnish into a wide-mouthed container, then dip the brush about one-half the bristle length into the varnish. Condition the brush first by dipping it into mineral spirits, then remove the excess solvent.

2 Press the brush against the side of the container to get rid of excess varnish. Never scrape the varnish off on the rim of the container because it will create bubbles.

3 Staring about 3 in. from an edge, brush the varnish to the end and lift off the brish slightly as you reach the edge to avoid drips.

4 Brush toward the other end. Hold the brush at roughly a 60-degree angle, and don't exert too much downward pressure. It should feel as though the varnish is flowing off the end of the brush. If the finish is not flowing, do not try to force it off the end of the brush by pushing down harder—this will create bubbles. Instead, reload it with more varnish.

5 Tip-off by holding a dry brush lightly at a 90-degree angle and dragging it across the surface. This technique evens out puddles and ridges and removes any air bubbles and dirt that got in the finish.

This results in less open time for dust to settle in the tacky finish.

When applying varnish, try to do so in a different room from where you sand the wood. Using air cleaners that remove fine dust particles helps. Varnishes are temperature-sensitive and should be applied at room temperature, with both the varnish and the wood at room temperature also. The ideal temperature is 70°F. Varnish should be stirred gently to mix up flattening compounds that sink to the bottom. It should always be strained and then poured into a separate, widemouthed container. The best brushes for the job are natural bristle.

The first coat of varnish is called the sealer coat, and it can be made from varnish thinned 50/50 with mineral spirits. You can also use shellac or varnish-based sanding sealer. This initial coat penetrates quickly into the wood, so technique isn't critical. Brush it on and sand it when it is dry with 320-grit sandpaper. Remove the sanding residue with a tack cloth.

Brushing Varnish on a Flat Surface

It's easiest to brush varnish on a flat surface. So if you can, disassemble your project as much as possible so that you can brush horizontally. Remove all hardware as well. Stir and strain the varnish. The consistency should be somewhere between maple syrup and honey. Thin it with mineral spirits if necessary.

Whack the dry brush against the edge of a table or your palm to dislodge any debris or loose bristle. Dip it all the way into mineral spirits up to the metal ferrule. This step makes the brush easier to clean later. Scrape off the excess thinner and wipe the brush with a clean rag.

Dip the brush into the varnish no more than halfway up the bristle. Lightly press off excess varnish against the side of

Brushing Varnish on Sides

1 Brush vertical surfaces by applying varnish horizontally, working from the bottom up. Load less varnish on the brush by dipping it only slightly in the varnish. When preparing the varnish, try not to thin it too much.

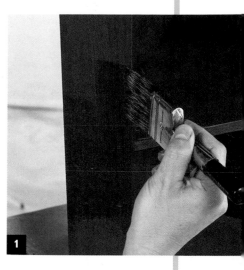

2 When you get to the edge, lift the brush up slightly to avoid dripping varnish down the sharp edge. If you get a drip, wipe it immediately, then brush it lightly to feather it in with the rest of the surface.

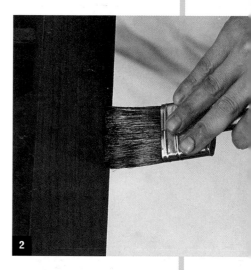

3 When you have finished applying the varnish, clean the excess off the brush and tip off the brush vertically. After several minutes, examine the surface in backlighting. Any sagging can be tipped off before the varnish starts to tack up.

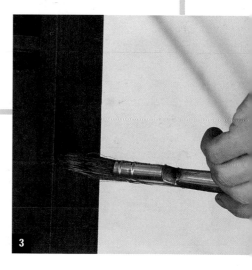

the jar. Do not scrape off excess finish against the rim. Start about 3 in. from an edge and brush lightly to the end. Starting where you left off, brush back toward the other end. Try not to exert too much pressure because it creates bubbles. As you brush, it should feel like the varnish is flowing off the brush (you don't want to feel like you're pressing it off).

Reload the brush when necessary and overlap your strokes by about ½ in. Do not worry about puddles or brush marks. Scrape any excess finish off the brush and wipe it with a clean, lint-free cloth. Holding the brush perpendicular to the surface, lightly drag it across the surface. Called tipping off, this technique evens out the puddles and brush marks. Examine the surface in backlighting to ensure that the whole surface is covered. Finally, do the edges.

Brushing Varnish Vertically

Brushing a vertical side requires an adjustment in technique. The varnish is applied less thickly and a technique called cross-brushing is employed. Cross-brushing involves applying the varnish horizontally then tipping it off vertically. It avoids drips and prevents sagging of the finish as it dries. Try to avoid overthinning the varnish when cross-brushing. The thinner it is, the more likely it is that you'll get drips and sags.

Start at the bottom of the vertical side, approximately 3 in. from an edge. Dip the brush about a third of the way up the bristle to load it. Brush the varnish toward the edge, then return to your starting point and brush toward the other edge. Continue this pattern, overlapping each stroke by about ½ in. and working all the way to the top. Then tip off vertically. As the brush loads up, wipe off the excess finish.

When cross-brushing more complicated vertical sides like a frame and panel, start at the deepest parts and work toward the higher parts. Do the raised field of the panel last. Wipe any drips lightly with a dry brush. Excess varnish pooled in corners and moldings can be wicked up with a dry brush.

Wiping Varnish

You can buy a wiping varnish, but manufacturers seldom disclose whether the finish is a thinned varnish or a varnish/oil mixture that would be less durable. For this reason, I prefer to make my own wiping varnish.

To make your own, choose an interior varnish (don't use spar or long-oil varnish unless it's an exterior project) and thin it 50/50 with naphtha or mineral spirits. Naphtha dries quickly, so if you think you'll need more time to apply the varnish before it starts to tack, use mineral spirits. It doesn't matter if you use an alkyd, phenolic, or urethane varnish. Pick the one that matches your needs. You can also use this technique to apply gel varnishes.

Sand the wood to at least 180 grit and make sure it's free from dust and sanding debris. I pour some of the thinned varnish into a tuna can or dispense it from a squeeze bottle similar to those used for dispensing glue. Any absorbent cloth-type applicator can be used, but I prefer non-textured paper towels folded up into squares. Simply dip the edge of the folded towel into the varnish or squirt some varnish from the bottle onto the square.

Wipe on the first two coats. They'll go on easily, and because the varnish is absorbed into the wood, they dry evenly and quickly, in about two to four hours. Once the second coat is dry, wipe on the third coat as evenly as you can, using a light touch and wiping with the grain of the wood. Let the third coat dry at least overnight.

Wiping Varnish

Use a piece of soft, absorbent cloth or a paper towel to wipe on the varnish. The first coats go on easily.

2 Use the corner of a folded piece of paper towel to get the varnish into crevices and edges.

3 On very complicated parts—like the mullions of a door—it's okay to use a small brush. Just apply the varnish thinly.

After several coats, lightly sand the flat surfaces. Use 0000 steel wool or an equivalent-grade cushioned abrasive on the complex and rounded parts. Be sure to remove all sanding residue and dust with a tack cloth.

5 You'll need your best technique and a light touch to apply the last coat of varnish. It helps to wipe it on in backlighting so that you can see what you're doing. Try not to miss any spots. If you have to redo the last coat because of a mistake and the varnish has tacked up, wipe off the last coat with a rag moistened with mineral spirits.

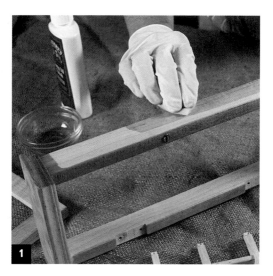

Padding Shellac

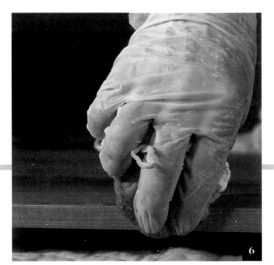

1 Make a pad by wadding up some soft, lint-free, absorbent cloth so that it fits easily in your hand and there are no seams or wrinkles on the bottom. Apply about an ounce of a 2-lb. cut of shellac to the bottom of the pad. (See p. 53 for more information on making shellac from scratch.)

2 To begin the basic padding stroke, bring the pad down at one end.

3 Land it lightly on the surface of the wood. Note how the board is raised off the table.

4 Continue wiping the shellac with the pad all the way to the other end.

5 As you reach the opposite end, start to lift up on the pad as you take it off the edge.

6 After recharging the pad, wipe the edges. If you have a complicated molding, conform the pad to the shape of the molding as you wipe it. The top should then be dry enough to start the padding sequence all over again.

Lightly scuff-sand the surface of the varnish with 320-grit sandpaper. If the paper starts to gum up easily, wait longer for the varnish to dry. It should powder easily when you sand it. Remove the sanding residue with a tack cloth, stiff brush, or vacuum if you have to.

Apply subsequent coats with a light touch and as evenly as possible. Once you have applied these later coats, do not go back and try to smooth them out. Unlike when you apply oils and oil/varnish blends, you want to leave a thin film on the surface of the wood rather than wipe off the excess. The temptation to go back and smooth things out is strong, especially if you see an area that's streaky or if you missed a spot. Don't do it! After the fifth and sixth coats, you should have a blemish-free, smooth surface on the wood.

Adjust the sheen of finish in one of two ways. First, if you used gloss for the building coats, you can apply a final coat of satin or flat. The resulting finish will be less glossy but better looking than if a satin varnish was used throughout the process.

The second option is to knock down the gloss by rubbing the gloss varnish with 0000 steel wool after the final coat has dried for at least a week. Use wax or rubbing compound if you want to bring up the gloss. (See Thin Finish Rub-Out on pp. 164-166.)

SHELLAC AND LACQUER

Shellac and lacquer are both fast-drying evaporative finishes with similar application characteristics. They dry fast enough so that dust that settles in the finish minutes after application can be wiped off. They cure hard enough to be sanded and rubbed out in a much shorter period of time than oil and oil-based products like varnishes. While shellac and most lacquers (excluding catalyzed lacquers) are less durable than varnish, they provide an attractive alternative.

Shellac can be applied by brush, by pad, or by spray. Lacquer can be applied by brush or by spray. The techniques for brushing and spraying shellac and lacquer are very similar, and once you learn how to spray one, switching to the other is easy. The technique of applying shellac with a pad—called padding—takes advantage of shellac's rapid drying time.

Both shellac and lacquer can be rubbed out to various levels of gloss, satin, and flat. In addition, both finishes are easy to repair if damaged.

Padding Shellac

Padding shellac is a method of wiping on shellac with a cloth pad. As with wiping varnish, the shellac is applied in thin coats. But because shellac dries so quickly, you can wipe more shellac over the dried shellac in minutes rather than after the hours or days varnish requires. A padded shellac finish can be applied easily over several days and rubbed out and waxed shortly afterward.

To apply the shellac, use a pad that is soft, absorbent, and as lint-free as possible. I use a product called padding cloth or trace cloth. Old T-shirts can also be used. Make a pad with a flat bottom by wadding up some cloth so that it fits easily in your hand. The bottom should have no seams or wrinkles. Squirt about 1 oz. of a 2-lb. cut of shellac onto the bottom of the pad. I like to use a squeeze-type bottle with a nozzle to dispense the shellac onto the pad.

Sand the surface to at least 180 grit and clean the dust and sanding debris. Disassemble the piece as much as possible because it's easier to pad a flat surface.

Retarding shellac and lacquer may make it easier for you to brush. Lacquer retarder will work for both. Pure gum turpentine (not the petroleum substitute) works for shellac only. Add about 1 ounce per quart.

Starting at the top of the board, bring the pad down lightly and drag it across the top and off the opposite edge. Come in from the other side and repeat the stroke.

Continue down the board in alternating stripes, with the grain of the wood. When you reach the bottom, start again at the top; it will be dry enough for you to repeat the same sequence. Keep doing this until the pad is dry, then recharge the pad with more shellac.

On tops, do the edges first after recharging the pad, then continue the same sequence as above. If there is a complex molded edge, conform the pad to the shape of the molding. Give the other parts of the piece—aprons, legs, and sides—a padding coat of shellac. When the board is tacky and the pad starts to stick, stop and let the surface dry.

Lightly sand the surface with 320-grit sandpaper when it has dried (approximately one hour later), then repeat the sequence, starting at the top of the board and working your way down. The pad should glide easily over the surface, and you should end up with an even coat of shellac on the surface. As the pad starts to dry out, you can switch from a stripe pattern to polishing in a circular pattern or a series of figure eights to get even coverage on the board.

Brushing Shellac and Lacquer

Shellac and lacquer require a different brushing technique than varnish. Varnish is flowed on the surface, then smoothed out with the tip of the brush before it sets to even it out. If you try to do this with lacquer or shellac you'll have problems. Because shellac and lacquer dry so quickly, the semi-cured finish will tear, or skin, if you try to rebrush it later.

I prefer to quickly brush on thin, light coats of shellac and lacquer, then feather out each coat before it dries. For shellac, use a 2-lb. cut first. If you have problems, thin it to a 1½-lb. cut. Most lacquers for brushing are too thick for this technique, so I cut the lacquer 50/50 with lacquer thinner.

Use a brush with fine, soft bristle for either finish. A fine, soft China bristle or a synthetic nylon artist's brush works fine. Buy the widest artist's brush you can, about 1½ in.

Work right from the can or pour the finish into a smaller can. Don't use plastic because the lacquer can attack certain plastics. Sand the wood to at least 180 grit and remove the sanding dust. Dip just the tip of the brush (about 1 in.) into the finish and press off any excess against the edge.

Starting about 3 in. from an edge, brush the finish to the edge. Come back to where you started and brush the finish to the other edge. Work in this pattern until the brush dries out, then replenish with more finish. When you start a new stroke there will be a puddle of thicker finish that you should immediately smooth into the rest of the finish with a flicking or whisking motion. Work the surface quickly and with thin coats. Because both lacquer and shellac dry quickly and because the coats are thin, you can come back almost immediately on a medium-size surface (24 in. by 15 in.) and start the next coat.

When the brush starts to stick, stop brushing and let the surface dry for at least an hour. Then lightly sand the surface with 320-grit stearated sandpaper. Press lightly on the edges because the finish will be thin. Rub the surface with 0000 steel wool or maroon-grade synthetic steel wool. Remove the sanding dust with a tack cloth.

Repeat the sequence of applying a thin coat of finish and letting it dry, but extend the drying time to overnight for the second

Brushing Shellac and Lacquer

1 Dip the brush about 1 in. into the finish and press off any excess. Thin the finish 50/50 with denatured alcohol if necessary.

2 Starting about 3 in. from an edge, brush the finish lightly to the edge. Use just the tip of the brush. At the beginning of the stroke, the finish should flow easily off the end of the brush.

Return to where you started and brush the finish to the other edge. Replenish with more finish as necessary, and work the finish quickly and evenly on the surface. You can work it with a whisking or flicking motion to even out puddles or brush marks.

Repeat the sequence until the surface is covered with finish. Go back to where you started; it should be dry enough to start the process again.

Use a smaller brush on edges and molding. Jab the edge of the brush into a corner to start the stroke, then pull it away from the corner. Try not to load too much finish on the brush on sharp edges or you'll get a drip.

If you do get a drip, wipe it immediately with your finger and rebrush the area.

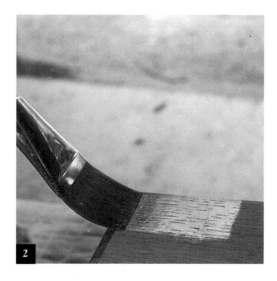

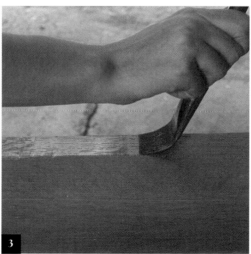

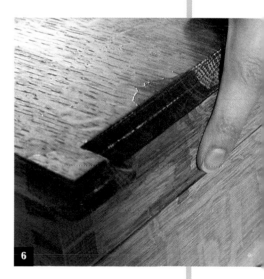

Spraying for the First Time

If you've never used spray equipment before, you can practice a bit and learn the controls by spraying plain water or solvent through the gun. Fill up the cup and turn all the controls on the back of the gun clockwise to close them off. Hold the gun so that you have light behind it and start opening the fluid-rate knob. A round, fine mist of water should start to appear. As you turn the knob more, a denser spray pattern will appear. Play with opening and closing the knob until you get the feel of the adjustment.

Next start to open the air-control knob (if the gun has one) and look at how the pattern gets wider as you open it. If the gun does not have this adjustment, turn the air cap to change the spray pattern. On guns with air-control knobs, turning the air cap changes the profile (vertical or horizontal) of the spray pattern.

Once you have the feel of the controls and where they should be set, try spraying water or solvent on a piece of cardboard or wood to get the feel for how far to hold the gun from the surface and how fast to move the gun (about three to five seconds per foot).

Now you can try finish in the gun. Fill it up with the properly thinned finish. Then hold the gun so that you can see the spray from the side and depress the trigger. You should see a fine mist of finish come out of the gun. If not, try adding more thinner to the finish, switch to a different nozzle/needle combo, or increase the air supply from the air source (if you can).

When you get it right begin spraying a flat piece of scrap wood. Play with the adjustments until you see a full wet swath of finish when you hold the gun 8 in. from the wood. Hold the gun really close to the finish as you spray another swipe and you'll see how the air from the gun puddles the finish. Now do another swipe and hold the gun far away from the wood, which produces a dry, rough finish.

The proper adjustments and technique will result in a smooth, even coat of finish once dry. Keep in mind that water-based finishes may look terrible until they dry for at least eight hours. Solvent-based finishes should look good after about an hour if your technique was right.

see pp. 24-27

WORKING SMART

The most helpful item you can have when spraying is a turntable. Screw a 12-in. lazy Susan-style turntable with steel bearings to a piece of plywood, then put a plywood plate on top (don't secure it). The plate will support various sizes of panels, chairs, and other items when you spray.

coat of finish. Build the finish to the depth that you like. For a durable, good-looking finish with great depth, try six or seven applications. Fewer applications will result in a more natural look.

Spraying Shellac and Lacquer

Evaporative finishes like shellac and lacquer are easy finishes to spray. If you've never sprayed before, you will find the good flow-out, fast-drying, dust-free qualities of these finishes hard to beat. Shellac and lacquer are also easy to repair.

The biggest problem is finding an appropriate area to spray. Both lacquer and shellac produce extremely flammable vapors. You need to spray in either a well-ventilated area free of potential sparks or in a specially designed booth to exhaust the spray (see pp. 24-27).

Spraying a flat surface If you've never sprayed lacquer or shellac, you should start by spraying a flat surface. This will give you an idea of the working qualities of the finish before you move on to more complex surfaces. The finish should be properly thinned and the gun set up to spray lacquer or other light-viscosity finishes. These finishes usually require the small nozzle/needle combination.

Thin lacquer with lacquer thinner, and thin shellac with denatured alcohol. When spraying shellac it's a good idea to add lac-

Spraying a Flat Surface

1 Spray the edges first to minimize overspray and dry spray on the top that will appear if you do them last.

2 Starting with the gun off the edge, depress the trigger before you hit the edge and move the gun slowly across the surface. How fast you move depends on the fluid-delivery rate adjustment, but you should deposit a wet film across the surface as you move it. About three to five seconds per foot is right. You should not move so slowly that the finish appears to puddle.

Continue the straight passes, overlapping each previous pass by about half. Work from the part of the surface closest to you and spray away from you to force the overspray off the edge.

4 Note how the gun is held so that it's 90 degrees to the surface. Try not to tilt the gun either up or down. This position is unnerving for beginners—you'll feel as though the finish will drip out the gun and spoil the work. As long as the top is tight and the seal is clean the finish won't drip.

Immediately after spraying the first pass, double-pass the first coat, meaning spray a second coat at a right angle to the first.

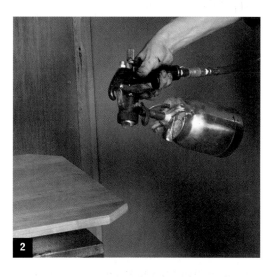

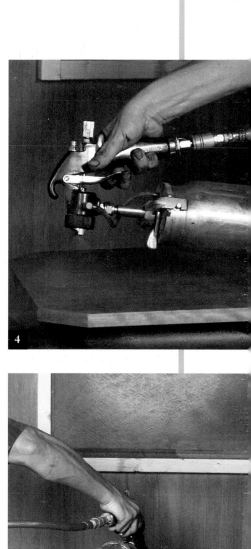

quer retarder to the shellac solution so that the shellac will flow out better and be less apt to blush. Add 1 oz. to 2 oz. per quart.

Starting off the edge and holding the gun 6 in. to 8 in. from the surface, depress the trigger and move the gun slowly across the surface. Try moving about 3 to 4 seconds per foot, but this speed may vary depending upon your fluid-delivery rate. You should see a wet film of finish being deposited. Overlap each pass by about half. When you get to the other edge, spray the surface in the same manner except at a right angle. This technique is called "second-coating," or "double-passing."

Spraying a complex surface Spraying a complicated surface like a chair or a cabinet presents some technical challenges with any finish. There are several things to

Spraying a Complex Surface with Any Finish

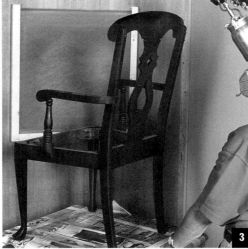

1 When spraying a complicated piece like a chair, it helps to spray from the inside out—meaning spray the least visible surfaces first, then work outward to the more visible parts.

2 Make sure you spray the undersides of arms and stretchers and the bottoms of legs.

3 After turning the piece over, start by spraying the outside of show surfaces, working from the top down. Spray the top of the crest, then work down and around the entire outside of the piece. Spin the piece on the turntable to get the finish on quickly and evenly.

4 Apply additional coats to areas of high wear, like arms, the front of legs, stretchers, and seat rails.

keep in mind. First, you should work from the inside out. On a chair that means you should do the inside of the legs and under the seat first, then flip the chair over and spray the more visible parts. Second, you should try and avoid over-thinning the finish. Many beginners over-thin lacquer and shellac because it seems to lay down and flow out better, but thin finishes will run easily and sag on complicated, vertical surfaces. Finally, you should make quicker passes and adjust the fluid rate to deliver less finish than when spraying a flat panel. Adjust the fan pattern for a medium-width pattern. The basic sequence is the same for any complex piece, but I'm going to use a chair as the example.

Start by spraying all the unseen areas like the bottoms of seat rails, the bottoms of legs, and the bottoms of stretchers. Spray the inside of the legs and the bottoms of the arms if there are any. Spray the underside of the top rail. Don't spray the top of the crest rail and the front apron; you'll need a dry surface to grab when you flip the chair over.

Start from the top and spray down. Spray the top of the crest and then down the splat. Spray quickly and turn the chair on the turntable quickly as you spray. I take quick, light passes, misting on the first coats, to minimize sags and runs. This is particularly important if you've stained the piece and need to lock in the stain. If you spray a thick coat on a vertical surface, the finish will run or sag, taking some stain with it.

Apply at least three coats with 1 hour drying time between each before sanding. Use sandpaper backed with your hand on flat parts and synthetic steel wool or some other type of cushioned abrasive on the rounded and curved parts. Remove the sanding dust and then apply more coats to

achieve the look you want. High-wear areas like the tops of crest rails, bottom stretchers, and the arms can be double-coated to provide a more durable surface.

Allow the last coat of lacquer to determine the sheen (a look called off-the-gun) because rubbing out chair parts is difficult. To prepare for this, remove all blemishes, runs, and other problems from the surface of the chair with a light sanding. Then rub the entire surface with gray-grade synthetic steel wool. Never use metal steel wool—it shreds and the tiny strands of metal are hard to remove from the finish.

Wipe the piece with a tack cloth and apply the final coat of lacquer in the sheen that you want. Try to work quickly and evenly so that you eliminate dry-spray, which is the dry finish overspray that settles on parts of the chair as you're spraying other areas. Working from the top down helps to eliminate dry-spray.

Spraying inside a cabinet Spraying inside a cabinet with dye or stain can cause problems. The vortex created at the tip of the gun prevents finish from getting into the crevices that form the corners. If the back of the cabinet is left on, the finish bounces back in your face.

First remove the back and finish it separately. An even better approach is to prefinish the parts of the cabinet separately before gluing them up. If neither option is possible, you'll have to live with some overspray, but it's still possible to get a good finish.

Start by spraying the four corners (assuming you were able to remove the back). Adjust the gun for a medium fan width and a medium fluid-delivery rate. Use the oval shape of the fan pattern to "draw" a line of finish into the four corners. You can reposition the air cap if necessary.

WORKING SMART

If lacquer or shellac drips while you're spraying, immediately wipe it lightly with your finger. Then spray over the area to blend it in with the surrounding area. If the drip starts to dry or you see it sag later, don't wipe it. Instead, let it dry until it's hard, then slice it level with a sharp chisel. Smooth it out with 400-grit sandpaper before respraying.

Spraying Finishes and Stains inside a Cabinet

1 Start by spraying all four inside right-angled corners. Hold the gun so that you can "draw" the fan edge of finish parallel to the edge. Try a small touch-up gun because it's less bulky and gets into tight spaces better. Do a single pass on the inside of the top next.

2 Move on to the first vertical side next. Note that the cabinet is oriented so the spray goes out the open screened window. If it's easier, change the air-cap position to reconfigure the spray pattern.

3 Spray the second vertical side. Try to depress and release the trigger as precisely as you can so the finish starts and stops right at the edges of the side panel.

4 The bottom is done last and may be double-coated if necessary. This sequence of working from top down eliminates dry spray on the bottom.

5 To produce an even finish transition to the front of the piece, spray the front of the cabinet immediately after spraying the inside. Start with the outer frame.

6 Move to the outside vertical sides and the top.

Then apply a single coat to the inside of the top and the two vertical sides. Try to depress the trigger precisely so that you begin and end each pass at the corner where the panels begin and end. Do the bottom last. You can double-coat it if necessary, because runs and sags won't be a problem.

If you cannot remove the back, cut back on the air pressure to the gun. Don't cut back too far, though; a reduction of only 5 psi may be all that's necessary. The lower pressure will alleviate bounce-back of the finish when the spray hits the back. Follow the same sequence as for a backless cabinet: draw the four corners first, then the top and two vertical sides. Then spray the back and finally the bottom. As soon as you're finished, blow out the cloud of over-spray from the cabinet with a blast of compressed air. A light touch on the trigger of most spray guns will work if you practice a bit; be sure to dispense air and not finish.

When you reduce the air, you may need to thin the finish a little more or add retarder to alleviate the chance of orange peel. If you have a turbine-driven HVLP gun with no air regulator, you'll have to do the best you can and live with the bounce-back.

Invariably spraying inside a cabinet involves some compromises, and you'll probably get dry, rough areas toward the back edges and in the corners. Prior to the last coat, sand all these areas flat with 320-grit sandpaper and then rub all the other areas with steel wool. Make your last coat your best and work with light passes to get the best application possible. You always have the option of rubbing out problems areas.

WATER-BASED FINISHES

Water-based finishes are here to stay. For those concerned with the fire and health hazards of solvent-based finishes, water-based finishes provide an attractive alterna-tive. They dry fast, can be applied by brush or spray, are widely available, and clean up easily.

People who want to spray at home or in facilities with limited exhaust systems can spray water-based finishes without fear of fire or explosions. Spraying a water-based finish is similar to spraying lacquer, but it requires some adjustments in technique and equipment setup. Multiple coats can be applied in a day, just like solvent lacquer.

Water-based finishes designed for brushing dry in 20 minutes or less, so dust is typically not a problem. While water-based finishes may not have the aesthetics of solvent-based finishes, they do provide you with some distinct benefits.

The downside is that water-based finishes don't fare well in cold, hot, or humid weather. On hot, humid days, avoid applying them. On cold days, first, get the finish as warm as you can, even if you have to place it near a heater or put it in a pan of hot water. Then try arranging a series of lights over or near the piece you're finishing to keep it warm. Keep air moving across the finish as it dries.

Brushing Water-Based Finishes

Water-based finishes are the most temperature sensitive of all finishes. Temperature and humidity are less of a problem when you brush water-based finishes, but you should try to finish at room temperature and in humidity below 70%. The finish and wood should be at room temperature. Because water-based finishes dry quickly, dust settling in the finish is not as much of a problem as with varnish, but finish in a clean, dust-free area if you can. Try to have fresh air flowing over the finish as it dries—a screened-in porch is ideal.

Prepare the wood by sanding to 180- or 220-grit paper. You can minimize grain raising from the sealer coat with one of two methods. Preraise the grain by sponging the wood with distilled water, letting it dry, and then resanding with your final grit. Or seal the wood with dewaxed shellac. The second option also increases depth and imparts an amber color.

Water-based finishes can be used straight from the can or thinned with water. Usually a small amount of water (5% to 10%) is all that's necessary. Some manufacturers make sanding sealers that contain an additive that makes the product chalk when you sand it. Any water-based finish can be used over itself as its own sealer, so you don't need a special product.

Use a fine, soft, synthetic-bristle brush to apply the finish. Chinex is a bristle that works well with most finishes (its name is stamped on the handle). But my all-around favorite is golden nylon. Before brushing, dip the brush in water to condition it, and wring out the excess. Strain the finish into a smaller container through a medium-mesh strainer. Then dip the brush about halfway into the finish and remove it. Let the excess finish fall off the end of the brush or press it lightly against the side of the container to push it out. As with varnish, do not scrape it off on the rim.

To apply the finish, start about 3 in. from the edge. Brush to the edge, then return to where you started and brush toward the other edge. Work the finish off the brush in smooth, even strokes. Make sure you maintain an even pressure and a wet edge. To maintain a wet edge, reload with more finish if anything but a full, wet swath comes off the brush.

Tip off the brush to remove small bubbles and to even out the finish. You'll see bubbles if you've worked the brush too aggressively. You have to act fast, though. Water-based finishes start to dry quickly

and may tear when you tip off; if tearing starts, leave the finish alone. Water-based finishes actually have slow-evaporating solvents that allow them to level themselves out—brush marks and all. Thin finishes might show brush marks worse than thicker finishes.

Unless you use shellac as a sealer, the first coat of finish will raise the grain, requiring you to sand the finish level before applying the next coat. Use wet/dry silicon carbide paper and a small amount of water to sand the finish level. Then apply another coat of finish.

Spraying Water-Based Finishes

The basic process of spraying water-based finishes is the same as for lacquer and shellac with two exceptions. You may need to change the setup of your gun and vary your technique slightly. Some water-based finishes are thicker than lacquers and shellac, so you'll need to use a larger nozzle/needle combination. I use anything between size 0.042 and 0.055 or a combination designed for medium-viscosity applications.

Because water-based finishes are higher in solids (they dry thicker), it's best if you apply them in thin coats and don't double-pass. Spraying thin, light coats also helps the finish to dry and flow out better.

You will not get acceptable results with underpowered HVLP spray equipment. The underpowered turbines simply cannot push the amount of air necessary to atomize a water-based finish adequately. A three-stage turbine is required when spraying water-based finishes.

Water-based finishes run or drip easily on vertical surfaces. It's very important to keep the coats light and thin. You can also minimize runs and sags by misting on a "tack" coat (a very quick mist coat) and then coming back within several minutes

Brushing a Water-Based Finish

1 Sponge the wood with distilled water to raise the grain. After the wood feels dry to the touch, resand it with the last grit you used for surface preparation.

2a Using a synthetic-bristle brush, apply the finish in smooth, wet strokes with the tip of the brush. Try to flow the finish off the edge without pressing down too hard on the bristle. Try to work in a warm room with plenty of air circulation to help the finish dry properly. After application, you can lightly tip off the finish, but only if it's still wet.

2b On large, flat surfaces, a short-napped pad is an option. Dip the pad in a shallow container of finish and apply it to the surface of the wood, moving it slowly.

2c Tip off the finish using the very edge of the front part of the pad. This evens out the finish and removes bubbles.

3 Lightly load the very tip of the brush and brush the edges.

4 For corners and other non-flat areas, lightly load just the very tip of the brush. Use just the tip for more precise control.

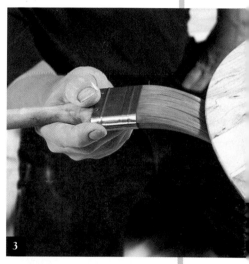

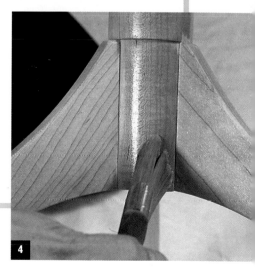

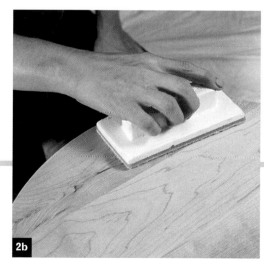

Spraying a Water-Based Finish

1 You must strain water-based finishes prior to spraying them. Water-based finishes are particularly prone to small bits of clumped resin or bits of dried finish that form around the top and fall back into the can when opened. Use a medium-mesh paper strainer.

2 Set up the gun with a larger nozzle/needle than for thinner finishes, like the one shown here for medium-viscosity finishes. Start spraying at the edge closest to you.

3 Move the gun across the work, spraying just enough finish so that the coat you're applying makes the wood look wet. It may appear cloudy or slightly bluish. If it's white it's too thick.

4 Move the gun away from you to force the finish off the far edge.

5 Coat the surface only once. Don't double-pass with water-based finish or it will be too thick and may have drying and curing problems.

with a wet application. The finish may look slightly cloudy or bluish as you spray it, but you should not apply the finish so heavy that it's white.

Water-based finishes have a peculiar characteristic: They look terrible when they're first applied and do not start to flow out and level quickly like solvent lacquer and shellac. Try to be patient and let the solvents in the finish do their job; it's not unusual to leave a hopeless-looking finish at night only to come back the next morning and see a perfectly flowed out, clear finish.

Strain the finish before spraying it through a medium-mesh filter. Set up the gun for a medium fluid delivery, and move it in a slow, steady motion perpendicular to the work, maintaining an even distance from the work. The finish should be wet and even as you apply it. Overlap each pass by about half its width.

The first coat should be hard enough to sand in about an hour. Because water-based finishes raise the grain, this coat needs the most aggressive sanding. On large, open-pore woods like oak, you may need to apply two coats before sanding. Use 320- or 400-grit silicon carbide wet/dry paper with water or a nonstearated paper. Remove all the dust from the surface with water and a clean, lint-free cloth (paper towels are best). Apply light final coats with about one hour of drying time between. You'll need only about two to four coats for a durable finish.

Warming Up Water-Based Finishes

Most water-based finishes look very different from oils and solvent-based finishes like lacquer, shellac, and varnish during and after application. They are either neutral in color, or they have a slight bluish tint, which is fine for some applications but less desirable on others.

This mahogany panel shows how to warm up water-based finish. The left panel is untreated. The center panel was stained an amber color with dye, and a small amount of the same dye was added to the water-based finish. The panel on the right was sealed with pale dewaxed shellac before the water-based finish was applied.

On certain woods like cherry, walnut, and mahogany, water-based finishes seem to lack the warmth and pleasant amber color that solvent-based finishes impart. On pickled or light-colored woods, this isn't a problem. In fact, the neutral color and non-yellowing characteristics are a benefit. For those situations where you want to warm up the color of a water-based finish, there are several ways to do it.

The first way is to dye the wood an amber color. Use a dye stain diluted to a yellow-amber color to approximate the color of a varnish or lacquer.

Another option is to seal the wood with shellac. This not only seals the wood and prevents grain-raising, it also imparts a warm amber color under the water-based finish.

You can also put color directly in the water-based finish. Adding a small amount of a compatible stain color to the finish warms it up. Some manufacturers even offer this as an additive. If they don't, use a honey-amber-colored stain and add it yourself. If you use a dry dye powder, mix it in a

Finishing Two Sides at Once

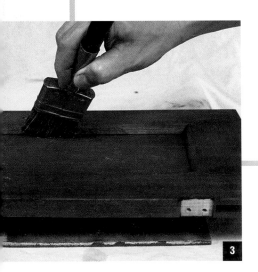

1 Finishing both sides of this frame-and-panel door at one time speeds up the finishing process and minimizes the possibility of finish dripping over to the other side. Begin by finishing the "non-show" side first. Do not brush the edges.

2 Holding the door by the unfinished edges, turn it over and place it finished-side down on the nail board. These four nails were located so they prop up the door at the four inside corners of the panel.

3 Brush the show side. Start at the deepest parts and brush to the highest parts, which on this door are the rails and stiles. Brush the edges last. Leave the door on the nail board to dry.

small amount of water to dissolve it before adding it to the finish.

My preference for warming up the color is to use shellac. It's easy to apply as a sealer coat and is available in a variety of colors. It dries fast and eliminates grain raising. When you use shellac, make sure it's dewaxed because wax prevents the waterbased finish from adhering well.

SPECIAL SITUATIONS

The reality of finishing is that no surface is flat (refer to p. 146 and 148). If it were, finishing would be much easier than it is. To complicate matters, there are two-sided doors, insides of cabinets with right angles, molded edges, and carvings, as well as small knobs, pegs, and other hardware to contend with.

Spraying makes finishing easier, but not everyone owns spray equipment. And even with spray equipment, you're still faced with myriad challenges, particularly with small items and the insides of cabinets where a spray gun has trouble reaching. You also have to contend with the prospect of how to hold different parts when spraying them.

One strategy is to finish all the parts of your project before you glue it up. Be sure to first protect areas that will get glued later, like tenons, and plug mortises so that finishing material doesn't interfere with later gluing. Prefinishing results in a cleaner appearance, speeds up the finishing process, and works very well for hard-to-reach cabinet insides on small projects.

Holding small parts and other objects can also be challenging. Over the years I've tried all sorts of custom holders and racks and wire grids, but I still keep coming back to the tried-and-true holders that I learned early in my finishing career: nail boards. These holders can be made in just a few minutes in a variety of shapes for holding various objects. I also use clothespins and drywall screws to hold awkwardly shaped parts and small items.

Finishing Two Sides at Once

You typically put a finish on both sides of doors, drop leaves, and lids. You can finish one side at a time, but there's a problem with this method. When you put a finish on only one side of a flat panel and wait for it to dry before you do the other side, it's possible that in hot, humid weather the unfinished side will absorb humidity while the finished side does not. The panel will warp and at best be difficult to fix (and more likely impossible).

The solution is to finish both sides at the same time. To do this, make a nail board, which is nothing more than a thin piece of plywood (¼ in.) with nails, brads, or drywall screws driven through one side. You finish one side of the piece, then place it finished-side down on the sharp points of the nails or screws to support it while you do the other side.

You can make a nail board in one of two ways. One method is to place the nails so they support the four corners of the panel in an inconspicuous spot. This works well for frame-and-panel doors. The other method is to drive enough nails into the plywood base that the weight of the panel is distributed evenly. When large, heavy objects are placed upon a large number of sharp nails, the weight is distributed evenly, there is less pressure, and the sharp nails mark less. This works well with items like drop leaves, backs, and larger doors.

Finishing Small Items

One of the challenges of finishing is holding small parts while you finish them. I use a variety of inexpensive solutions including clothespins, drywall screws, and small

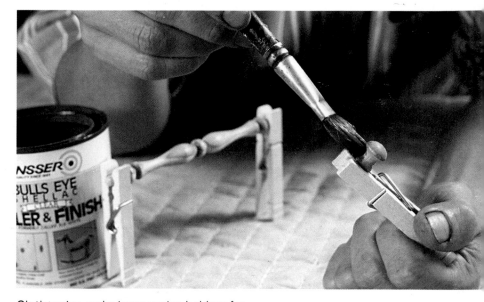

Clothespins make inexpensive holders for small knobs and spindles

custom-made nail boards. Finishing small parts before you glue them in or attach them will result in a cleaner look.

Clothespins can be used to hold small objects like spindles, knobs, and other irregularly shaped parts. Tape off tenons on spindles with masking tape so that you don't interfere with a good glue bond later. You can use clothespins as miniature supports on long spindles, or use them as miniature clamps to hold small knobs and other items when brushing or spraying them. Other devices such as paper clips and spring clamps can be used in the same way.

When you have a lot of knobs to finish, you can drill a series of holes the same size as the tenon to hold the knobs while you finish them. Knobs that are held by screws from the inside are treated a little differently. Twist the knobs down onto sharp drywall screws driven through a piece of plywood. The sharp points of the drywall screws grab the knob securely without damaging the screw hole. You can then hold the board full of knobs at various angles to brush or spray.

To hold small knobs while you stain and finish, screw them down onto the sharp points of drywall screws driven through a piece of plywood.

Once the knobs are on the screws, it's easy to brush them.

With irregular or round objects, spraying finish is the best method. To hold the object, place it on a miniature bed of nails.

Dipping is an efficient and easy way to stain and finish a lot of small parts. Clothespins make inexpensive holders for dipping the items into stain or finish, and they hold them upright to dry later as well. When dipping large numbers of objects, replenish the stain frequently to avoid progressively lighter colors.

To finish awkward items like round balls, use a small nail board. Space as many small brads through a piece of thin plywood as you can fit. The numerous brads distribute the weight evenly so you won't see any marks. Try to spray round objects because it's impossible to get a brush around the entire circumference of the ball. Aerosol versions of just about any finish

When you have a lot of small parts, dipping them into the stain or finish is the fastest way to finish them. Clothespins make great holders both for the dipping and as the parts dry.

To finish the interior of a small cabinet, brush on shellac or lacquer with a small artist's brush or a bristle brush with a sharp, square tip.

are available, or you can purchase small pressurized sprayers at paint stores to spray any liquid finish or stain.

Finishing Interiors

Interiors and insides are best finished before assembly. You can take apart drawers to finish the bottoms separately on many designs, and most cabinets have backs and shelves that can be removed. Remove the tops on case pieces and tables for access to the insides, and finish table leaves and tops separately.

When finishing the insides of cabinets and drawers, I recommend that you avoid oil and oil-based finishes. These products take a long time to thoroughly cure, even

Taking apart a drawer and finishing it in pieces results in a cleaner appearance when it's reassembled.

157

TROUBLESHOOTING FINISHES

PROBLEM	CAUSE	REMEDY
Oils		
Oil not drying	Raw linseed oil used Too much oil left on surface Temperature too low	Use boiled linseed oil Wipe surface clean after oil application Raise temperature
Oil bleeds*	Too much oil applied to open-pore wood	Wipe oil every three to four hours until it stops bleeding or apply thin seal coat
Oil smells on inside of drawers and cabinets	Odor unable to dissipate	Let item cure in open air as long as possible or seal with shellac or lacquer
Oil gets sticky and is hard to remove*	Oil/varnish blend drying too fast	Remove with mineral spirits, reapply, and wipe off sooner
Varnishes		
Bubbles in brushed varnish	Can was shaken right before use Pressing down too hard on brush or working varnish too hard with brush Varnish too thick	Let can sit for one to two hours after shaking Adjust brushing technique Thin varnish 5%-10%
Varnish won't dry	Temperature too low Manufacturer changed formulation Oily wood like rosewood, cocobolo, and other tropicals contain chemicals that inhibit curing	Raise temperature Switch to another brand or add Japan drier Switch to a different finish or seal with shellac before application
Varnish fisheyes (crawls into craters)	Silicone contamination	Wipe off varnish, seal with shellac, or add fisheye remover
Varnish won't level, showing brush marks	Varnish applied too thick Varnish drying too fast	Thin varnish Add mineral spirits

*Oil/varnish blends only

after the top of the finish is dry and hard. In an enclosed space, the solvent smell will linger for a long time. In addition, the solvent smell can be transferred to linens and clothes. If you want to oil the insides even with those potential problems, apply a light coat of oil, let it dry, and seal it with shellac or lacquer. Or apply only shellac or lacquer to the insides to seal the wood. The third option is to leave the insides unfinished.

While the third option seems contrary to sound woodworking practice, it's all right to leave secured sides and tops finished on one side only, as long as you allow for normal movement of the wood with the grain. Drop leaves or other unsupported items should always be finished on both sides or warping is likely.

When finishing very small interiors, I recommend a small artist's brush with a chisel edge like a golden-nylon brush or a fine soft-brush bristle with a chisel-cut tip. I usually apply several coats of lacquer or shellac using the technique described earlier and then rub out the surface with 0000 steel wool and wax. The wax imparts a silky "friendly" feel to the surface when your hand touches it.

TROUBLESHOOTING FINISHES (continued)

PROBLEM	CAUSE	REMEDY
Shellac and lacquers		
Turns white after application	Moisture trapped in film	Apply thinner over finish and add retarder
Lacquer finish fisheyes (crawls into craters)	Silicone contamination	Strip and add fisheye remover
Pores show small pinholes	Previous stain or finish not dry	Strip and refinish
Drips, runs	Finish applied too thick	Wipe immediately and reapply or let dry and cut off with chisel
Shellac finish doesn't dry	Shellac past its shelf life	Strip and use fresh shellac
Finish cracks	Coat too thick; didn't dry between coats Shellac sealer is old Too much lacquer sanding sealer used	Strip and apply thinner coats Strip and use fresh shellac Strip and use less sealer
Shellac finish is thicker at edges	Forms "fat edge" as it dries	Apply thinner coats; use additive; ease edges with sandpaper
Water-based finishes		
Bubbles in brushed finish	Applied too vigorously with brush or wrong brush used	Adjust brushing technique or change brush
Finish won't dry	Humidity too high or temperature too cold	Wait another day to finish
Rough textured surface (orange peel)	Not enough atomization	Boost air pressure on spray gun
Finish pulls up stain	Solvents redissolving dye	Seal dye with shellac
White clumps in finish	Finish not strained	Sand or remove finish with water, strain, and reapply
Finish peels off	Stain or sealer incompatible	Strip and reapply
Black specks in wood	Steel or metal particles embedded in wood or finish	Strip and remove black wood mark with oxalic acid
Finish fisheyes (crawls into craters)	Silicone contamination Stearates from sandpaper left between coats	Strip and add fisheye remover Remove finish, wipe clean with water, and reapply

RUBBING OUT

The final coat of finish rarely behaves exactly the way you want it to. Bubbles, dust, and other debris may lodge in the surface of the finish. Brush marks and patterns from spraying leave an irregular surface, particularly on gloss finishes. Rubbing out a finish removes these imperfections, evens out and smooths the surface, and establishes a consistent sheen to the finish. The first step is to remove defects and level the finish. The second step is to polish the finish to the sheen you want. Not all finishes need to be rubbed out, but a rubbed out finish has a visual and tactile quality that's hard to beat.

TO RUB OR NOT TO RUB

Any film-forming finish can be rubbed out. Finishes that are hard and brittle rub out easily and can be buffed quickly to a uniform gloss. These finishes include shellac, solvent lacquer (nitrocellulose and acrylic), short-oil varnish, most water-based lacquers, and catalyzed lacquers. Finishes that are soft or tough and flexible can be rubbed out, but they don't always take a uniform sheen and are difficult to polish to gloss. These finishes include oil-based polyurethane, water-based polyurethane, and catalyzed varnish. Oil finishes and oil/varnish blends do not form a hard film and are too soft to be rubbed out.

Any gloss finish can be rubbed out to flat or satin, but the difference between a flexible finish and a brittle finish becomes evident when you try to polish it back up to gloss. Tough and elastic finishes deform and tear when you abrade them, and it's impossible to establish a well-defined, even pattern of scratches. Hard, brittle finishes leave a well-defined scratch pattern, so you can continually make the pattern of scratches smaller to eventually polish to gloss.

Not all finishes need to be rubbed out. Most of the time, semi-gloss, satin, and flat finishes can be left alone. And a carefully applied padded shellac finish, oil finish or varnish may look fine right off the applicator.

CHOOSING MATERIALS

The materials change as you move through the steps. You'll need sandpapers to remove imperfections and flatten the finish. Then you'll need steel wool, synthetic steel wool, and abrasive powders to polish to the desired sheen.

Sandpapers

Silicon carbide wet/dry papers are traditionally used for removing imperfections and leveling the finish. They should be used with a lubricant, either mineral spirits or soapy water.

The Stages of Rubbing Out

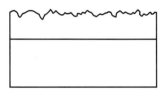

Finish has hollows and bits of debris lodged in it.

Abrading away part of the finish removes defects and levels finish.

Polishing to sheen puts very fine scratches in the surface.

How Is Sheen Created?

Sheen is a measurement of how much light is reflected off a surface. When a large percentage of light is reflected we call the sheen gloss. In a gloss finish the reflection of an item behind or above the surface is distinct and sharply outlined. When a low amount of light is reflected we call the sheen flat. In a flat finish, the reflection of a close-by item will appear fuzzy or indistinct on the surface. In between these two extremes are semi-gloss, satin, and eggshell sheens.

Sheen is created in clear finishes one of two ways: with flatteners or with very fine scratches. Flatteners are very fine, transparent particles in a finish that float to the top of the surface of the finish as it dries. These particles break up the surface of the smooth, dry film, causing some of the light to be diffused away. The more flatteners in the finish, the more light is diffused and the less glossy the surface will be.

For the same effect you can put very fine scratches in the finish once it has been applied. These fine scratches also break up the smooth surface of the finish and diffuse light. The size of the scratch determines the sheen. The scratches produced by very fine sandpaper (400 to 600 grit) produce a flat finish. Finer abrasives or polishing compounds create smaller scratches, so less light is diffused and the finish becomes glossier.

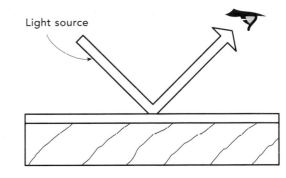

A surface appears glossy when at least 80% of the light hitting it is reflected to your eye.

Light source

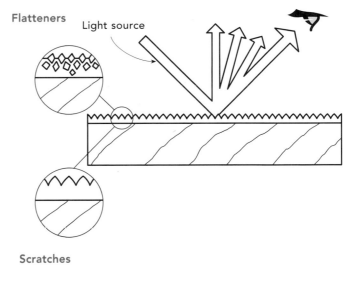

A surface appears satin or flat because flatteners or scratches diffuse light away from your eye.

Flatteners Light source

Scratches

For dry-sanding, stearated sandpaper is always. They can clog quickly with finishes like solvent lacquer, shellac, varnish, and some water-based lacquers. However, on tough finishes like polyurethane and two-part lacquers they don't clog as quickly. The advantage of dry-sanding is that you have better control because you can see what you're doing. Lubricated wet/dry papers create a slurry, which gives a false illusion of a thick finish. It's easy to sand through to sealer or color coats with wet/dry paper.

Steel Wool and Synthetic Steel Wool

Steel wool and synthetic steel wool are used after wet-sanding or dry-sanding to establish a consistent scratch pattern for flat and satin finishes. The scratches made by steel wool are different from those made by a sharp abrasive particle, and the result is a slightly different looking sheen. The cushioned nature of both materials makes them ideal for rubbing round and complex surfaces.

Abrasive Powders

Abrasive powders are used for polishing up to the desired gloss after sanding and using steel wool. Traditional powders are pumice (powdered volcanic glass) and rottenstone (powdered decomposed limestone). These powders are minerals and composed of sharp, angular fragments that scratch the finish. Pumice is sold in grades from 1F (coarse) to 4F (fine). Rottenstone is finer than pumice and is sold in only one grade, which is fine enough to polish a surface to gloss.

These abrasive powders and others like fine silica or tripoli can be combined with a carrier and other ingredients to produce liquid polishes or pastes that can be used by hand or machine. You can find these products at automotive-supply shops.

THIN FINISH RUB-OUT

Because rubbing out involves removing a portion of the finish, the procedure for rubbing thin finishes is different from thicker finishes. You might rub out a thin finish in two situations. The first is when you apply a hard finish that's built up only slightly on the surface of the wood. Because there is only a little finish on the surface, you risk sanding through into the stain or bare wood if you sand aggressively. The other situation is when you apply thin finish coats with a reactive finish like varnish. These coats do not fuse together, so aggressive rubbing of the last coat may go through, making the outline of the previous coat visible.

To rub out a thin finish, start with a very fine abrasive paper and back it up with your hand. I usually start with 600 grit, never use anything lower than 400 grit, and never use a backing block. I prefer to dry-sand thin finishes with stearated paper. It allows you to see what you're doing, and you get a better

Rubbing Out Thin Finishes

On a thin finish, either evaporative or reactive, scratches from aggressive rubbing out will go through the finish into the wood below.

With reactive finishes, sanding scratches can go through thinly applied coats of varnish because reactive finishes don't melt together. When this happens, a line appears called a "witness line."

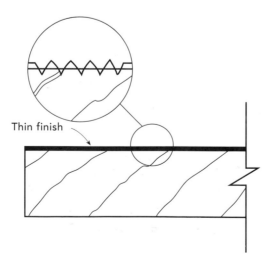

Thin finish

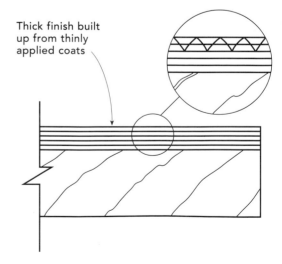

Thick finish built up from thinly applied coats

Rubbing Out a Thin Finish

1 Using sandpaper backed with your hand, sand the surface of the finish lightly, just enough to scuff the surface and remove defects. The finish should powder easily, so if it gums, let it dry longer.

2 It's easy to sand through sharp corners if you're not careful. Hold the paper as level as you can, work the edges in short strokes, and avoid pushing down on the paper at the end of the stroke.

3 Don't sand moldings. Instead, make a small pad from a piece of 0000 steel wool and conform it to the molding as you rub. Use this technique for carvings and turnings as well.

4 After sanding, use a 0000 steel wool pad backed with your hand. Work the edge perimeter separately from the top with short strokes of the pad. Feather this into the rest of the flat surface until you have a uniform, dull surface. If you see low, shiny spots, bear down harder with the pad.

5 To bring up the sheen to satin, apply a coat of paste wax with a piece of 0000 steel wool dampened with mineral spirits. Use a dark-tinted wax if you don't like the light color of natural wax or if you want to add contrast to open-pore woods like this oak. For a gloss look, use polishing compound or rottenstone. Dark-colored polishing compounds can be used on dark woods.

feel for how much finish you're removing because you can see the finish powder up as you sand.

To size paper for sanding, cut a sheet into quarters. Then fold one quarter sheet into equal thirds by folding the ends in toward each other. This way one abrasive side does not touch another abrasive side, which would prematurely wear the abrasive.

Begin sanding with the grain. The finish should powder and not gum. If it gums, the finish isn't dry, so let it dry longer. A rule of thumb is that fast-drying, evaporative finishes should cure at least several days before sanding, while oil-based varnishes should cure for at least a week. Sand just enough to remove any application marks and dust pimples. In most cases, one or two passes should be enough. At the edges, hold the paper perfectly flat so that you don't cut through the edge. Do not sand intricate moldings, turnings, or carvings.

Wipe off the dust with a cloth dampened with mineral spirits or water. Unravel a piece of 0000 steel wool, then fold it up into quarters to maximize the surface area and extend the life of the pad. Be sure to unravel the pad before you start rubbing because trying to unravel a pad that's loaded with finish dust, solvent, or wax is impossible.

Rub the flat areas with the steel wool. You'll see the dull pattern left by the sanding scratches if you examine the surface in oblique lighting. Shiny spots will appear as you rub, and these are the bottom of pores and low areas. Bear down a bit with the steel wool until these spots disappear. To avoid rubbing through the edges, do these separately. Take short, quick rubs with the steel wool around the perimeter until it's dull like the rest of the surface. Then blend all the areas together with a couple of quick passes over the entire surface.

To increase the shine, apply some paste wax and buff it when dry. Or apply some rottenstone or fine polishing compound with a soft cloth. On open-pore finishes make sure you use a dark wax or polishing compound if you don't like the light color of the wax or compound.

To rub moldings, turnings, and carved areas, rub lightly with the steel wool, just enough to knock down the gloss a bit. You can tear off small pieces of steel wool to make pads that conform to the shape of moldings and are easier to use.

THICK FINISH RUB-OUT

Thick finishes are rubbed out differently than thin finishes. The goal is the same—to remove imperfections and control the final sheen—but with thick finishes you can level the finish more aggressively to get a perfectly flat surface. Once you level the finish, you bring it up to the desired luster by creating a pattern of progressively finer scratches with steel wool, abrasive powders, or liquid pastes. Before you start rubbing, though, there are several important points to consider.

The first is surface flatness. You'll get the best results if you start with a perfectly level sanded wood surface. Poor sanding leaves an uneven surface that's exaggerated when the finish is applied and rubbed out. Complex surfaces like moldings, carved and turned legs, and rounded surfaces should never be level-sanded with a backing block. Back up the sandpaper with your hand instead.

The second consideration is the pores. Gloss finishes look best when the surface appears as a flat, uninterrupted surface. If you plan on a gloss finish for open-pore woods like mahogany, walnut, and oak, fill the pores with a paste wood filler. A open-pore gloss finish is difficult to buff and doesn't look as elegant as a filled-pore finish.

The next consideration is cure time. You should always let the finish cure. Cured finishes buff up better and faster than finishes that aren't fully cured. The longer you wait the better. Shellac, solvent and water-based lacquers, and two-part finishes should cure for at least a week. Oil-based varnishes and polyurethane should cure for at least two weeks. If the finish is gummy and loads up the paper at the level-ing or polishing stage, it's not dry enough. Let it cure longer.

The final consideration is the finish itself. The greatest danger from rubbing through the finish top coat occurs when you are leveling. To prevent this, I build up the finish with several coats of finish (after all the final coloring and paste wood fill-ing) and then level-sand it. For varnish, I apply two full coats after the final coloring

Rubbing Out a Thick Finish

Wrap wet/dry sandpaper around a soft block made of felt, cork, or rubber. Rub the surface in the direction of the grain until the defects are removed. Then, using the same grit or higher, level the surface until it has a uni-form, dull appearance. Wet-sand to 600 grit.

2 For the edges, use a fine-grit wet/dry paper backed up with your hand. 600 grit works for most situations. Use a light touch to avoid rubbing through a sharp edge.

Unravel a piece of 0000 steel wool and then fold it back up into quarters to maximize the sur-face area of the pad.

4 Rub the surface in long strokes until an even, dull sur-face appears. Do the edges first, in short, choppy strokes, then blend the edges into the rest of the sur-face with longer strokes. You can leave the surface flat or go onto rubbing to satin (see p. 170) or to gloss (see p. 172).

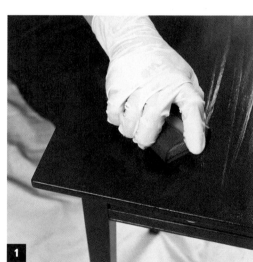

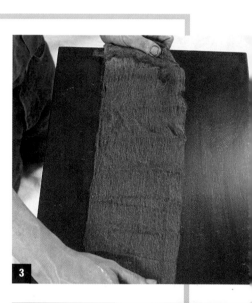

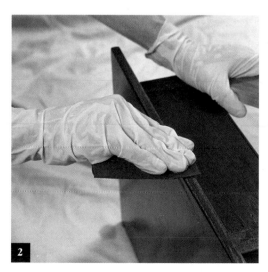

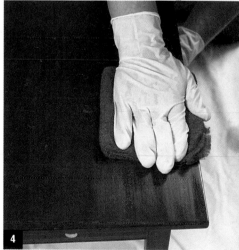

WORKING SMART

To determine the sheen as you rub out the finish, check the quality of the reflection of an overhead light or of an object at one end. A clear, distinct reflection indicates gloss. A slightly fuzzy image means semi-gloss or satin. A completely indistinguishable image means a flat finish.

step, level-sand with 320-grit sandpaper (always sanding with the grain), then apply a full wet coat of finish.

For shellac and lacquers, I apply three or four full wet coats after the final coloring step (staining, toning, or glazing), then level-sand with 320-grit sandpaper, and apply three or four coats of finish, allowing one hour of drying time between coats. I do the same for water-based lacquer. However, because some water-based finishes do not melt into the previous coat, I change the final step, applying three to four light coats in rapid succession with only 10 to 20 minutes of drying time between coats. Following these steps creates a level base for the last top coat(s) so there's less finish to remove during rub-out.

To remove the imperfections efficiently, start rubbing out with a low grit wet/dry sandpaper. I usually start with 400 or 600 grit, but will go as low as 320 grit if the surface has heavy brush marks or orange peel. If the surface has minor dust pimples, 600 grit is sufficient. Wrap the paper around a backing block and sand just enough to remove the tops of pimples so that they're level with the rest of the finish. With orange peel and brush marks, try to sand them as level as you can. Soapy water can be used as a lubricant on most finishes but it can cause problems with shellac, which requires mineral spirits instead. At this point the surface should have alternating dull and shiny spots when viewed in backlighting.

Once the high spots, drips, and other defects are removed, you'll switch to leveling. The goal of this step is to establish a consistent scratch pattern across the entire surface of the wood. Start with the grit you used in the previous step or one grit finer.

Rubbing Out Thick Finishes

On a thick evaporative finish like shellac, there's no danger of cutting through to the wood.

You won't rub through a reactive finish if you apply a thick enough final coat.

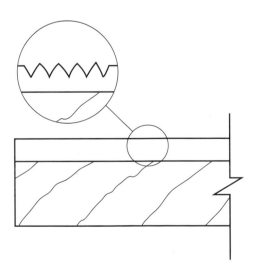

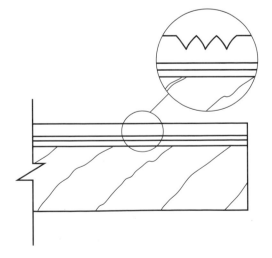

Wrap a quartered sheet around a soft block and start at the edges. Work the edges all the way around the perimeter of the top. When the edges are done, switch to the center of the board and work it in manageable sections. Check the surface of the paper often. If it starts to clog, shift it to expose fresh grit or change it. Don't try to economize by using clogged paper.

Brush aside the slurry and look at the surface in backlighting. You should see a dull scratch pattern. More than likely you'll also see areas that are still shiny. Work slowly and deliberately until the entire surface is dull. Don't worry about any small shiny areas, which are probably partially filled pores or low spots. They'll blend in when the entire surface is polished.

When you're satisfied with leveling, move up to the next grit of wet/dry sandpaper and follow the same pattern listed previously, starting with the edges then switching to the center of the board. Continue increasing the grit until you reach 600 grit, then switch to dry 0000 steel wool and rub the surface until all the shiny spots are gone and the surface has an even, dull sheen. Now you have a choice. You can leave the surface as it is, which would be a dull sheen, or continue on to satin or gloss.

THE SATIN LOOK

Rubbing to satin begins once the surface has been level-sanded to at least 600 grit. Unravel a pad of 0000 steel wool and fold it into quarters. Squirt some soapy water on the board, then apply some steel-wool rubbing lubricant (Wool-Lube or Murphy's Oil Soap) on the pad or the board.

Rubbing with the grain and bearing down hard with your hand, make three complete passes over the surface, slightly overlapping each pass with the next. The

amount of pressure you put on the pad is anywhere from 20 lb. to 30 lb. (you can press down on a bathroom scale to judge the pressure). Switch to a fresh part of the pad and repeat two times for a total of nine passes. Brush aside the slurry periodically to check that you're putting down a uniform scratch pattern. You may have to let the board dry to see if you've got it right. If you want the surface to have a silky, waxed feel, let the slurry dry, then buff it off, just like wax. When viewed in backlight, the surface should look like brushed metal.

If the sheen is still not shiny enough for your tastes, continue rubbing using one of two techniques. The first is to sprinkle some 4F pumice powder and soapy water onto the surface of the wood. With a white synthetic steel wool pad, rub the surface with the grain using the same techniques you did for the previous step above. Or you can use a fine rubbing compound and a soft cloth wrapped around a soft block like cork or felt. Always rub with the grain, never in a circular motion.

When viewed in backlighting the surface should appear flat and have an even sheen created by a very fine scratch pattern. You may discover problems at this stage like errant, large scratches, low spots, and areas near the edges where you may have rubbed through and exposed the stain. To fix large scratches, return to the dry steel wool step and rub the surface to remove the scratch. Do not work in just the problem area, though; instead, periodically feather into the rest of the surface to blend and avoid a depression or hollow. To fix low spots, resand with 600-grit or 400-grit wet/dry sandpaper and then feather into the rest of the surface. Then rub with dry steel wool and continue with the rest of the steps for rubbing to satin. To fix multiple light scratches or to revive a

WORKING SMART

To get a sheen that's somewhere between satin and gloss, try using wax thinned 50/50 with mineral spirits as a lubricant. The wax fills in the tiny hairline scratches left by the steel wool pad so the sheen is higher.

satin finish, wet-sand the entire surface, rub with dry steel wool, and continue with the steps for rubbing to satin.

If you rub through an edge while leveling or rubbing, avoid the area until you've finished rubbing the rest of the surface. At that time, brush some dye or pigment mixed with shellac onto the revealed bare wood if it was stained. Then cut a slit about the size of the rub-through in the middle of a piece of thin cardboard. Tape

or hold the cardboard so that the rub-through is visible through the slit, and spray some satin lacquer or varnish over the rub-through. Spray several coats and let it dry. When it's dry, use 0000 steel wool, feathering the line of the new finish into the old finish with some light strokes.

THE GLOSS LOOK

The difference between rubbing to satin and rubbing to gloss is that you make finer

Rubbing to Satin

1 Using 0000 steel wool with mineral spirits, soapy water, or a rubbing lubricant, like Wool-Lube or Murphy's Oil Soap, rub the surface using long, even strokes. Back up the steel wool with your hand and use moderate pressure to press down (20 to 30 lbs.). Do this after sanding to 600 grit.

2 After three passes, open up the pad and switch to a fresh surface. Do the same after each additional three passes, up to a total of 12 passes.

3 Make sure you rub under the top overhang as well as the sides. As finishes are generally thinner in these areas, make several passes.

4 On legs and other small surfaces, be careful not to rub too aggressively, and go light at the edges. Just use a small portion of the pad, and back it up with one or two fingers.

scratches. By polishing the surface of the finish with increasingly finer abrasives, the scratch becomes so small that it cannot diffuse light. When this happens the surface is glossy.

To rub a surface to gloss, level the surface with 600-grit sandpaper, then wet-sand up to at least 800 grit. If you want to avoid a lot of work with polishing compounds, wet-sand to 1,200 grit.

Sprinkle some 4F pumice on the surface of the wood, then squirt some soapy water or rubbing oil over the pumice. Wad up a clean, dry cotton cloth and, working in any direction, polish every square inch of the board. Apply a good deal of pressure and replenish the pumice and water as it dries. Let the slurry haze over, then wipe it all off with a damp rag. Switch to rottenstone and follow the same steps until the finish is as glossy as you want.

You can substitute commercial rubbing compounds, pastes, or liquids for the pumice and rottenstone. Start with a compound that will remove the last scratch pattern from your rubbing schedule. If you sanded the surface to 800 grit, start with a heavy or coarse compound. If you sanded up to 1,200 grit, start with a finer grade.

Rubbing to satin by hand is easy, but rubbing to gloss by hand is a lot of work. You can save a lot of time by investing in a power buffer if you have to rub out large surfaces. Power buffers are only used on gloss finishes; satin finishes still have to be hand-rubbed.

The best buffers are right-angle orbital polishers with at least two set speeds (2,000 and 3,800 RPM are about right). These machines are used with a wool bonnet-type foam pad. To use an orbital buffer put on an apron and move the piece you're buffing to an area where flying compound won't be a problem. After wet-

sanding to at least 800 grit, squirt some stripes of compound material down the center of the surface about 8 in. apart. If you have an old pad on the buffer, you'll need to spin off the old compound by holding a stick against it while the buffer is spinning. Then with the buffer turned off, smear compound all over the surface of the finish. Hold the buffer on the surface at a very slight angle and turn it on. Move the buffer across the surface of the finish slowly, trying not to stay in one area too long. I do the edges first, then work the buffer toward the center.

There is a natural fear of using a buffer, but if you follow some simple guidelines, you shouldn't have any problems. Try not

The surface on the right was rubbed to satin with 0000 steel wool, and the surface on the left was rubbed to gloss with fine polishing compounds and a cloth. Note how the gloss side has more depth and a deep color.

Rubbing to Gloss

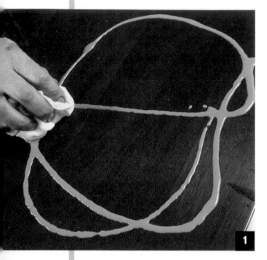

1 To produce a gloss sheen, squirt some rubbing compound on the surface after wet-sanding it to at least 800 grit. Use a medium- or heavy-cut compound first to remove the scratches from the wet-sanding as efficiently as possible.

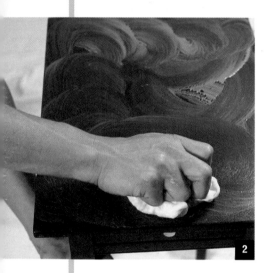

2 Rub the compound with a soft cloth. Rub in any direction because the scratches left by this compound will be removed with the next. When you're done, remove all excess compound with a clean, dry cloth.

3 Smear the final compound—a finer polish to bring up the gloss—all over the surface. Rub it until a deep gloss appears. When the compound hazes over, remove it with a dry, soft cloth. For a wet gloss finish, follow this compound with a glaze.

to jerk the machine; concentrate on working the buffer in smooth, confident strokes. When working edges, pay attention to the angle and rotation of the buffer. Angle the buffer so that the part of the pad in contact with the surface spins away from an edge, not into it. On large objects, like dining room tables, you can work the top while it's attached to the aprons and legs. On small, light items like nightstands you may need to remove the top and secure it.

The scratches from sanding disappear as you buff. Overhead lighting or backlighting will highlight errant scratches, and you can work any missed areas with more compound. Let the compound haze, then wipe it off with a soft cloth and examine again. It's important to remove all scratches with the initial compound. If you don't and you discover visible scratches with the next compound, you'll have to go back to the first compound again and start over.

Switch to polishing material when you've finished with the rubbing compounds. Apply the polish using the same techniques described above. I like to change to a different pad. A deep gloss should appear quickly at this stage. Cover the entire surface, let the compound dry, and wipe it off with a soft cloth.

At this point you can apply a product called a glaze or a swirl remover. Glazes contain an oil or polymer emulsion, and they fill in the tiny hairline scratches left by the previous compound. Swirl removers contain a very fine abrasive and/or a resin. I apply both products by hand to eliminate the chance of swirl marks caused by an orbital buffer. If you have a clean pad, you can dry-polish the surface instead by misting it with soapy water and then buffing it at a slow speed (around 2,000 RPM).

TROUBLESHOOTING RUBBING-OUT PROBLEMS

SYMPTOM	CAUSE	REMEDY
Finish gums or tears when you wet-sand or polish with compounds	Finish not cured hard enough	Let finish dry longer
Finish polishes unevenly	Wrong type of finish to rub out	Rub to as even a sheen as you can with dry steel wool, then apply wax or switch to a different finish
White spots in pores or cracks	Polishing compound dried white in open pores and cracks	Use a dark-colored buffing compound or wax; cover up residue with dark oil-soluble dye or wax
Buffer cuts through the finish	Not enough finish applied Buffed too long in one place	Apply thicker top coats and rebuff Adjust technique
A line appears when you buff or rub out (witness line)	The coats of finish do not melt together (reactive finishes)	Apply a thicker final top coat
You consistently cut through the finish on edges	Finish is thinner at edges or edges are too sharp	Keep the paper level around edges; use hand to back paper; if spraying, double-coat the edges; ease edges with sandpaper
White residue appears in crevices and moldings	Buffing compound residue	Remove with a damp cloth or a soft toothbrush and soapy water
Deep scratches appear when you buff to gloss	Scratches left by oversize grit particles in sandpaper	Wet-sand the scratches with 800-grit sandpaper or dry steel wool, then rebuff
Scratches aren't even on satin finish	You're arcing your hand when you rub with steel wool	Rub steel wool in even, straight strokes

To rub out complex surfaces to gloss you have to change your technique slightly. For moldings, wrap 800-grit wet/dry sandpaper around small rubber or wooden sanding blocks to approximate the convex and concave curves of the molding. After drying, rub the molding with 0000 steel wool and wax or fine polishing compound. When dry, the wax can be buffed up to approximate the sheen of the rest of the surface.

On turned legs use 800-grit wet/dry sandpaper on the flat areas, then use 0000 steel wool and wax thinned with mineral spirits or a fine polishing compound on the curves. Avoid hard rubbing because it will cut through the finish on sharp details.

Carvings should not have a lot of finish applied to them because it destroys detail. Rub lightly with 0000 steel wool to knock down the gloss to satin. If you want to apply wax, use a soft cloth and buff it with a soft brush. Use dark-colored wax on dark woods, or just leave these woods "off the gun" (no buffing).

When you're buffing to gloss and you rub through an area, use the procedure outlined previously except use gloss finish. When the finish has dried for a day or so, use rubbing and polishing compounds and feather them into the rest of the finish.

CLEANING AND REPAIR

Wood finishes vary in protection, durability, and aesthetics, but they all react to the forces of light, moisture, air, and general wear and tear. Finishes may yellow or oxidize, become brittle and crack, or simply get scratched, dented, or scraped. Certain finishes fare better than others, but all finishes eventually need some type of maintenance.

There are three kinds of protection and maintenance: general prevention, cleaning and appearance maintenance (including restoration of surface luster and shine), and repair work (fixing the evidence of everyday use).

PREVENTATIVE MAINTENANCE

The first step in maintaining your finish is to prevent avoidable problems. Sunlight and oxygen combine in a process called photo oxidation, which causes most of the damage to finishes as well as to the wood itself. Photo oxidation causes dyes and some pigments to fade and finishes to become brittle, resulting in cracking and crazing. This causes a dull appearance. Strong sunlight produces heat that will warp wood and cause it to split and crack, and may eventually bleach out the natural color of the wood. Prolonged exposure to high moisture causes glue joints to fail and may turn finishes white or cloudy. High heat combined with moisture turns some lacquer finishes a dark yellow.

The answer to these potential problems is simple. Keep your furniture out of strong sunlight, high heat, and damp areas like basements. If you have large picture windows, consider curtains or window blinds to keep colors from fading.

CLEANING AND APPEARANCE MAINTENANCE

Cleaning and maintaining the appearance of a finish can be done in one of two ways—with wax or polish.

Waxes

Waxes are suitable for use on most finishes, but there are two situations where wax could cause a problem. The first is on a buffed gloss finish. Waxes tend to smear easily on a slick surface and are hard to buff out to a consistent sheen. Emulsion polishes or glazes are better on these finishes.

The second problem occurs with waxes that contain a strong solvent (toluene),

Applying wax with 0000 steel wool will smooth the finish and apply the wax at the same time. It helps to thin the wax with mineral spirits.

The Myths and Realities of Wax

Waxing furniture is filled with myths about what the wax actually provides in terms of protection. The truth is that wax provides little—if any—added protection to a finished surface or when used as a finish on its own. Wax is easily softened by heat and can be easily permeated by water. While it does have the advantage of being easy to apply, its real advantage is more the aesthetic and tactile benefits it provides. The properties of wax differ depending on its use.

Wax is sometimes used as a finish for bare wood. Multiple coats of wax are applied to the surface at regular intervals. This is the least protective finish you can apply to wood. While wax makes water bead up, it also allows water to permeate after a short time. The most popular use of wax as a finish is for English country pine furniture.

Wax doesn't make a good cleaner. The solvent in wax will dissolve and break up oil-soluble dirt and grime, but the mixture of grime and wax will dry softer and gummier than the wax alone. It's much better to clean the surface first with mineral sprits, then with water. This removes both water- and oil-soluble grime and will provide a clean base for the wax.

Wax can be used for scratch protection. It will deflect scratches by making the finish slicker so that sharp objects tend to slide on the surface. However, if you want scratch resistance on a high-traffic area, like a floor or a dining table, it's better to use a finish that's hard to scratch, like polyurethane.

The best use of wax is to improve the luster and shine of old or slightly damaged finishes. It's an easy, reversible method for sprucing up antiques and old finishes. It hides scratches better than polishes because it fills up the scratches. Also, wax is a better product to use on crazed or cracked finishes. Polishes will wick through the cracks and turn them dark, but wax will not.

which will soften finishes that aren't fully cured and will remove oil finishes. In these situations, it's better to use a wax that has mineral spirits as the solvent. Look for mineral spirits in the ingredients list on the can. If you can't find a wax with mineral spirits, ask for help. Mineral spirits has a recognizable odor so the salesperson should be able to identify a wax with it, or you can contact the manufacturer.

The color of the wax is a big consideration. Waxes that are sold as natural or neutral usually dry to an off-white or beige color. If these waxes are applied to dark-stained woods or open-pore woods, the light color of the wax usually looks strange. In these situations, it's better to use a dark-colored wax, or you can tint a wax yourself. Use dry pigments or oil-soluble dyes dissolved in mineral spirits for tinting.

To apply wax, start with a clean surface. You should wipe the surface with a rag dampened with mineral spirits or with soapy water to remove dirt and grime. On very dirty or old surfaces, you may need to use steel wool moistened with mineral spirits to get rid of the grime. Once the surface is clean, you can apply the wax. Make a wax applicator by placing a hunk of wax in the center of a cloth and then wrap the ends over the wax. This applies the wax evenly, making it easier to buff out to a consistent appearance. Work on one manageable section at a time.

It's time to buff the surface when the wax starts to haze over. The time frame in which the wax hazes is determined by the type of carrier and the temperature. Fast-evaporating carriers and dry weather will flash the solvent quicker, so you'll have less time to go back and buff it. If the wax dries hard, just go over it with a rag moistened with mineral spirits to redissolve it.

You can also apply the wax with 0000 steel wool, which has the added benefit of smoothing the surface of the finish as you apply it. If you have trouble applying the wax, it may help if you thin it a bit with mineral spirits. You can also add mineral spirits if the wax is old or if the lid was left off or not tightly sealed. You can add as much solvent as you wish, but remember that thinner reduces the amount of hard wax that's left on the surface.

Polishes

Polishes are the easiest and most effective product to clean furniture, hide minor

A colored wax fill stick will easily and quickly fix a small gouge on an edge that doesn't get a lot of wear and tear.

scratches, and temporarily change surface luster and shine. Few polishes contain wax (or very little if they do), so they do not form any film on the surface of the finish.

If a polish is clear, it may contain oil, mineral spirits, dye, and fragrance. It may not have any oil and just be mineral spirits with fragrance. These products clean fingerprints and any oil-soluble dirt like a crayon mark. They also clean dust and restore a temporary surface shine and luster to the finish.

If the polish is milky looking, it's an emulsion of water and mineral spirits. It may also contain oil and fragrance. These products are better cleaning aids than clear polish because they clean both water-soluble and oil-soluble dirt. They also remove dust. They are best used on buffed gloss lacquer finishes.

A colored polish is a mixture of mineral spirits and color, which is usually asphaltum or an oil-soluble dye. The polish may also contain a mineral oil or fragrance to disguise the smell. These products are like clear polishes in regard to cleaning but have the extra advantage of hiding scratches on dark furniture.

Polishes are simply wiped on and wiped off. You can apply polish to a cloth and wipe the surface, or you can apply polish to the surface and wipe the excess off.

I have two reservations about polishes. First, it's not a good idea to use dark polishes on seats and any other furniture parts that will come in contact with clothes. Many dark dyes contain the colorant asphaltum, which is a nondrying, tarlike substance that can stain clothes. Second, polishing finishes that are badly cracked or crazed to the point where the cracks go

Filling a Large Gouge

1 Rub the wax crayon into the gouge to fill it. Or cut off a piece and press it into the gouge with your finger or a piece of wood. Pare off the excess wax until it's level with the wood.

2 Smooth the filler level by rubbing it with the smooth side (back) of a piece of sandpaper.

through to the bare wood can be a disaster. If the polish contains any nondrying oil like mineral oil it will wick into the bare wood and turn it dark, exaggerating the crack. Once this happens the only cure is to strip the finish.

FIXING GOUGES AND DENTS

Gouges and dents are repaired by filling the depression with a colored substance that imitates the color of the surrounding wood. There are a variety of substances that can do this, but the easiest two are colored wax crayons and stick shellac (also known as burn-in sticks). Of the two options, colored wax is the easiest to use. Wax is soft, so it's best used for areas that won't get a lot of handling or get bumped. Stick shellac is harder, so it's better for areas that will get more wear and tear. Both options are available in a wide variety of colors.

If the gouge is part of a corner, try to use wood to fill in the depression. Wax is too soft for a corner that may get bumped, and stick shellac is too brittle. Pare away the damaged corner with a chisel until you have a flat surface, then glue an oversize piece of wood to it. Pare away the excess until it's flush with the original surface, then stain it the same color and apply finish.

To use colored wax on a small dent or gouge, rub the wax crayon along the gouge. Then rub off the excess with a soft cloth wrapped around a small block of wood. If you rub it too much, you'll remove the wax, so rub just until it's level.

To fill larger gouges with wax, rub the area with the crayon or cut off a small piece and jam it into the depression. Then use a "chisel" made from a small piece of wood to pare off the excess wax until it's level with the surface. Finally, take a piece of fine sandpaper (320 or 220 grit) and rub the wax level with the surface using the back of the sandpaper, not the abrasive side.

Fixing a Scrape

1 Scrapes that remove both finish and color usually leave both ragged and bare wood, so the first step is to smooth the edge with 240-grit sandpaper.

2 Apply the color to the bare wood. You can apply several colors together to achieve different colors, apply two coats with drying time in between, or lighten it by wiping it immediately with mineral spirits if it's too dark.

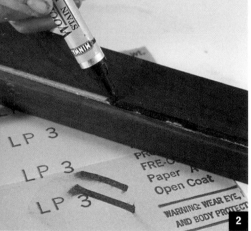

3 Seal the color in with finish to protect it, and smooth it with fine steel wool to blend it in. Pigment pens have binder so they'll dry hard, but it's still a good idea to seal in the color.

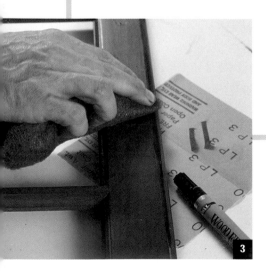

Burn-in sticks are more difficult to use, and it's easier to damage the surface around the gouge or dent if you're not careful. The general procedure is to melt, or burn in, the stick into the depression with a hot knife or soldering iron. Then quickly press down with your finger to push the resin into the depression.

If the resin is shellac, the repair is best leveled with a piece of muslin wrapped around a small piece of wood. Wet the muslin slightly with alcohol and rub the repair. If the surface is shellac or the repair material is another type of resin, level the stick by sanding very carefully with fine sandpaper lubricated with mineral spirits. Top coat repairs made with burn-in sticks with more finish to protect the repair.

FIXING SCRAPES AND SCRATCHES

Scrapes and scratches are repaired in different ways, depending on the depth of the scratch, whether it goes through stain to bare wood, and its location. While many deep scratches or scrapes on the surface of wood can be repaired by stripping, sanding, and refinishing, there are several other repair techniques that can mitigate or completely disguise damage.

The type of finish and the sheen affect how visible a repaired area is. Evaporative finishes like lacquer and shellac are the easiest to repair, because new finish will melt into the existing finish. On the other hand, reactive finishes like varnish are hard to repair invisibly. Also, flat and matte finishes are easier to repair than high gloss finishes and hide repairs better. Finally, a scratch or scrape on the side of a piece or toward a corner will be easier to repair invisibly than a dent in the center of a table.

Scrapes

Scrapes usually appear as large areas of finish and/or color removed from edges. Scrapes on an edge can usually be repaired easily. Large scrapes that occur in the center of a side or top are harder to repair, and it's best to strip and refinish the area.

To determine if a scrape has removed only the finish or also the stain or dye color, wet the damaged area with naphtha. If the wet surface blends in with the rest of the finish, only the finish has been damaged. To make the repair, simply spray or brush on more finish, let it dry, then smooth it with fine steel wool to blend it in. You can match the original sheen of gloss, satin, or matte by rubbing with 0000 steel wool. Or spray the finish with an appropriate sheen on the scrape.

If both color and finish are missing, the scrape will appear lighter than the rest of the finish when you wet it with naphtha. In this case, you'll need to replace the original color first, then apply finish. The easiest way to replace color is with touch-up repair pens, but you can also mix some dry pigment with shellac and paint it in with a fine artist's brush. Pens are far easier to use and are available in paint and hardware stores. The color selection is limited, but you can apply several different colors or lighten dark colors with solvent (naphtha works best) to achieve matches with most wood tones.

Touch-up pens are available in two types: pigment and dye. Dye-based touch-up pens have a felt, chisel-edged tip similar to magic markers. Pigment-based pens can be identified by instructions telling you to shake the pen before use and to push down on the tip to dispense the color.

Although dye-based pens are far easier to use, the pigment-based pens are more

lightfast and have binder in them to adhere the color to the repair area. This is important when the scrape has removed part of the finish and toner, but the wood is still sealed with finish. Dye-based pen color can be wiped off by polishes unless it's applied to unsealed wood. If the pen color won't stick to the wood, sand through the exposed area with fine sandpaper to expose fresh wood and the color will adhere better.

A general rule to follow when you apply the color to the wood is to leave it lighter than the finished wood surface because most color deepens when finish is applied over it. If the color is too dark, you can apply more color. If you apply it too dark, wipe it immediately with a rag to lighten it. If the color is wrong, apply another color over it or remove it. A naphtha-moistened rag will remove most colors completely. When the color is dry, seal it in with finish of the appropriate sheen or rub it out to gloss.

Scratches

There are three ways to fix scratches depending on their location and depth and on your skill level. If the finish is thick enough and the scratches are light, you can remove them by sanding them out. Deeper scratches or scratches on thin finishes can be repaired by adding more finish

One of the easiest ways to fix a scratch is to use a product called scratch cover. Scratch cover is actually mineral spirits with a colorant added. Like oil polish, it may also have mineral oil and a fragrance added to disguise the petroleum smell. Unlike traditional oil polishes, though, the asphaltum does not evaporate— it stays behind to keep the scratch disguised. Scratch cover only hides or partially disguises the scratch; if the scratch is deep, it will be visible at certain viewing angles.

> **WORKING SMART**
>
> Dark waxes can be used to disguise scratches, scrapes, and crazed finishes. If the color isn't quite right, add a bit of dry pigment to the wax.

Using Scratch Cover

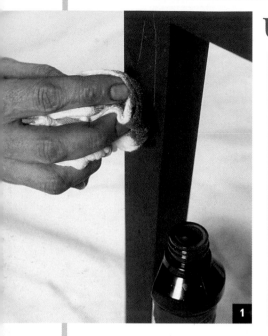

1 To apply scratch cover, drizzle some of the polish onto a soft cloth and apply it directly to the scratches.

2 The scratches should disappear. Then wipe the surface clean with a dry, clean rag.

Nonetheless, the ease of application makes scratch cover an attractive option. You wipe it on and let it sit for a minute or so, then wipe off the excess. You can apply it to a cloth and then wipe it in or apply it directly to the wood. You can apply it selectively, just to the damaged area. It is best applied to legs, aprons, and other non-critical surfaces. Because it doesn't actually repair the scratch, at best it should be considered a quick fix. Do not apply scratch cover if the finish is badly crazed or cracked.

If the finish is thick enough or if the finish is reactive, like varnish or polyurethane, your best bet is to try to sand out the scratches. The process for doing this is exactly the same as leveling and polishing when rubbing out a finish (see pp. 166-169). Using the lowest grit capable of removing the scratch will save a lot of work later.

I generally start with 600 grit and have rarely gone below 400 grit to remove a scratch. Follow the wet-sanding with rubbing with 0000 steel wool for satin finishes or polishing compounds for gloss. If the scratches are light, you can work the scratched areas selectively with 600-grit sandpaper. But if the scratches are deep, you may want to wet-sand the entire area to avoid hollows created by working one area too aggressively.

For thin scratches that are too thin to sand out without going through the finish, it's best to apply more finish. You can also use this method if you're not sure how thick the finish is or whether there are color coats of glaze or toner underneath the clear finish (damage to one of these requires stripping and refinishing). If the finish is an evaporative finish like lacquer or shellac, scratches will disappear and blend in with the new finish, as long

Using Finish to Repair a Scratch

1 Using a small, red sable artist's brush, build up deep scratches first with new finish.

2 When the finish is dry, level-sand the filled scratch, then rub it out. Apply more finish to the whole area to blend it in better.

as the scratches are not too deep. For oil finishes that are lightly scratched, apply more oil and wet-sand it in to remove the scratch. Because oil finishes don't build significantly on the surface, rub lightly or you'll cut through any stain or surface patina.

For deep scratches, it's best if you fill the scratch with finish before applying more finish over the entire surface. This only works for lacquer and shellac finishes and with most water-based finishes. Using a red sable artist's brush, fill the scratch with lacquer or shellac. Several applications with overnight drying between each coat may be needed. Don't allow the finish to get too thick or it may not dry correctly; instead, build it up slowly. When the scratch has been filled, level-sand it with sandpaper, then apply more finish to the

whole area. When the finish is dry, rub it out to the sheen that you want. If the scratch is deep and white, and the finish is varnish, catalyzed lacquer, or water based, you'll be better off stripping and refinishing if you want a perfect repair.

Sometimes you may encounter a situation where you're not sure of what the finish is. A small drop of alcohol in an inconspicuous spot will make shellac sticky within a minute or two. A small drop of lacquer thinner will make lacquer sticky and will soften most water-based finishes. If neither has an effect, the finish may be varnish or catalyzed lacquer. It's always best to put the same type of finish over the existing one when repairing scratches. It helps to avoid incompatibility problems and means you can expect the same durability from the new finish.

> **WORKING SMART**
>
> If the scratch is cross-grain and the wood is stained, do not apply the original color dye. The scratch will stain darker because it's end grain. Instead, apply a lighter color stain or just finish.

Rings and Water Marks

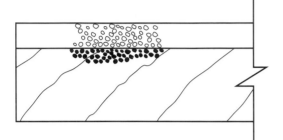

A

Black Rings
Water permeates the finish and turns wood black or gray under the finish (the finish may also be damaged).

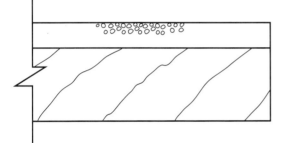

B

White Rings on Top of Finish
Heat, water, or both damages the top of the finish, turning it white.

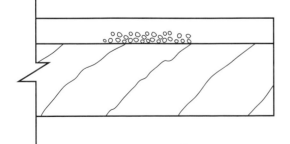

C

White Rings on Bottom of Finish
A hot object placed on the surface of the finish causes water held in the wood to turn the finish cloudy. This happens on the bottom of the finish where it meets the wood.

RINGS AND WATER SPOTS

Aside from scratches, rings and water spots are the most common damage to finishes. How easy they are to remove depends upon where the damage is (the wood or the finish) and how the damage was done. The color of the ring will tell you what to do.

If the color is black or gray (drawing A at left), the damage is from water that has permeated the finish and discolored the wood below. The most common cause of this damage is pots or vases with slight cracks in them that allow water to wick under the base of the pot. The water is not seen until the pot or vase is removed, and by then it's too late. To repair this damage you have to strip the finish, sand the wood, and bleach it with oxalic acid (see Bleaching, beginning on p. 91). Clean off any residual bleach before you refinish the surface.

If the ring is white, the damage is from water or heat and is to the finish only. The damage may appear on top of the finish (see drawing B) or at the bottom (see drawing C), where the finish meets the wood. Top damage is easy to repair, but if the damage is at the bottom, it's from heat and is rarely repairable. There's no easy way to tell where the damage is, so you'll have to try a sequence of steps to see what works.

Most superficial heat or water damage can be rubbed out with steel wool and oil, rubbing compound used with a soft cloth, or fine wet/dry sandpaper used with mineral oil or soapy water. The whiteness disappears fairly quickly, and once it's

TROUBLESHOOTING WAXES, POLISHES, AND REPAIRS

PROBLEM	CAUSE	REMEDY
Waxes		
Wax dries to a light color in pores and crevices	Natural color of wax trapped in pores	Switch to a dark-colored wax
Wax hazes too quickly	Fast-drying carrier	Add some mineral spirits to slow down drying or work on more manageable sections
Wax is hard to buff	Wax dried before you could buff it	Redissolve wax with mineral spirits
Wax shows fingerprints	Too much wax left on surface	Buff out wax more or remove it with mineral spirits and rebuff
Polishes		
Polish smears or streaks	Too much polish left on surface	Wipe off polish with a clean rag or mineral spirits
Polish turned dark in cracks	Polish wicked through finish to bare wood	Try scrubbing wood with naphtha; if this doesn't work, strip the finish
Repairs		
Repair product appears too dark on scratches or scrapes	Wrong color used or cross-grain scratches stain darker	Lighten up by wiping with mineral spirits or clear polish
Scratches don't disappear when more finish is applied	Scratches are on varnish or catalyzed lacquer and don't remelt	Wet-sand scratches or strip the finish
White marks don't rub out	Marks are too deep	Strip the finish

removed, the finish can be rubbed out to the original sheen. If the finish is lacquer or shellac, a light wiping with a rag moistened with alcohol will remove the white spot. Dampen the rag enough so that it feels like the tip of a dog's nose, not dripping wet, and use a back-and-forth pendulum motion to remove the white spot. If neither of these methods work, strip the finish or find a good-looking vase to hide it.

SPECIALTY FINISHES

Sometimes you see a finish on a piece of furniture in a store or in someone's home and wonder how that look was done. Or you may have a picture in your mind of exactly the finish you want, but after countless samples and dozens of stains and finishes, you still can't get it quite right. In this chapter you'll learn how to pull together the materials and techniques discussed earlier in the book to produce the look you want on real furniture projects. I've collected 14 of the most popular and requested finishes and distilled them down to a series of manageable steps. You can pick the look you want and follow the steps to get it.

ARTS AND CRAFTS

The large pores of oak create dramatic contrast on this timeless finish. The combination of an oil-based pigment stain and a gel varnish makes this an attractive and easy finish for beginners.

Beginner

MATERIALS
Pigment stain

Gel or wiping varnish

TECHNIQUES TO REVIEW
Applying pigment stains (p. 81)

Wiping varnish (p. 139)

DISASSEMBLE BEFORE STAINING ❶

To make staining easier, disassemble the piece before you start if it's held together with screws. Staining disassembled also creates a cleaner appearance once the piece is reassembled.

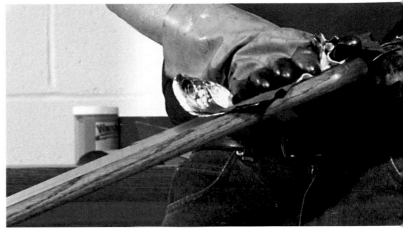

3 **WIPE OFF THE STAIN**
Using a clean rag, wipe off the excess stain. If the stain is too dark, wipe it with mineral spirits. If it's the wrong color, apply another color of stain. Prop the stained pieces against a wall or use a nail board while they dry.

2 **APPLY PIGMENT STAIN**
Apply a dark brown pigment stain with a brush or rag. Stain all the individual parts at once, including the bottoms.

4 **REASSEMBLE THE PIECE**
When the stain has dried enough to handle (overnight is best), put the piece back together. Work on a soft blanket so you don't mar the piece as you work on it.

STAIN THE SCREW COVERS **5**
These screw covers are tapered for a pressure fit—they're not glued in. Pound them back in with a soft-faced mallet and then stain them using a small artist's brush. It's OK if you get some stain on the previously stained surface—it will wipe off cleanly. Wipe the excess stain off the covers and let them dry thoroughly.

APPLY A VARNISH ⑥
Using gel or wiping varnish, apply the first coat evenly on the surface, working in any direction. Then immediately wipe it with the grain in smooth, even strokes.

⑦ SAND BETWEEN COATS
After applying one or two coats of varnish, use 400-grit sandpaper to remove dust nibs, then use 0000 steel wool to smooth the finish. Go easy on the edges, as the finish will be thin. Wrap the steel wool around the contour of the edge as you rub.

APPLY THE FINAL COAT ⑧
Apply the last coat as evenly as you can, wiping with the grain. If the varnish is too glossy, rub it out with steel wool after it has dried, or apply the final coat of varnish in the sheen of your choice.

LIMING AND PICKLING

The large, distinct pores of this quartersawn footstool make an easy liming and pickling project. A polyurethane top coat means the finish will withstand years of even the toughest use.

Beginner

TECHNIQUES TO REVIEW

Applying pigment stains (p. 81)

Brushing varnish on a flat top (p. 136)

Brushing varnish on sides (p. 137)

Rubbing out a thin finish (p. 165)

MATERIALS

Liming or pickling stain

Gloss polyurethane

CLEAN THE PORES ❶

Sand to 180 grit, then clean the sawdust from the pores and the surface with a brush or vacuum.

APPLY THE STAIN 2

Apply the stain to the surface with a stiff-bristle brush that works the stain into the pores.

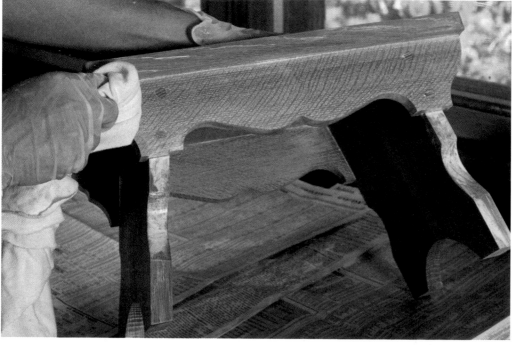

3 WIPE THE STAIN

With a clean cloth, remove the excess stain from the surface. If the stain has started to set and is hard to remove, use a rag moistened with mineral spirits.

APPLY GLOSS POLYURETHANE 4

Apply a thinned 50/50 mix of polyurethane and mineral spirits with a good-quality natural-bristle brush.

⑤ SCUFF-SAND THE SEALER
Using 320-grit stearated sandpaper, lightly sand the polyurethane sealer coat smooth on all surfaces.

REMOVE THE DUST ⑥
Wipe the surface clean of dust and sandpaper residue with a tack cloth. A clean cloth dampened with a bit of thinned polyurethane makes a good substitute for a tack cloth.

⑧ RUB OUT THE FINISH WHEN DRY
After lightly sanding the surface with 400 grit, use 0000 steel wool to rub the polyurethane flat. For a bit more gloss, use thinned wax or Wool-Lube on the steel wool.

⑦ APPLY A SECOND COAT
With a brush, apply a second coat of polyurethane (this time unthinned). Coat the edges of the top last so you have a dry surface to grab to turn the piece around.

OIL, SHELLAC, AND WAX

This simple, understated finish brings out the grain and figure in any wood. It's pictured on unstained cherry, but it can be used on most natural or stained woods. Be sure to reapply wax every year or so to keep the piece looking its best.

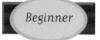
Beginner

MATERIALS
Boiled linseed oil or oil/varnish blend

Shellac (any type)

Paste wax

TECHNIQUES TO REVIEW
Applying oil finish (p. 133)

Padding shellac (p. 140)

Brushing shellac and lacquer (p. 143)

Waxes (p. 176)

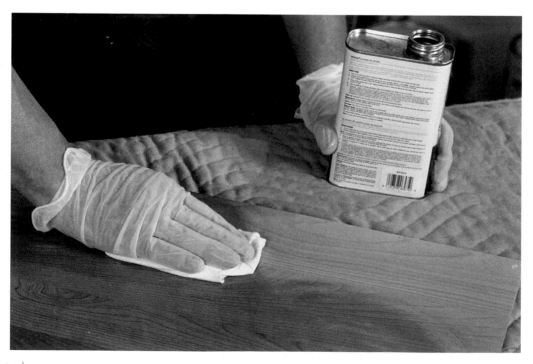

1 APPLY THE OIL
Apply a coat of boiled linseed oil or an oil/varnish blend to the surface. Apply just enough to make the wood wet—don't flood it. Wipe the surface briskly with a clean cloth after application. Allow the oil to dry.

PAD SHELLAC ON FLAT AREAS

After the oil has dried for one day, apply a 2-lb. cut of shellac. Pad it on large, flat areas, like the top. Apply several coats on both sides and the edges.

BRUSH SHELLAC ON CURVED AREAS ③

It's easier to brush shellac on curved areas. Use a small brush and load it lightly to avoid drips. Brush the undersides of the piece as well. Apply two coats.

④ APPLY SHELLAC TO THE INSIDE

Apply shellac, not oil, to the insides of drawers. Apply a 2-lb. cut of shellac here as well.

SAND THE SEALER ⑤

The first coats of shellac seal the wood. Sand with 320-grit sandpaper and a light touch, backing up the paper with your hand. When finished, remove the sanding dust and debris with a tack cloth or a dry rag.

6 PAD THE WHOLE PIECE

Now use the padding technique to finish the shellac application. Pad the entire piece with at least several more applications, building the shellac to the thickness you want.

SAND 7

Sand the entire
piece with 400-grit stearated
sandpaper, then remove the
dust. Rub with 0000 steel wool.

APPLY WAX 8

Paste wax provides
protection from scratching
and a silky feel as well. Use
a natural-colored wax for
light woods. On the cherry
table here, a light brown wax
was applied with a piece of
0000 steel wool. After the
wax hazes (5 to 15 minutes),
buff it out with a clean cloth.

EARLY AMERICAN MAPLE

This classic finish duplicates the look of maple antiques from the late 1700s. Created with dye and glazing, this finish pops the figure in highly figured maple or makes plain maple stunning. If you've never tried dyes or glazing techniques, this is a perfect way to start.

Intermediate

MATERIALS

Water- or alcohol-soluble dye (about 1 pint mixed)

Dewaxed shellac

Vandyke brown glaze

Varnish or polyurethane

TECHNIQUES TO REVIEW

Applying water-soluble dyes by hand (p. 82)

Applying alcohol-soluble dyes by hand (p. 83)

Brushing shellac and lacquer (p. 143)

Wiping the glaze (p. 115)

Brushing varnish (p. 137)

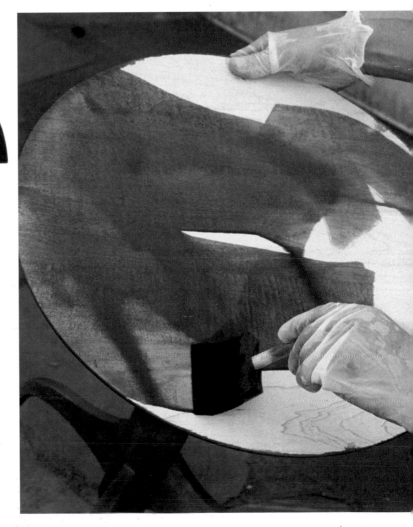

APPLY THE DYE ❶

Apply the dye with a brush or rag. I'm using a water-based dye here, so I flood the surface evenly, then blot up the excess. The dye raises the grain, so preraise the grain with distilled water first.

③ SMOOTH THE SEALER
Sand the shellac sealer coat to provide some tooth for the glaze. Use 320-grit paper on the flat surfaces and maroon synthetic steel wool on the curves. Remove the residue with a tack cloth.

② BRUSH ON SHELLAC SEALER
Brush on a 2-lb. cut of dewaxed shellac to seal in the dye and stiffen the fibers. Use a lightly loaded brush to avoid drips.

APPLY THE ④ GLAZE
Using a stiff-bristle brush, apply the glaze over all surfaces, including the undersides. If you're using a fast-drying glaze, work on the base first and wipe it before applying glaze to the top.

⑤ WIPE THE GLAZE CLEAN
With a clean, wadded-up rag, wipe off the excess glaze. Leave some in the crevices to mimic patina. Turn the rag frequently to expose fresh, clean cloth. Let the glaze dry thoroughly (at least overnight).

6 **APPLY THE TOP COAT**
Tabletops get lots of wear and tear, so they need a coat of varnish or polyurethane. A fast-drying product dries dust-free in about 30 minutes. A slower-drying polyurethane needs more time and should be protected indoors while it dries.

7 **SAND THE FIRST COAT**
Use stearated 320-grit sandpaper to sand the polyurethane smooth and level. Watch the edges of the paper, and use your hand to back it. Remove the sanding debris with a tack cloth.

8 **APPLY THE FINAL COAT**
With a good-quality brush, apply one final coat of satin varnish or polyurethane to the whole piece. Brush in smooth, even strokes, and tip off the brush when done. If your brushing technique isn't up to snuff, an alternative is to wipe on one or two coats of satin polyurethane thinned 50/50 with mineral spirits or naphtha.

EBONIZED FINISH

An ebonized finish provides a striking contrast to light natural wood colors like maple. A water-based lacquer helps keep the creamy, white color of maple from yellowing.

Intermediate

MATERIALS
Black water-soluble dye

Pale dewaxed shellac

Water-based lacquer

TECHNIQUES TO REVIEW

Applying water-soluble dyes by hand (p. 82)

Brushing shellac and lacquer (p. 143)

Brushing water-based finish (p. 151)

Spraying water-based finish (p. 152)

Rubbing out a thin finish (p. 165)

Rubbing out a thick finish (p. 167)

RAISE THE GRAIN FOR THE EBONY FINISH

1

To minimize grain-raising after dyeing, preraise the grain. Apply distilled water to the wood, then resand with 180- or 220-grit sandpaper when dry.

 APPLY THE DYE
Flood the surface evenly with black water-soluble dye, then blot the excess. Do the underside first, then turn it over and do the top. A second coat may be necessary to get a positive black. When the surface is dry, lightly sand it with maroon synthetic steel wool.

③ SEAL THE DYE
Apply pale dewaxed shellac to seal the dye. This prevents the dye from bleeding into the water-based top coats.

④ SCUFF-SAND THE SEALER
Scuff-sand the shellac sealer with 320-grit sandpaper on the flat surfaces and maroon synthetic steel wool on the edges.

⑤ RAISE THE GRAIN FOR THE NATURAL FINISH

Apply distilled water to the area you want to look natural. When it's dry, sand with 180- or 220-grit sandpaper. Clean the residue with a rag lightly moistened with distilled water.

APPLY CLEAR COATS ⑥

Brush or spray on clear finish to the natural-looking area. Use gloss, flat, or satin and a synthetic-bristle brush. Lightly scuff-sand between coats.

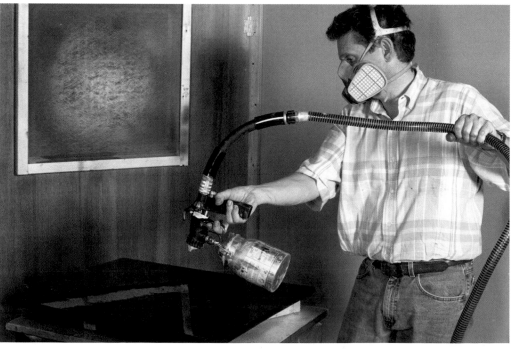

⑦ FINISH THE EBONIZED AREA

Spray or brush gloss water-soluble lacquer on the top, and lightly sand between the second and third coats. Leave it "off-the-gun," with the final coat in the sheen you want, or rub it out.

ANTIQUE PINE

Almost anything goes in distressing a pine top to mimic years of wear and tear. You can finish the base the same way or paint it, which adds nice contrast to the top.

Intermediate

TECHNIQUES TO REVIEW

Applying alcohol-soluble dyes by hand (p. 83)

Applying glazes (p. 114)

Brushing varnish (p. 137)

Rubbing out a thin finish (p. 165)

MATERIALS

Alcohol-soluble dye (about 1 cup mixed)

Burnt umber glaze

Oil-based varnish

Wax

APPLY THE DYE ❶
Apply an alcohol-soluble dye to the piece (except where you will paint). It should be a yellow-orangish color. Let the dye dry for at least several hours.

2 APPLY VARNISH SEALER

To lock in the dye and provide a base for the glaze, apply a generous coat of thinned gloss varnish (1 part varnish to 1 part mineral spirits). Try two coats and allow several hours between the first and second coats for drying.

DISTRESS THE 3 SURFACE

To mimic the dents and dings of time, lightly dangle a key ring full of keys on the surface. This is a good chance to use all those stray keys you've saved over the years.

5 ROUND OVER CORNERS

Using the shank of a screwdriver, round over and burnish sharp edges where the piece would get the most wear and tear. The front edge and corners are the most likely spots.

4 CREATE WORM HOLES

Pound an awl or a drill in the top to produce the look of tiny worm holes. Don't do the whole surface—just near edges and on the moldings.

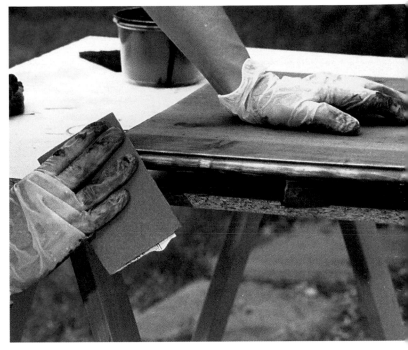

7 SAND
With 120-grit sand-
paper, sand through the glaze
and dye in areas that get
wear and tear, like the front
edges. Sand lightly, and don't
overdo it.

6 APPLY A DARK GLAZE
Apply burnt umber glaze to the entire surface, working it
into all the dents and holes you've made. Wipe it clean with a rag
before it dries.

**APPLY TWO
COATS OF VARNISH 9**
Once the glaze is dry, apply
two coats of gloss varnish.
When the final coat is dry, rub
it out with 0000 steel wool
for a flat look. Or apply flat
varnish for the final coat and
use a cheap brush so that
brush marks show.

8 HIGHLIGHT WITH GLAZE
Apply glaze selectively to molded edges to simulate the
buildup of grime and wax. Before the glaze dries, strike off some
from the high spots of the molding.

LIGHTLY DISTRESSED PAINT

A light distressing adds a touch of charm without making the piece look too worn. A red stripe around the top adds a touch of simple elegance. I call for milk paint, but you can substitute water-based latex paint.

MATERIALS

Paint (milk paint or latex)

Dewaxed shellac

Dark brown glaze (water based)

Striping tool

Red paint

Satin water-based finish

TECHNIQUES TO REVIEW

Brushing a water-based finish* (p. 151)

Spraying a water-based finish* (p. 152)

Brushing shellac and lacquer (p. 143)

Applying glazes (p. 114)

Antiquing (p. 123)

* The techniques for applying clear finish are the same as for applying paint.

Intermediate

2 SEAL WITH SHELLAC
Apply a 2-lb. cut of shellac to seal in the paint and provide a base for the glaze coat. A pale-colored dewaxed shellac is the best to use under the water-based glaze and top coats.

1 APPLY BASE OR PRIMER COAT
For milk paint, apply two coats, lightly sanding in between them. For latex, use a primer coat designed for latex paint.

SCUFF-SAND 3
Lightly smooth the shellac with 320-grit sandpaper to provide some tooth for the dark glaze.

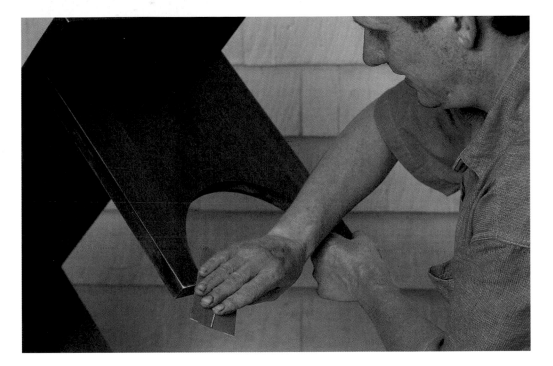

LIGHTLY DISTRESS THE SURFACE

Using 180-grit sandpaper, lightly rub through the edges of the base and around the top. Try to rub through where damage would be the likeliest to simulate actual wear.

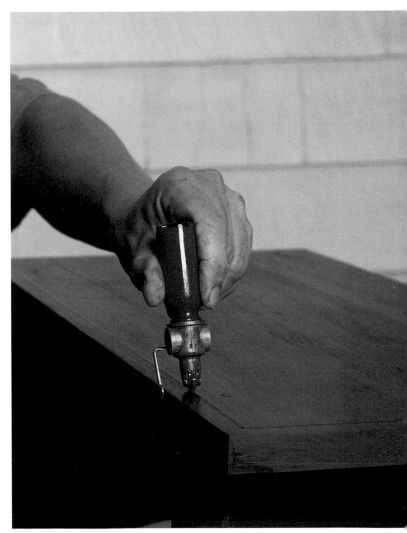

 APPLY GLAZE

Apply a dark brown water-based glaze like dark walnut over the whole piece. You can also use a thinned concentrated color like raw umber or Vandyke brown. Experiment with the colors because each will produce different effects over the base coat color.

ADD A STRIPE

With a striping tool, make a red line around the perimeter of the top. You can also tape off an area with masking tape and paint in the line with a small artist's brush. When the line is dry, apply two coats of water-based finish of the desired sheen.

HEAVILY DISTRESSED PAINT

A heavily distressed paint creates a rustic and plain, but charming, look. Twenty years ago people were paying to have these cracked, old finishes stripped and the piece refinished. Now they are paying to have the old look duplicated.

Intermediate

MATERIALS

Milk or latex paint

Paste wax

Dark glaze

Clear flat finish (water based, oil, or solvent)

TECHNIQUES TO REVIEW

Brushing a water-based finish (p. 151)

Applying glazes (p. 114)

Antiquing (p. 123)

1 APPLY A BASE COAT OF PAINT

For the base coat, choose a color that you want to show when you flake off parts of the second coat. Here, a dark base coat will be followed by a lighter top coat, but you can easily reverse the colors.

DAB ON PASTE WAX 2

Dab the ends of a bristle brush in a can of paste wax so you load just the tips. Then flick it over areas where you intend to flake off the second coat of paint.

3 APPLY THE SECOND COAT

Choose a color that contrasts with the base coat and apply it over the entire piece. Thick applications or water-based paints are repelled by wax, so you may need to apply several thin coats atop these areas. Allow the second coat to dry for at least one day.

4 FLAKE THE PAINT

After the second coat is dry, flake away the paint in the areas that you waxed. Use your fingernail or a razor blade.

APPLY A 6 DARK GLAZE

Apply a dark glaze over the surface. If you want less overall color with the glaze, seal the surface first with clear finish. Work the glaze into the distressing marks with the brush. When the glaze has dried, seal it with a flat finish. Use varnish or solvent lacquer over oil-based glaze and water-based lacquer over water-based glaze.

5 DISTRESS THE SURFACE

Dangle some keys on the sur-face to simulate tiny dents and dings. You can also use other objects, like rocks, bricks, or a file. Smooth the surface with gray synthetic steel wool.

WHITEWASH

Whitewashing deposits a thin layer of translucent white paint over a surface. A nonyellowing lacquer finish keeps it white. This is a great project for practicing your spray techniques.

MATERIALS

Pickling stain

Specking glaze

Nonyellowing lacquer (acrylic lacquer, CAB acrylic, butyrate, or water-white two-part lacquer)

TECHNIQUES TO REVIEW

Applying pigment stains (p. 81)

Faking the damage (specking) (p. 123)

Spraying a complex piece (p. 146)

Intermediate

1 STRAIN THE STAIN
Mix the stain thoroughly, then pour it through a medium-mesh strainer. You can use a stock pickling and liming stain or thinned white paint.

2 TAKE THE PIECE APART

A complex piece like this is easier to spray if you take it apart. Remove the screws that hold the swivel plate to the base to break it down into two pieces.

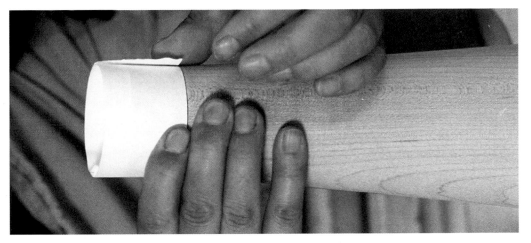

3 TAPE OFF

Use masking tape to tape off any areas that you don't want to stain, such as the cast-iron collar for the chair swivel.

4 APPLY THE STAIN

Spray or brush the base first. If spraying, set up the gun to deliver a medium to light fluid delivery and a medium-wide fan pattern. Apply even, light coats. (You'll get more stain to stay on the surface if you sand to only 150 grit.)

5 **WIPE THE STAIN**
Before the stain dries, wipe it off with a clean rag (above). You should be meticulous about this because any areas you miss will show up later when the clear finish is applied. Go over all surfaces several times.

SPRAY A SEAL COAT **6**
Spray the first coat of nononyellowing lacquer (above right). Set up the gun for a medium fluid delivery and a medium-wide fan pattern. Spray light coats to avoid drips.

7 **FLY-SPECK**
Fly-specking a medium or dark glaze over the white-wash produces an interesting effect (left). For a subtler effect, pick a glaze that's closer to the color of the white stain.

SPRAY THE **8**
FINAL COATS
Spray at least three more coats of finish, lightly scuff-sand, and rub out with gray synthetic steel wool. Then spray the final coat of finish (right). You can leave the sheen as is or rub out a gloss finish to the look you want.

DECORATIVE FILLED-PORE FINISH

The large open pores of oak or ash can be filled with a colored glaze that contrasts with the color of the rest of the wood. Filling pores with colored glaze is a technique that every finisher should learn. Once you master the basics of this finish, you open up a range of effects limited only by your imagination.

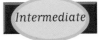

TECHNIQUES TO REVIEW

Dye stains (p. 82)

Spraying inside a cabinet (p. 148)

Glazing basics (p. 114)

MATERIALS

Water-soluble dye

Lacquer sealer (sanding sealer or vinyl sealer)

Glazing stain

Clear lacquer

APPLY A DYE STAIN **1**

Using a water- or alcohol-soluble dye stain, spray the inside of the cabinet and work to the outside. If you're using a water-soluble dye, raise the grain first with distilled water.

213

2 SAND THE DYE

Lightly sand the first coat of dye to smooth the raised grain even further.

REAPPLY THE DYE 3

To ensure even coverage of the stain, apply a second coat of water-soluble dye. Saturate the surfaces completely, then blot the excess dye, which tends to collect in corners.

4 SEAL THE DYE

Using lacquer sanding sealer, apply several light coats to all surfaces. Work from the inside out. Apply the first coat, let it dry for 30 minutes, then apply a second coat. When dry (usually 2 hours), scuff-sand the sealer coat smooth with 320-grit sandpaper.

5 MIX A CONTRASTING GLAZE

Mix a contrasting glaze using a thick glazing liquid so it collects in the pores better. Here a black glaze is mixed with just a touch of green.

6 APPLY THE GLAZE

Using a bristle brush, apply the glaze to all surfaces. Work on one section at a time and wipe the glaze clean before it sets up. When using lacquer, you can top-coat the glaze as soon as it hazes, usually within several hours.

7 APPLY A BASE COAT TO THE BACK

Begin by painting with a base coat. Here off-white paint was tinted with some Japan color.

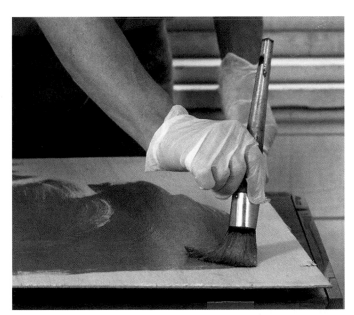

8 APPLY THE GRAINING COLOR

Uninteresting wood like this birch back looks better if it's grained. Apply a graining glaze color to the surface. Here, a section was taped off with masking tape to better imitate the effect of boards glued together to make a larger panel.

9 CREATE GRAIN

Draw a paper towel, rag, brush, or graining tool through the glaze. Different tools produce a variety of effects. To duplicate the pore structure of the oak, try paper towels. When the glaze dries, seal it with several coats of lacquer.

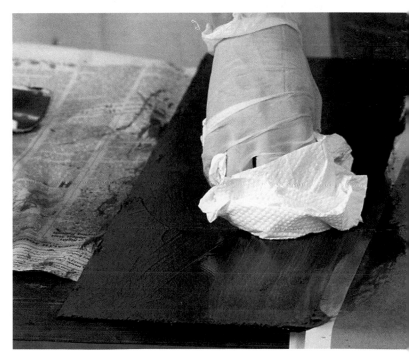

BLOND MAHOGANY

In the '40s and '50s, blond mahogany was a popular finish on walnut, cherry, and mahogany. The natural color of the wood is removed with two-part bleach. This may seem like heresy with such beautiful woods, but the results are quite elegant.

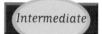

Intermediate

MATERIALS

Two-part bleach

Golden-oak or raw sienna stain (raw sienna color)

Clear gloss lacquer

TECHNIQUES TO REVIEW

Bleaching with two-part bleach (p. 93)

Applying pigment stains (p. 81)

Spraying shellac and lacquer (p. 144)

Rubbing out a thick finish (p. 167)

1 BLEACH THE WOOD

Using a two-part wood bleach (A/B bleach), bleach the wood to the color of bone or light straw. Two bleachings may be necessary. Neutralize the bleach afterward by wiping vinegar on the wood.

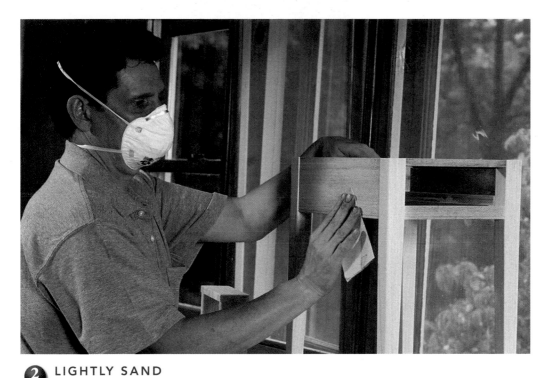

2 **LIGHTLY SAND**
Two applications of bleach will raise the grain. Use 320-grit sandpaper on the flat areas to smooth it down. Don't sand too hard or you'll go through the bleached surface to the dark wood.

CLEAN **3**
THE WOOD
Using a vacuum cleaner with a soft brush attachment, vacuum all the dust and sanding debris from the surface.

4 **APPLY**
THE STAIN
Stain the wood with a mustard-colored stain like golden oak or raw sienna. Make sure you do all the show surfaces as well as the ones that don't show (like underneath).

5 **WIPE THE STAIN CLEAN**
Wipe off the excess stain with a clean cloth. The clean wood should be the color of straw. Note the difference between the stained wood and the bleached wood in the background.

6 **APPLY CLEAR LACQUER**
Using aerosol lacquer or a spray gun, apply three coats of clear gloss lacquer. Apply light coats to the base to avoid drips.

7 **SAND**
After three or four coats of clear lacquer, sand the lacquer flat with 400-grit wet/dry paper backed with a hard block on the top. On the base, back the paper with your hand to avoid rub-throughs. Clean the residue, then apply three more coats of gloss.

RUB OUT **8**
Rub out the lacquer by wet-sanding. Start with 400-grit wet/dry paper, move on to 600 grit, and follow with steel wool for satin or polishing compounds for gloss.

FILLED-PORE MAHOGANY

Dyed mahogany has a deep, rich appearance, and a paste wood filler provides a glass-smooth surface when rubbed out to satin or gloss. The process is time-consuming, but it's worth every minute when you're finished.

Advanced

MATERIALS

Dye stain (alcohol or water soluble)

Paste wood filler (oil based)

Clear gloss lacquer (solvent or water based)

Toners (dark brown, red)

Specking glaze

Cowtailing brush

TECHNIQUES TO REVIEW

Dye stains (p. 82)

Using oil-based fillers (p. 105)

Spraying shellac and lacquer (p. 144)

Toning (p. 128)

Faking the damage (cowtailing) (p. 123)

Rubbing out a thick finish (p. 167)

APPLY THE DYE ❶

Apply a dark reddish brown dye to the top and base. Be sure to dye the insides of the piece and underneath. If you apply a water-soluble dye, preraise the grain with distilled water and resand when dry with 180- or 220-grit paper.

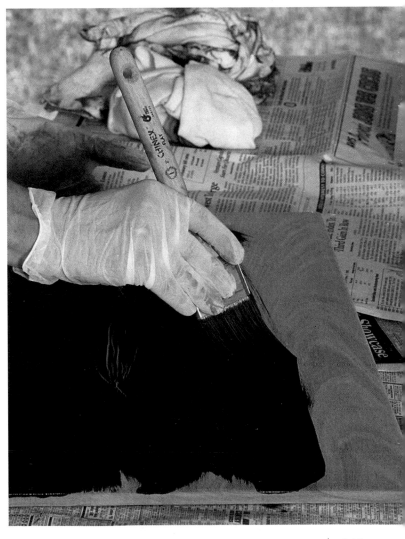

② SEAL THE DYE

Seal the dye with sealer or thinned finish. Spray a light coat, then let it dry for 30 minutes. Apply a full, wet (thicker) coat and let it dry for at least several hours before sanding lightly with 320-grit paper.

③ APPLY THE FILLER

Remove all sanding dust, then apply a dark brown paste wood filler with a stiff-bristle brush to the top, base, and drawer front. Remove the excess with a squeegee, then wipe it clean with burlap when it hazes. Allow the filler to dry for several days.

④ SAND THE FILLER

When the filler is dry, lightly sand it. Use 320-grit sandpaper on the flat surfaces and maroon synthetic steel wool on the legs. Apply a mist coat of sealer, wait 15 minutes, then apply a thicker single-pass coat.

⑤ SPECK AND TONE

Fly-speck, cowtail, and distress when the sealer has dried. Then tone or shade if necessary.

6 **APPLY TOP COATS**

Apply three double-pass coats of lacquer. Wait 1 hour between coats. Make sure you finish the inside of the drawers and the undersides of the base. When spraying the base and vertical sides, make only one pass.

7 **WET-SAND THE FINISH LEVEL**

Using 320-grit wet/dry paper, wet-sand the finish level until the pores are no longer or just barely visible. Use soapy water or mineral spirits as a lubricant.

APPLY FINAL COATS **8**

Apply three or four more coats of lacquer and allow the piece to dry for at least a week. Then wet-sand the finish with 400-grit wet/dry paper until the outlines of the pores are no longer visible. Switch to 600 grit and rub to satin or gloss.

COLONIAL CHERRY

To get the aged look of commercial cherry furniture with enhanced grain and color, follow these basic steps. You can also use this finish on birch, maple, or poplar to make it look like cherry, or follow the same steps to match another finish.

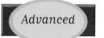

Advanced

MATERIALS

Amber-colored water- or alcohol-soluble dye

Oil-based glaze

Toners

Lacquer sealer (vinyl or sanding sealer)

Clear lacquer

TECHNIQUES TO REVIEW

Dye stains (p. 82)

Glazing basics (p. 114)

Faking the damage (cowtailing) (p. 123)

Toning and shading (p. 127)

Spraying shellac and lacquer (p. 144)

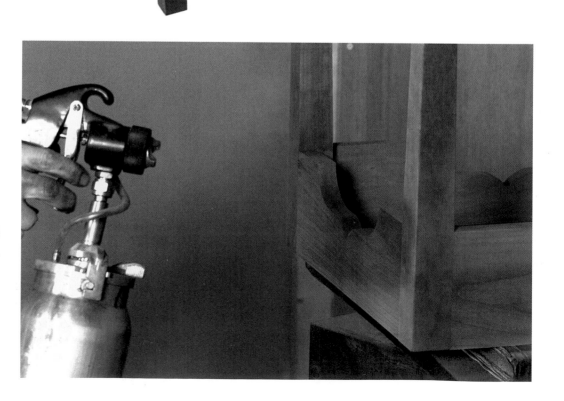

APPLY AN AMBER DYE STAIN ①

Apply a light honey-amber colored dye on the table to even out the tonal variations between boards and to help blend in sapwood. You can spray it or apply it by hand. After it has dried, seal it with vinyl lacquer sealer.

2 APPLY THE GLAZE

After sanding the sealer with 320-grit paper, apply a dark reddish brown glaze. The color of the glaze helps establish the overall color, so use a dark brown glaze like Vandyke brown for dark colors or burnt sienna for lighter colors.

3 GLAZE THE BASE

When glazing the base, make sure you do all the interiors and bottoms of the aprons. If you don't, they'll show as lighter areas later.

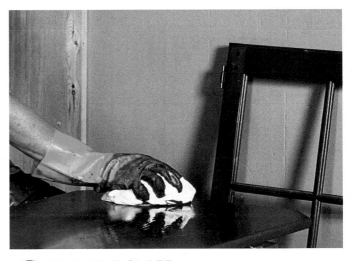

4 WIPE THE GLAZE

Wipe the glaze clean with a rag. Do the bottom of the top first, then turn it over to wipe the show side. Then wipe the base.

TONE ⑥

Tone to establish the final color. Use a combination of colors to sneak up on the final color. I use red first, then a dark brown. To neutralize a red color, use a green toner. Apply the toner lightly in a wide fan pattern.

⑤ CHECK THE COLOR

If you're matching another piece of furniture (like the door in the photo), keep the piece nearby to see how the color is coming along. Changing the color of the glaze or lightening it up will make it easier to finalize the color later. Seal the glaze with another coat of vinyl sealer. When it's dry, do any surface distressing. (like fly-specking or cowtailing).

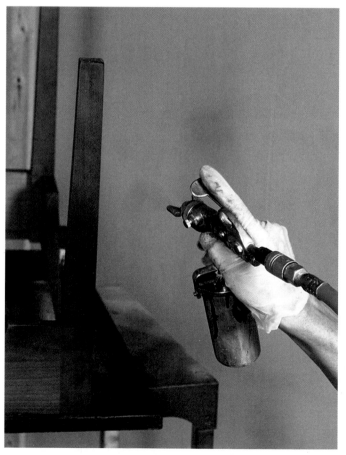

⑦ SHADE

If necessary, selectively shade areas, like the sapwood on this leg or to add a dramatic contrast to the edges. A touch-up gun is ideal for shading.

⑧ APPLY CLEAR TOP COATS

Apply three coats of clear gloss lacquer, then level-sand with 320 grit. Apply another three or four coats and rub out the finish to the desired sheen using wet/dry paper, steel wool, or polishing compounds.

PEARLED ASH

This plain ash nightstand is transformed into something extraordinary by this finish. The look employs most of the techniques discussed in this book. When done properly, the finish mimics the blue-pink pearlescent effect of natural pearls.

MATERIALS

White lacquer paint (water or solvent based; premixed or made from white color and finish)

Pink glaze

Blue glaze

Nonyellowing lacquer (water or solvent based)

TECHNIQUES TO REVIEW

Spraying a complex piece (p. 146)

Making a glaze (p. 126)

Applying glazes (p. 114)

Faking the damage (specking) (p. 123)

Rubbing out a thick finish (p. 167)

Advanced

APPLY WHITE PAINT ❶

Lightly apply a white base paint so that the grain shows through. Use an aerosol paint or make a white toner by adding colorant to a clear finish. You can also use thinned white paint. Don't wipe the paint.

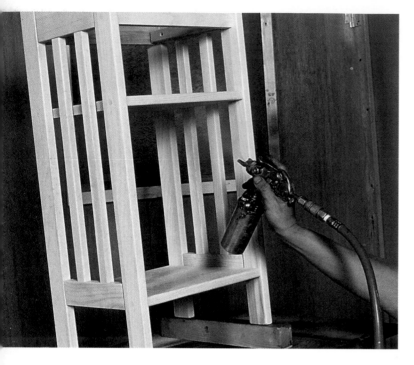

② SEAL THE PAINT

Seal the paint with a clear finish. The touch-up gun in the photo is great for getting into tight places.

SCUFF-SAND ③

Lightly sand the sealer coat with 600-grit sandpaper (600 grit is a good choice if you want the glaze to go into only the pores). Avoid sanding through the edges. If you do, you can touch up with another application of paint.

④ MAKE A PINK GLAZE

Make a pink-colored glaze by adding just a touch of red and white to some clear glazing base. The thick consistency of the glazing base makes it hang in the pores better. (Use water-based glaze if you're using a water-based finish.)

⑤ APPLY THE GLAZE

Using a brush, apply the glaze. Then wipe it off with a clean cloth across the grain so that it stays mostly in the pores. On a complicated piece like this, work on one section at a time.

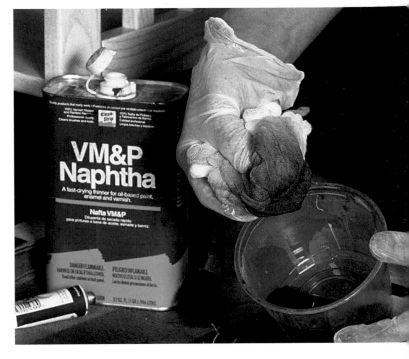

 SEAL THE GLAZE
Seal the pink glaze with a coat of clear finish. You can switch to a larger gun to speed things up a bit or stay with the smaller touch-up gun if you prefer.

MAKE A BLUE GLAZE **7**
To make a thin blue glaze, thin some concentrated color. I thinned artist's oil (Prussian blue) with enough mineral spirits to make a water-thin glaze.

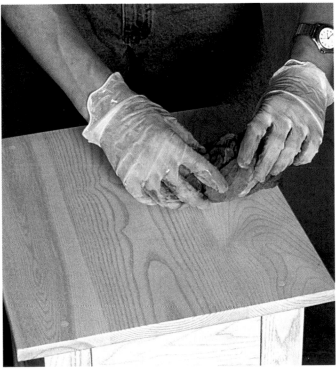

SPECK **9**
Using the same blue glaze, speck fine, tight drops on the surface. Practice first on a piece of white paper to get the right pattern.

SPRAY FINAL **10**
COATS
Spray at least three coats of finish and then level-sand with 400-grit sandpaper. Remove the dust, spray three more coats, and then rub out to a gloss or satin sheen.

8 **STIPPLE THE GLAZE**
Dip a rolled-up rag into the glaze and lightly roll it on the surface to produce a mottled-translucent effect. If you make a mistake, wipe off the glaze with mineral spirits and start over. The color of the glaze should be barely discernible, as it will darken up when a clear finish is applied.

Resources

A concerted attempt was made in this book to use products that are easily available through hardware stores, paint stores, and home centers. However, some products may not be available locally and must be purchased from specialty suppliers. These are listed below.

GARRETT-WADE
161 Ave. of the Americas
New York, NY 10013
(800) 221-2942

HOMESTEAD FINISHING PRODUCTS
1935 W 96th St., Unit Q
Cleveland, OH 44102
(216) 631-5309

MERIT INDUSTRIES
1020 North 10th St.
Kansas City, KS 66101
(800) 856-4441

M. L. CAMPBELL
224 Catherine St.
Fort Erie, ON, Canada L2A 5M9
(800) 364-1359

ROCKLER WOODWORKING AND HARDWARE
4365 Willow Dr.
Medina, MN
(800) 403-9736

SHERWIN WILLIAMS CO.
(800) 331-7979 (for product information)
(800) 4-SHERWIN (to find a store near you)

WOODCRAFT SUPPLY
210 Wood County Industrial Park
P.O. Box 1686
Parkersburg, WV 26102
(800) 225-1153

WOODWORKER'S SUPPLY
1108 N. Glenn Rd.
Casper, WY 82601
(800) 645-9292

Index

Note: References in bold indicate a photograph; references in italic indicate a drawing.